IN THE NAME OF THE MOTHER

RE-MAPPING THE TRANSNATIONAL
A Dartmouth Series in American Studies

Donald E. Pease
Avalon Foundation Chair of Humanities
Founding Director of the Futures of American Studies Institute
Dartmouth College

The emergence of Transnational American Studies in the wake of the Cold War marks the most significant reconfiguration of American Studies since its inception. The shock waves generated by a newly globalized world order demanded an understanding of America's embeddedness within global and local processes rather than scholarly reaffirmations of its splendid isolation. The series Re-Mapping the Transnational seeks to foster the cross-national dialogues needed to sustain the vitality of this emergent field. To advance a truly comparativist understanding of this scholarly endeavor, Dartmouth College Press welcomes monographs from scholars both inside and outside the United States.

For a complete list of books available in this series, see www.upne.com.

Samuele F. S. Pardini, *In the Name of the Mother: Italian Americans, African Americans, and Modernity from Booker T. Washington to Bruce Springsteen*
Sonja Schillings, *Enemies of All Humankind: Fictions of Legitimate Violence*
Günter H. Lenz, edited by Reinhard Isensee, Klaus J. Milich, Donald E. Pease, and John Carlos Rowe, *A Critical History of the New American Studies, 1970–1990*
Helmbrecht Breinig, *Hemispheric Imaginations: North American Fictions of Latin America*
Jimmy Fazzino, *World Beats: Beat Generation Writing and the Worlding of U.S. Literature*
Zachary McCleod Hutchins, editor, *Community without Consent: New Perspectives on the Stamp Act*
Kate A. Baldwin, *The Racial Imaginary of the Cold War Kitchen: From Sokol'niki Park to Chicago's South Side*
Yuan Shu and Donald E. Pease, *American Studies as Transnational Practice: Turning toward the Transpacific*
Melissa M. Adams-Campbell, *New World Courtships: Transatlantic Alternatives to Companionate Marriage*
David LaRocca and Ricardo Miguel-Alfonso, editors, *A Power to Translate the World: New Essays on Emerson and International Culture*
Elèna Mortara, *Writing for Justice: Victor Séjour, the Mortara Case, and the Age of Transatlantic Emancipations*

SAMUELE F. S. PARDINI

IN THE NAME
OF THE MOTHER

Italian Americans,
African Americans,
and Modernity from
Booker T. Washington
to Bruce Springsteen

To Jabie,
January '17
with gratitude for all the support
you provided me with to complete
this book.

DARTMOUTH COLLEGE PRESS
HANOVER, NEW HAMPSHIRE

Dartmouth College Press

An imprint of University Press of New England

www.upne.com

© 2017 Trustees of Dartmouth College

Manufactured in the United States of America

Typeset in Sabon by Integrated Publishing Solutions

For permission to reproduce any of the material in this book, contact
Permissions, University Press of New England, One Court Street, Suite
250, Lebanon NH 03766; or visit www.upne.com

Chapter 3 brings together two articles: one titled "In the Name of the
Father, the Son and the Holy Gun: *The Godfather* and Modernity,"
which appeared in *Americana: E-Journal of American Studies in
Hungary* 12.2 (2015); the other appeared in *Critique: Studies in
Contemporary Fiction* 57.2 (2016), accepted for publication by Taylor
& Francis LLC (tandfonline.com), with the title "From Wiseguys to
Whiteguys: The Italian American Gangster, Whiteness, and Modernity
in Don DeLillo's *Underworld* and Frank Lentricchia's *The Music of the
Inferno.*" A portion of chapter 5 appeared in *Italian Americana* 28.1
(2010). They are reprinted, slightly modified, with permission.

Library of Congress Cataloging-in-Publication Data available upon
request

5 4 3 2 1

To Tara and Dante
To my mother, Dania Baldaccini (1941–2015)
And in memory of Leslie A. Fiedler

CONTENTS

ACKNOWLEDGMENTS

I HAVE THE DUTY and the great honor to thank the many colleagues, friends, family members, students, and institutions that helped me to research and write this book. First and foremost, I want to thank Frank Lentricchia and Fred Gardaphé, who provided advice and mentorship for years and supported this book from beginning to end. They read the entire manuscript, made invaluable suggestions, and were instrumental in bringing it to University Press of New England. In short, without them this book would have not been possible. I am grateful to Thomas J. Ferraro, Kenneth W. Warren, and Eric Lott, who read portions of the manuscript and offered useful comments. Ken also made me think about the importance of a better title for chapter 3. In addition to reading a portion of the manuscript, Janet Zandy (and her husband Bill) offered logistical support for my research at the University of Rochester's Department of Rare Books and Special Collection. Likewise, Geoffrey Green and Michael Frontani read portions of the manuscript and offered recommendations on how to improve it. As much as I value their professional expertise, and I value it immensely, I cherish even more their continuous encouragement and support during several difficult years of my work life. They have been there all along since we met years ago, and became two of my dearest friends, which I consider a great privilege. Werner Sollors provided me with a video of a lecture that Jerre Mangione delivered to one of his classes at Harvard and discussed with me *Mount Allegro* on the occasion of his visit to my professional home, Elon University, for a talk on Italian Americans and ethnic modernism. I am sure that, however unconsciously, some of that discussion found its way into the book.

I am especially grateful to Antonio Ricci, Anthony Fragola, Dominic Candeloro, Joseph Sciorra, Don Pease, James Cocola, Marcia Green, George Guida, and Al Gravano, who gave me the opportunities to present portions of this work in various settings at Indiana University, UNC Greensboro, Loyola University in Chicago, the John D. Calandra Italian American Institute in New York City, the Futures of American Studies Institute at Dartmouth College, the annual meeting of the MLA's Italian American Literature Discussion Group, the Humanities Education Research Association, the American Italian Historical Association, and the Italian American Studies Association general meetings respectively.

A heartfelt thanks to my students at SUNY Buffalo, Vanderbilt, and Elon University who discussed with me in various classes and seminars some of the ideas that inform this study. Teresa LePors, Shannon Tennant, Lynn Melchor, Anna Zwingelberg, Tony Weaver Jr., and Dan Reis at Elon University's Belk Library provided me with all the materials and technical support I needed in a very timely fashion. So did Phyllis Andrews and Melinda Wallington in the Department of Rare Books and Special Collections at the University of Rochester's Rush Rhees Library, where, from time to time, I established residency to dig in the Jerre Mangione archives, one of my favorite things to do during the research process of this book. Gabie Smith, dean of Elon's College of Arts and Sciences, and Tim Peeples, Elon's associate provost for faculty affairs, made available the financial support and a semester teaching sabbatical necessary to conduct research trips and to complete the manuscript. Tim has been a steady supporter of my work since my first day at Elon, for which I am grateful. I am delighted to acknowledge my fabulous colleagues in the small but robust American Studies Program at Elon that they gave me the privilege to lead, as well as my colleagues in the Department of World Languages and Cultures. The experience and directness of my editor Richard Pult and his collaborators at University Press of New England have made the process of getting this book done much easier, especially when it came to copyrights and other technicalities, for which I believe I have a genetic aversion. I am extremely thankful to Glenn E. Novak, who went above and beyond when it came to the copyediting work on the original manuscript. In addition to simplifying several passages and taking care of my previously mentioned aversion to all things technical, Glenn made several observations about the content that were essential in clarifying my argument.

I am at a loss to express in words my gratitude for the unconditional love and encouragement of my mother-in-law Phyllis Shannahan, my father-in-law Paul Shannahan, my brother Stefano, his wife Cristina, my brother- and sister-in-law John and Molly Rosenecker, my nieces Deborah, Ava, and Irene, and my father Giorgio. Perhaps because the Buffalo Soldiers gave him back the freedom that the fascists and the Nazis had taken away from him; perhaps because he witnessed the segregation of African American citizens in Virginia in the late 1950s; or perhaps because of both these experiences, my father filled our home with black music and together with our mother taught me and my brother to value difference and respect the other ever since we were little kids. In a way, I think he is the main inspiration for this book.

One of the greatest blessings of my life, both professional and personal, was to meet, work, and become very close with Leslie Aaron Fiedler, the most phenomenal teacher and mentor one can hope to have. He and Sally, his wife, opened their home and, at times, their wallet for me while I was a graduate student at my beloved SUNY Buffalo. Whatever I did for them, it does not even get close to resemble everything they did for me. Although this book is not directly the fruit of the work Leslie and I did together for six unforgettable years, his influence is everywhere in it, whether through some of his scholarly writings or, more importantly, the countless stories and memories about our countries, our writers, and our artists that he told me during those memorable years. I like to think that somehow his voice resonates in these pages.

My mother Dania, who unfortunately did not live long enough to see this book in print, instilled in me the love for literature when she started bringing books back from work to an apartment that did not have many of them in the first place. As my love and passion for literature and culture grew, so did her unfailing support, even when that meant seeing one of her sons crossing the Atlantic for good. *Mannaggia l'America* indeed!

In the end, however, neither this book nor much else in my work life would have been either possible, or especially enjoyable and gratifying, without my wonderful wife Tara and the joy of our life, our nine-year-old son Dante. They have been supporting me and continue to support me in every possible way. More importantly, they fill my life with all the joy and love one can hope for, even when I drive them crazy, which the writing of this book has contributed to do aplenty! If *In the Name of the Mother* were nearly as wonderful as they both are, I could really stand shoulder by shoulder with "il grande fiorentino." Once again, "l'amor che move il sole e l'altre stelle."

IN THE NAME OF THE MOTHER

I AM GOING TO start with a personal story that frames the larger one that I tell in this book. One morning in the late spring of 2000 I was doing research for my doctoral dissertation at the central branch of the Buffalo and Erie County Public Library in downtown Buffalo, New York. Two African American female middle-school students were working on a project at a desk near mine. At one point, one of the girls turned toward me and politely asked if I had a pen that she could borrow, which I had and happily gave her. A few minutes went by, and the pen that I was using to jot down notes stopped working. Thankfully, I had one last pen left in my case. A few more minutes passed, and two African American boys of about the same age as the girls walked into the area of the library where the girls and I were. Those boys were on a mission. They approached the two girls, and one of them asked for, of all things, a pen. The girl who had borrowed my pen answered that neither she nor her friend had one. In fact, she told him, she was using a pen she had borrowed from me. Noting a smile on my face, the boy approached my table, leaned toward me, and asked me if he could borrow a pen. I replied that the one on my desk had just stopped working and, unfortunately, I did not have another one to lend him. He turned around, walked away and said, "It must be nice being white. I'd like to be white." Instinctively, I thundered back, "No! It's not, and you wouldn't like it!" The kid stopped and walked back toward me. He had the look of someone who had been caught off guard, even disturbed by my answer. He hesitated for a second. Then, he asked me with a bullying tone, "What are you, Irish? Polish?" "Italian," I replied. "Why, you gotta a problem with that?" He stared into my eyes speechless, stunned by my defiance. Suddenly, he flashed a big smile and told me, "I knew you weren't white!" and walked away.

In the Name of the Mother seeks to unearth, understand, and map the reasons that led that African American kid to tell me I am not white *because*

I am an Italian American. As a way of theoretical and historical introduction, as well as a hint as to how the book tries to achieve this goal, let me take a close, contextualized look at that boy's words, the same strategy I use to read the material that I have selected for this study. To begin with, the kid's answer gave me an identity, one that at once he defined along racial lines on the basis of his blackness and that transcended the color of my skin because I am Italian American. By so doing, he established a correlation between the two factors, which constitutes the overarching focus of this study. If there is one thing that we learned from Ralph Ellison's *Invisible Man*, it is that the way others see or do not see us (the latter being a way of seeing too) is just as, if not more important than the way we define ourselves. We are never what and who we think we are. Our identity depends just as much on how others see and think of us as it depends on how we see ourselves, which in turn explains the nonsense of cultural insularity as well as my comparative approach in this work. To this black teenager my identity as an Italian American transcended the color of my skin. He associated being Italian with not being white. In this way, he, an African American, positioned me, an Italian American, out of the category that makes a person white in the United States at the beginning of the twenty-first century in a urban, multiethnic, and multiracial environment such as that of Buffalo, an "All America City," as the sign along Highway 90 before entering the city reads. Secondly, that kid used the past tense, "I knew." The premise of his understanding and subsequent definition of my identity as nonwhite because I am an Italian American lay in the past, or at least his version of the past, which is to say, a version of the past seen from the perspective of an African American that in turn defines his present. The young age of this African American person is irrelevant. If anything, it speaks volumes about the contemporaneity of such past, the pastness of the past, as T. S. Eliot would put it. Regardless of the kind of knowledge upon which he based his understanding and definition of my identity, whether it was life experiences, his historical memory, or stories that he heard or that he was told, his knowledge preceded my verbal unveiling of my Italian American identity and reacted to it. Only *after* I told him that I was Italian was he able to dig into his past, his experience and his history, and define me as nonwhite, unlike other white ethnic groups of European origins, such as the Irish and the Polish (the other major European Catholic ethnic groups—though non-Mediterranean—to which he attributed an antagonist whiteness in the first place).

The disclosure of my identity as an Italian American triggered a mechanism in this black person. It is not difficult to understand the reason for it. He defined me as an Italian American by negation because as a black person he knew that, in prototypical modern fashion, he was defined by negation too. He knew that his blackness mattered and defined him because of some-one else's whiteness and because of his country's whiteness. In his eyes, the eyes of a person who knows what not being white means in the United States, being Italian meant not being white, which obviously to him meant somehow sharing a not-aligned subject position as nonwhite people that did not solely depend on color; having a commonality; belonging to a way of being not shared by white people of European origins. Nonetheless, being Italian American did not equal being of another color.

I doubt that that Buffalo kid knew that his definition of an Italian American by negation resembled Robert Orsi's theory of the "in-betweenness" of the Italian Americans, a term that the historian of Catholics in the United States borrowed from John Hingham's *Strangers in the Land: Patterns of American Nativism, 1860–1925*. Orsi uses the term to underscore how "Italian-American history began in racially inflected circumstances every-where in the United States" (314). Drawing on folklore, social history, and his fieldwork on what used to be the section of New York City called Italian Harlem, as well as his background as a second-generation Italian American from the Bronx, as a northeasterner, Orsi concludes that the Italian immi-grants to the United States became Italian Americans once they learned that becoming white in America granted privileges that were otherwise denied to them. Italians learned how to become white and changed accordingly in order to acquire those privileges. This transition into whiteness indicates that on the one hand being white is not uniquely a matter of pigmentation. Like any identity, this too is an unfixed, unstable identity, one subject to change. On the other, that transformation tells us that being Italian and living according to what such identity historically entailed at the time of the major Italian immigration to the United States between the late nineteenth and the early twentieth centuries signified a vicinity to those excluded from the benefits of being a white individual in America. This proximity of ways of being and living, we might say of civilization, extended beyond the color line just as the kid's definition of my identity and, conversely, his identity linked the two aspects.

I examine this proximity and the resulting association first of all by focus-ing on the investment of black male writers in Italian Americans and the response of Italian American writers and artists to blackness in the twenti-eth century. More specifically, I link both this investment and the response to it to the popular humanism of the Mediterranean civilization, the every-day-life ways of being and acting that the Italian immigrants brought with them from Central and Southern Italy, where the vast majority of them came from, and read them against the white intellectual tradition that convention-ally defines modernism and transatlantic modernity. All this, I argue, is what made Italian Americans attractive to African Americans. In essence, my view is that this historically overlooked and, for the most part, critically unexamined encounter offers a hybrid, transnational model of modernity capable of producing democratic forms of aesthetics, social consciousness, and political economy, including an enlarged, non-solely color-based notion of race. This concept of modernity avoids the trap of the theorization of a postracial society whose main goal is to do away with the classist structure of a capitalist society of which race is a constant reminder.

The story of this engagement is a modern story, one that belongs to twentieth-century modernity, the dynamic process upon and to which it depends and responds. It is what Marshall Berman defines as a vital experience of "space and time, of the self and the other, of life's possibilities and perils," a "unity of disunity" typical of a society that operates within the constraints of a capitalist regime of production, consumption, and commodification of social relations that increasingly tends to flatten and shrink the view of modernity and what being modern can signify (15). From different angles and in different ways, this tendency seems to be crucial in the critical evaluations of the relationship between modernity and culture in the Western world. For example, in *The Black Atlantic*, Paul Gilroy invites his readers to go beyond the canonical black-and-white dichotomy of our humanism, what he refers to as "the symbolism of colour," and argues for the recognition and the promotion of the hybridization of modern cultural formations (1). Gilroy sees the struggle of black people to be perceived "as people with cognitive capacities and even an intellectual history" as one of the problems of Western humanism altogether, thus extending chronologically and culturally the restricting tendency of modernity that Berman conceptualizes (6). From a strictly theoretical position, Agnes Heller agrees that this is precisely the distinctive feature of modernity in the West. Its universalization is "the elimination of distinction," which explains also the reasons as to why she writes that modernity is already postmodern. "The postmodern perspective could perhaps be best described as the self-reflective consciousness of modernity" (46, 4). This preoccupation with the condition of our modernity is also behind Kenneth Warren's attempt to declare an end to African American literature in *What Was African American Literature?*

The idea to dig up the story of the engagements of two groups of people commonly considered the opposite of one another responds to the intent of thinking differently about the possibilities of modernity. In this respect *In the Name of the Mother* is not properly a study of ethnicity and race, let alone of Italian American and, to a lesser extent, African American identity. To assert otherwise would be to fall prey to the same diminishing view that I argue against. Insofar as this book attempts to deal with Italian American and African American identities, it does it in the Gramscian sense of the "historical process" that according to the Sardinian-born intellectual deposits in people "an infinity of traces, without leaving an inventory" that "must therefore be made at the outset" (326).[1] The story of Italian Americans and African Americans that I present here is one of the traces of the inventory of the twentieth century.

The lack of any substantial critical study of this topic, from the perspective of either side in question, seems to me equally symptomatic of the previously mentioned modern tendency as well as of the degree of contemporaneity of Gramsci's reflection. It also highlights the necessity to start filling this gap, especially with regard to the experience of the Italian Americans in the United States. More than twenty years after Orsi's article and in spite of the flourishing of both African American and Italian American studies as academic disciplines, we lack still a critical study in the field. One would think that the sheer number of Italian Americans and African Americans in the country, almost forty-five million people,[2] would be a good enough reason to demand an account of their interactions or lack thereof. More to the point, it would be next to impossible to deny the artistic and literary accomplishments of these two groups, which along with their Jewish American peers have left indelible marks on twentieth-century American culture.

Fred Gardaphé provides a short summary of the paucity of works of this subject in a short essay called "Invisible People: Shadows and Light in Italian American Culture." As the title of the essay indicates, Gardaphé recognizes how crucial blackness and the initially contested racial status of Italian Americans still are in the life of this group today. Gardaphé contends that the refusal of Italian Americans to account for this defining aspect of their past results in their self-propelled invisibility: "Italian Americans are invisible people. Not because people refuse to see them, but because, for the most part, they refuse to be seen" (1). Italian Americans are willfully oblivious of the racial otherness of their past and pass as white because they do not want to be seen as nonwhite, which is exactly how the African American kid in the Buffalo public library saw me as soon as I told him that I was Italian. Gardaphé questions Richard Gambino's thesis of the incompatibility of the African American and Italian American communities because of their supposed "diametrically opposed value systems" (3). Gardaphé recalls historian Rudolph J. Vecoli's thesis on the incompleteness of the Italians' whiteness in his essay "Are the Italian Americans Just Plain White Folks?" However, he also points out that the Italian Americans achieved whiteness. And yet, Gardaphé notices how the institutional medial representation of Italian Americans hardly projects an image that evokes full assimilation, let alone white respectability, the ultimate cipher of whiteness. Indeed, such representations often display a persistent, subtle, and vastly unacknowledged contemporary form of cosmetically well-packaged prejudice. Italian Americans, Gardaphé concludes, are accepted as white folks as long as they behave accordingly, accept their distorted image in the media, and obey corporate America's structurally racist culture. This, along with the loss of the Italian language, and, I would add, the many dialects that the immigrants spoke, is the price of the ticket for Italian Americans: hiding who you were and your past and, therefore, who you are and your present in exchange for the benefits that whiteness guarantees in the United States.

Whereas Orsi thematizes the impact of blackness and modernity on Italian Americans along the line of identity, Gardaphé historicizes it. Both scholars recognize the centrality of blackness for Italian Americans at some level, as if America and modernity granted to them in the first place a racial status, one that they learned to adjust to, at least publicly. Neither of these scholars, however, conceptualizes this triangulation. What happens when we account for the racial part of the Italian Americans' past in relation to the larger issue of the reducing proclivity of twentieth-century modernity and the subject position of Italian Americans in relation to that of African Americans? One methodological way to go about this task is to look at how Italians benefited from the structure of whiteness, which is Thomas A. Guglielmo's thesis in *White on Arrival*. As informative and accurate, as well as geographically and theoretically localized, as this study is, it does not add much to what we already know in terms of the conceptualization of the issues in question. What seems to me more beneficial is to look at what happens when the other by definition in the United States, African Americans, look at Italian Americans. What do they see in them? How do they see them? What does this tell us about Italian Americans and America? Does this approach increase our knowledge of African American culture? And, if it does, how is this achieved? What is at stake in this interplay with regard to the overall modern development of the United States? Conversely, how does this dialectics intersect the identity of the two groups? How did the Italian American presence alter the racial mosaic of the United States and, consequently, the way African Americans think about themselves, perhaps even see themselves? Last but not least, in what forms does the otherness of the Italians manifest itself when we see the Italians through the lenses of African Americans?

To answer these and other questions I pursue what used to be called contextual criticism. I try to set the literary works of art, the cultural artifacts, and the performances of popular musical acts in their wider contexts, at once historical and psychological as well as geographical and economic. My goal is to evaluate the artistic vision that the material under examination projects as well as its underlying political economy. Ideally, this approach would like to start recuperating history to a project that envisions a humanism from below that does away with the modal typological type of liberal democracy that translates in either Success-America (in whatever form: assimilation, rags-to-riches story, cult of gratitude, achievement of middle-class status) or failure (damnation, marginalization, left-behind). I favor the idea of an ever-evolving humanism, conscious of its limitations and imperfections, that consequently entails conflict. Such humanism does not expect to do away with its tradition. Neither does it propose an antitradition of traditionlessness à la Whitman or Twain. In this perspective, I have found it beneficial to pay attention to the symbols, the symbolic forms, and the symbolic domains that the cultures in question expose and negotiate. I am not by any means claiming or invoking a return to the School of Myth and Symbol, although, as a scholar trained in comparative literature, I claim this school's opened view of culture, intimate knowledge of literatures other than American literature in English, acquaintance, if not mastery of languages other than English, and familiarity with international critical traditions as well as the centrality of capitalism as a system of social relations in the analysis of Western cultures and literatures.

If anything, my emphasis on symbols, symbolic forms, and symbolic domains is concerned more with the materiality of their modes of production. In *Symbolic Economies*, Jean-Joseph Goux points out how modern society "has divorced economic practices from their diffuse symbolic valences" (122). What Goux extracts from what might otherwise appear to be a common observation is the notion that modes of exchange and of production are also *"modes of symbolizing"* that uncover hegemonic formations, what he calls a "socially dominant form of consciousness which is determined by a specific mode of symbolizing" (68, 75–76). The French theorist argues that these modes repress other ideologies and forms of consciousness, another example of modernity's propensity to reduce and limit. Thus, by reversing Goux's assertion, by looking at how modes of symbolizing are also modes of production and of exchange, we might be able to begin to see the dimensions of other ideologies and forms of consciousness that the Italian immigrants brought to the United States and their offspring experienced and, at least at times, internalized and transformed in the American scene as they confronted blackness.

I am also mindful of Peter Stallybrass and Allon White's observation on the construction of subjectivity by way of exclusion of the other, which results in the *"socially* peripheral" becoming "so frequently *symbolically* central" (5) and their adaptation of Barbara Babcock's notion of symbolic inversion, which "may be broadly defined as any act of expressive behavior which inverts, contradicts, abrogates, or in some fashion presents an alternative to commonly held cultural codes, values, and norms be they linguistic, literary or artistic, religious, social and political" (quoted in Stallybrass and White, 17).

The semantic fluidity of the cultural formations and interplays that I discuss throughout the book demands an equally fluid notion of class—especially pertinent in a comparative work whose content is defined by migratory movements that affected the physical as well as the mental relocation and dislocation of millions of people, both Italians and African Americans, an element that reverberates in generation after generation of descendants of the original migratory people, however differently. This notion E. P. Thompson defines in *The Making of the English Working Class*. Class, writes the British social historian, is "a historical phenomenon, unifying a number of disparate and seemingly unconnected events, both in raw material of experience and in consciousness." Thompson does not see class "as 'structure,' nor even as a 'category,' but as something which in fact happens (and can be shown to have happened) in human relationship . . . the notion of class entails the notion of historical relationship" (9). I find this definition especially useful in order to look at the Italian American experience and the ways in which it related to African Americans and vice versa in a self-constituted narrative intended to form modern people.

Central to this self-constitution is the figure and the position of the Italian American proletarian woman and mother trope, which I consider as a social identity that specific social and cultural codes determined. One especially important code is her relationality of origins that I trace back to her cosmic, Mediterranean view of the world and human life, a view that includes the impossibility of partitioning motherhood and sexuality and her unmediated relation to her body, which made her especially disturbing and a radically subversive figure because it clashed with the social and cultural codes of whiteness. As such, it also provided a link to African Americans in the way this feminine relationality is internalized by design by her male descendants in order to cross the color line especially, although not exclusively, in the realm of popular music. A quick example is when in *Mount Allegro* Jerre Mangione recalls the horrified looks of white Americans as they see Italian American women breastfeeding their children in the public park of Rochester, New York. Mangione's anecdote entails the historical return of the repressed that stands in between the maternal and the sexual in early twentieth-century America. We can also look at Mangione's recollection as the cipher of the social and psychic conflict that the Italian American woman and mother can and, at times, does unchain, which we will examine by following her evolution from emigrant to Italian American.

Such discomfort, to put it mildly, should not surprise. Historically, in the United States the relationality of the sexual and the maternal is especially subversive. Politically speaking, we are a father-centered nation that constantly celebrates its patriarchal origins. We have Founding Fathers and not Founding Mothers. We promote individualism (never mind the definition of it) as a male product that the mythology of the self-made man signifies. The historical omission spills into the social realm rhetorically, as the mirror of social policies. Notoriously, we have welfare queens, or so we are told, but not welfare kings, although politically we constituted ourselves by way of rebelling against a kingdom, which confers to this antifemale rhetoric an egregious psychic dimension. Even our swearing vocabulary, the cipher of a people's common culture, is indicative of the extent to which the sexual and the maternal unsettle the national subconscious. A symbol of the seeming inviolability of the mother, our favorite expletive testifies instead to the sacredness of the man's incorporative agency over the woman, her concomitant sexual neutralization, and what Sacvan Bercovitch has called *The Puritan Origins of the American Self* (1975), as the title of his grand study of colonial American literature reads. Even the enduring success of Francis Ford Coppola's *The Godfather*, to stick with one of the cultural artifacts that I am working with here, speaks to the religiously inflected erasure of the sexual and the maternal.

Where is, so to speak, our *The Godmother*? Or, better yet, why have we not been able to see the (God)mothers we actually have? One possible explanation is that a vision of modernity from the proletarian female and maternal standpoint might enact subversive processes of modernization and a humanism that gradually reposition subject positions in the development of twentieth-century modernity. Contrary to the stereotypical image of the homebound mother tending to her family, the hegemonic male-dominated white culture of Protestant origin perceived the Italian immigrant women and mothers as subversive figures, especially because of the politics of sharing that guided their everyday life practices. The communitarian, inclusive, and other-directed practices these women brought to this side of the Atlantic along with their cosmic view of the world that did not separate people and their environments, neither concretely nor mentally, might represent a repository of ways of viewing and being in the world that foster a way of being modern that solicits inclusion and rejects the view of modernity as the total sum of productivity, self-interested individualism, and consumption. Their consciousness originated in the practice of mutuality and reciprocity that is antithetical and incompatible with such a view of modernity. In other words, their "I" contained many "we"s. Let me be clear on this specificity of the

Italian immigrant women. I am not arguing in favor of an Italian immigrant women exceptionalism that is magically subversive and makes these women unique and unlike any other women and mothers. Neither, of course, am I arguing that other immigrant and ethnic female figures lack a specificity of their own. What I am after, rather, is a map that shows the incompatibility between these women's way of being and seeing the world and twentieth-century capitalist modernity in the United States, which resulted in a specific kind of female subversion.

In this respect, the reader may wonder why a book whose title and theoretical presuppositions indicate a seeming gender preference deals with a substantial, although by no means exclusive, male authorship. There are several reasons, some of which I would like to enumerate, however briefly. To begin with, there is the question of who produces and publishes what and whom, over which I have no control, except dealing also with less common texts and authors. To think that cultural criticism can counterweigh the power of major publishing corporations or Hollywood is the worst form of intellectual and political self-delusion. This, of course, does not mean to abdicate the role of the critic as opener of new critical spaces, which is how I envision the critic's role. It means being conscious of the material circumstances under which one works. It also means to recognize that media are developments of the forces of productions that shape social relationship, archives of the ideology of reality. Thus, one has to address what haunts the public psyche. The first and the second *Godfather* movies inhabit the popular imagination as hardly any other Italian American work of art does. As such, they are inescapable artifacts that must be confronted, especially if one aspires to do away with certain issues that they raise.

This inevitability, as it were, raises the question of the canon. Any work of criticism responds to the established canon. At the same time, any such study has the potential to produce a canon of its own by way of types of reading one presents along with the additions and subtractions of certain texts. This exercise is the outcome of one's politics and aesthetic sense. *In the Name of the Mother* is no different. Thus, I offer less common, if not entirely unorthodox, readings of canonical works such as Mangione's *Mount Allegro*, Puzo's and Coppola's *The Godfather* and the latter's *The Godfather Part II*, and Don DeLillo's *Underworld*. Equally atypical is my reading of some canonical African American texts written during Jim Crow such as James Weldon Johnson's *The Autobiography of an Ex-Colored Man*, along with less studied ones such as Richard Bruce Nugent's *Gentleman Jigger*, where I focus on the representations of Italian Americans rather than black Americans. Some of the authors or performances that I have selected, instead, have gone and continue to go unjustifiably unrecognized, if not entirely forgotten. For example, Michael DeCapite's novel *Maria* continues to lie, covered in dust, on the shelves of the libraries that are lucky enough to have a copy of it. DeCapite's first book is the perfect example of the ways that first-rate male authors and artists portrayed women. It also offers the possibility to see the subversive potential as well as the political limits of the question of female and maternal relationality and the structures of twentieth-century modernity as hardly any Italian American female novelist succeeded in doing. Trying to understand what male writers and artists do when they speak in the name of the mother does not necessarily mean to deny female subjectivity. On the contrary, it can be an opportunity to come to terms with the political history of twentieth-century modernity that might help display the overwhelming obstacles that women, including women writers, encountered in getting their voices heard. To quote once again Goux, "between woman and mother there is nothing but a rift that tells the whole story *of the masculine history of the symbolic*" (243; his emphasis). From this perspective, the culture here under examination becomes a method to look at the masculine history of the symbolic. Ultimately, however, the idea underlying my reading and selection of literary texts, cultural artifacts, and popular performances is to put the voices of their makers in a continuous dialogue that responds to the idea that no culture, no matter the hegemony, is ever monolithic and separated in autonomous, inward directed, and noncommunicative spheres.

It is on this turf and along these conceptual and methodological lines that I work out the encounter between Italian Americans and African Americans and the development of their relationship. In terms of chronology, we have a first example of such a meeting in William Dean Howells's 1872 *Suburban Sketches*. Thematically speaking, however, the connection appears for the first time with a prominent role in Mark Twain's *Pudd'nhead Wilson*, the intriguing and complicated novel that Mr. Clemens sent to the press in 1893. The book belongs to what Henry Nash Smith, in a noted article on the future of American Studies, called the phase of Twain's career when he wrote from "the perspective of alienation," a dramatic shift from the times of *Adventures of Huckleberry Finn*, which Twain completed only three years before *Pudd'nhead Wilson* (6). According to Smith, Twain's shift "has long been a capital problem of criticism" and "is an equally important problem of cultural history," two problems that he intertwined and that in his view cannot be solved separately (6). Despite the scholarship industry on Twain produced since 1957, the year of publication of Smith's essay, the Texan critic's point seems to me still relevant as cultural history, perhaps less so with regard to criticism.

One of the reasons for *Pudd'nhead Wilson*'s lasting significance is the role of the Italian twins Luigi and Angelo Capello in the novel's overarching theme, which is that most modern theme of appearance and reality, illusion and facts, self-deception and the truth. The Italian twins, who initially represent European bourgeois humanism, end up embodying the regressing racial realities of post-Reconstruction America that the rest of the text discloses as the central paradox of modern America. This paradox Twain was culturally unequipped to reckon with. It was one thing to reject the old European culture and tackle the public issue of slavery as he did in *Adventures of Huckleberry Finn*. It was a totally different question to deal with the new racial and political realities of post-Reconstruction. They required literary tools totally different from the ones available to Mr. Clemens, as the ambiguous presence of the Italian twins in the tale indicates.

Twain was neither a true realist nor a naturalist writer, as he knew all too well. For this reason he reversed the clock of the novel backward in time to 1830, the time of slavery in the little town of Dawson's Landing, Missouri, situated on the Mississippi River. In a way, it was his best attempt at naturalism. In another, perhaps more significant way, he reminded his readers living the post-Reconstruction racial crisis of the late 1800s that the westward expansion of the early part of the century, which gave all white male citizens the right to vote, was predicated on the slave system just as Jeffersonian democracy was. It might be profitable to recall that when the novel was published, slavery was no longer the central public issue of the nation, and the western frontier had been officially declared closed for three years. The year the novel reached the marketplace, historian Frederick Jackson Turner published his seminal essay on the significance of the frontier in American history. Of course, setting chronology back is also an old literary trick that a writer employs to address current political realities and situate them historically. One such example is Alessandro Manzoni's *The Betrothed* (1821), a novel that might have been in Twain's mind. After all, he wrote most of *Pudd'nhead Wilson* while he was living in Florence. However, there was another, more compelling reason as to why Italy was much in his mind when he composed the book.

This reason was the concomitant political crisis between his native and his hosting countries, caused by the lynching of eleven Italians and Italian Americans in New Orleans. In 1890, an unidentified group of men killed New Orleans chief of police David Hennessy, a thirty-two-year-old man with serious political ambitions. Richard Gambino writes that the chief's would-be rescuer, Billy O'Connor, reported that before his last breath, Hennessy whispered in his ears that "the dagoes" had shot him (4). As often in history, words turned into bullets or, in this case, ropes, as they unleashed the ferocious anti-Italian sentiment prevalent in the Crescent City at the time and on the rise in the rest of the country. Anti-Italianism had strong economic and racial underpinnings in New Orleans. Since their arrival in Louisiana in the early 1870s, the Italians, for the most part Sicilian peasants, had turned lands that native landowners considered worthless into profitable enterprises. Slowly, the Italians had become a relevant economic group in New Orleans, further altering the original power structure of the white elite that the early phase of Reconstruction had somewhat already disrupted. What made matters worse in the eyes of the white ruling class was that a significant aspect of the economic growth of the Italians was their mutual commerce with African Americans, which, in typical American fashion, turned the Italians from "dagos" to "*black* dagos." The Italians' crossing of the color line did not stop at the cashier. In 1888 the daily *Lantern* lamented that any Sicilian girl falling for a black man was one too many even for what was considered the sexually promiscuous New Orleans. Whether this kind of interaction was calculated economic advantage or natural human tendencies, or both, the white elite perceived it as an alteration in the existing social and economic relationships at a time when the white solidarity movement aimed at erasing all the progress that Reconstruction and the rising labor movement had achieved since the Civil War. Historian George E. Cunningham has concluded that Italians were perceived as a "hindrance to white solidarity," as the title of his essay has it.

When the jury acquitted the nineteen Italians and Italian Americans that had been expediently rounded up after the killing of Chief Hennessy, anti-Italianism turned into bloodshed. Cunningham writes that some of the leaders of the city's white elite led the assault of a mob of over twenty thousand people, including some blacks and women, on the city's prison where the "dagoes" were kept for security reasons, with what a reporter of the *Times-Democrat* described as "low, repulsive countenances" and in "slavery attire" (26). The result was the greatest lynching in American history. Richard Gambino states that the killing of the Italian men was especially gruesome, to the point that gender made no difference: "Some of the women of the city came and dipped their lace handkerchiefs in their [the victims] blood as souvenirs" (87). By the time Twain sent *Pudd'nhead Wilson* to the press, the lynching had become both a national and an international affair. The lynching provoked the Italian government's formal protest. Rumors of war circulated on both sides of the Atlantic hemisphere. People from all over the United States as well as from Ireland and England volunteered to enlist in the American armed forces in the event of a war with Italy. As it is often the case, this time too American foreign policy was the projection of unresolved national issues. Seemingly, a foreign policy affair with strong anti-Italian underpinnings had reunited the North and the South. In reality, racism had reunited what racism had divided.

The lynching was mythologized immediately. Richard Asbury recalls that a popular song called "Hennessy Avenged" referred to the Italians as "assassins . . . from a foreign soil" and praised the white people of Louisiana who had shown "our Southern blood" (421). A more racially nuanced theme instead underscores the popular short story based on the event titled "The New Orleans Mafia; or, Chief of Police Hennessy Avenged," which appeared in number 439 of the first volume of the *New York Detective Library* on April 25, 1891, a little over a month after the lynching. The short story associated the dark complexion of the Italians with their supposed natural predisposition to violence, the defining trait of their Mediterranean identity in the mind of white Americans. However, this description includes a religious underpinning, one that aims at locating the Italians outside of Christianity, which, of course, in the United States means outside of Protestantism, or, better yet, to identify Christianity with Protestantism: "Sicilians have always been the most bloody-minded and revengeful of the Mediterranean races. These traces were probably owing to their Saracen origin, murder and intrigue being natural with them" (9).

Mr. Clemens never forgot that he had two hands. With one he wrote fiction, journalism, and, occasionally, literary criticism. With the other he kept count of his perennially unstable finances. In other words, he always kept a close eye on the economy of the places where he lived and those he visited. When he stopped in New Orleans in 1888, the year the *Lantern* lamented the Italian girls' infatuation for black men, he must have taken notes with both hands as he observed that the city was economically thriving, a fact that partly reflected the rising racially and ethnically mixed economy, whose racial ramifications he tried to exploit in *Pudd'nhead Wilson*. Eric J. Sundquist has put it in this way: "It is inconceivable that Twain was not impressed by the Italo-American crisis and the light it cast on the blurring of the color line caused by the non-Anglo immigrant races," a comment that in the first place points toward the intertwining of the political dimension of the racial status of the Italians in the United States and the social impact of their racial identity (69).

That Twain wrote with the New Orleans lynching in his mind seems to me more than conceivable—it seems likely. The engine of the novel is the swapping of two infants. Roxy, a slave woman who looks white because she is only one-sixteenth black, fears that her master will sell her and her son Chambers, who is one-thirty-second black and whiter than she is, "down the river." Thus, she decides to swap Chambers and Tom, the son of her master, who are of the same age and look remarkably alike. By so doing, she frees Chambers from slavery and guarantees him a life of privilege. Tellingly, privilege turns the "new" Tom into a selfish and dissolute "white" person with a gambling habit that gets him into serious debt. After Tom kills the man who adopted him after "his" father died, his uncle Judge Driscoll, and engineers the plan to accuse Angelo and Luigi as the real murderers, Twain comments: "The town was bitter against the unfortunates [the Italian twins], and for the first few days after the murder they were in constant danger of being lynched" (119). Initially, Twain introduces the twins as singers of Florentine noble heritage, reflections of the typical Northern European bourgeois romanticized *image* of Italy as a cultural product to consume, which the citizens of the little town do by listening to the twins singing, and therefore of immense fascination to those same white citizens of Dawson's Landing, where no tourist has ever stopped before. "Italians! How romantic! Just think, ma—there's never been one in this town, and everybody will be dying to see them, and they're all *ours!* Think of that," exclaims Rowena to Aunt Patsy, the woman who is going to lodge the twins (32). This, of course, is a mask that Twain puts on the twins, as he tells us further into the tale. When Tom verbally scolds Luigi, not coincidentally the darker of the twins, during a political meeting between pro- and anti-rum parties, Twain writes, "Luigi's *southern* blood leaped to the boiling-point in a moment" (70; my italics). The adjective serves to indicate the geography of origin of the twin. As such, it also functions as a tool to unveil Luigi's racial identity and the (stereo) typical traits inscribed onto the racialization of the Italians.

Not even the most rabid American nativist of the late 1890s, in fact, would consider Dante's hometown a part of Southern Italy. In other words, Luigi is neither from Florence nor of noble heritage. He is wearing a mask. He is a Southern Italian. That is to say, he is by nature prone to violence, irrational, even animalistic because his skin color is not much fairer than that of his one-thirty-second-black accuser that the reality created by virtue of "law and fiction" turned white, and, therefore, of lower class than his accuser. Once the mask is down—and the mask comes down when, just as in New Orleans in 1890, a powerful white man, a man of an institution theoretically devoted to preserve the social harmony of a community, Judge Driscoll, is killed and somebody makes false accusations—so are the intricacies of whiteness. Tom laments to Wilson, the young lawyer who eventually will unmask Tom's real racial identity, that his uncle wanted him "to challenge that darned Italian savage," which he, wearing the white mask he knows at this point in the book that his mother put on him, will not do (78). When he tries to convince Wilson that the five-hundred-dollar Indian knife that the twins say has been stolen, a knife that he has in fact stolen, does not exist, he tells Wilson, "But they are strangers making their way in a new community" (95). Finally, Tom convinces his uncle that the only reason why he did not challenge Luigi is that Luigi is a "confessed assassin," the perpetrator of an unfortunate but noble act that Luigi's brother, Angelo, confirmed his twin brother committed (96).

The trajectory of the Italian twins goes from plural to singular; from welcome Florentine nobles and singers who embody a romanticized image of Italy, to strangers making their way in a new community, to assassins. This path starts with sought-out white respectability necessary to be accepted in the white world of Dawson's Landing and ends with a non-solely color-based form of racial discrimination, as Judge Driscoll's closing speech of his political campaign against the twins toward the end of the book points out. The Judge scoffs at Luigi and Angelo on the basis of their otherness. He singles them out as "adventurers, mountebanks, side-show riff-raff, dime museum freaks." He assails "their showy titles with measureless derision" (104). Finally, he delivers the ultimate blow, the one that matters the most here, when he takes down their mask and, by so doing, *his* white mask: "He said they were back-alley barbers *disguised* as nobilities, pea-nut peddlers *masquerading* as gentlemen, organ-grinders bereft of their *brother*-monkey" (104; my italics). This is not 1830s political rhetoric. This is end-of-the-nineteenth-century nativist anti-Italian hysteria turned into bloody reality in the 1891 New Orleans lynching, a reality that continued for decades, especially in the South and the West of the country.

One of the elderly men who according to Leslie Fiedler defines Dawson's Landing as a society "defined by the fathers" intent to preserve their Anglo heritage, Judge Driscoll takes the mask away from the twins and replaces it with another one as part of the constant theme of the double that Twain enjoys throughout the book (81). The new mask is a combination of class devaluation, status degradation, and subtle racism that associates the twins with the animal character that the society of fathers traditionally projected onto black Americans. In other words, in the white eyes of the society of the fathers, black Americans and the Italian immigrants belong to each other, or at least to the same sociocultural ovaries, so to speak. The society of fathers locates the Italians along the "other" side of the chromatic racial mosaic of America. Equally important, the Italian twins set in motion a kind of racial conflict within the society of fathers of Dawson's Landing that locates blackness onto the Italians through the assassination of the Judge. Blacks and Italians become partners in crime.

In the end, Twain did not develop this issue. A secularized southern liberal Calvinist working in the North, he found it comfortable to turn the twins into birds of passage and send them back to Europe, although, conveniently and tellingly, neither to Florence nor another named location. Yet—and this is the reason of this brief textual analysis of *Pudd'nhead Wilson* in this introduction—he provided some of the information for the thematic map of

the encounter between Italian Americans and African Americans that we
will draw in what follows. First of all, the Italian Americans' acceptance is
contingent upon fluctuating social components and fixed power structures.
Second, such contingency signals also a passage into the world of the fathers
that sexual impotence and death connote. Third, in the society of fathers that
fails and is failed by its sons, the Italian American man replaces the black
man as an agent of deadly violence, which is also a form of racial alignment
and the defining feature of Italian American masculinity. In absence of a
black man, the Italian American will step up to the stage for the white audience and play the surrogate black murderer. After all, the nonbiological parricide of *Pudd'nhead Wilson*, which is to say the social parricide of the norms
and the behaviors upheld in the novel, is perpetrated with the knife of the
Italian twins. One of the ways we can read the twins' role in *Pudd'nhead
Wilson* is as a fictional parody of the New Orleans lynching, which was directed toward the Italians in order to continue the ongoing economic and
political disenfranchisement of black Americans as well as, nightmare of all
American nightmares, the forging of a working-class interracial and intra-
cultural alliance between the former slaves and the immigrants that represented a "hindrance to white solidarity."

Paradoxically—and paradoxes are good historical indexes—one of the
persons who feared the most such a hindrance was the most powerful black
man at the time of the Italian immigration to the United States between the
end of the nineteenth and the onset of the twentieth centuries, Booker T.
Washington, whose account of his visit to Europe and Southern Italy in a
rarely discussed book titled *The Man Farthest Down* opens the first chapter
of this study. In it, I compare Washington's observations of Southern Italy
and Southern Italian women and Emanuele Crialese's 2006 film *Nuovomondo* about the immigrant saga of a Sicilian family, a comparison that
serves to lay out the theoretical presuppositions of the book as well as its
periodization. Washington's volume inscribes within the modern discourse
of the West a new geo-cultural, Afro-Mediterranean region by way of linking Southern Italy to Africa, and Southern Italian women to black slaves in
pre–Civil War America. Symbolically and rhetorically, he detaches Southern
Italy and its poorest inhabitants from Europe and the Eurocentric, patriarchal dominant discourse of the time. However, Washington reinscribes this
discourse within the eugenics-inflected instrumental logic that governs the
bio-politics of immigration to the United States that he proposes as the liberating force of modernity. Fortunata Mancuso, the female protagonist of
Crialese's movie, destabilizes and subverts the boundaries of this bio-politics
of immigration. Symbolically speaking, this woman epitomizes the foundational position of the Italian proletarian immigrant woman in her relation-

ship to modernity—the New World of the motion picture's title—which the other female figures analyzed in these pages develop and define.

In chapter 2, I read Jerre Mangione's memoir *Mount Allegro* as the encounter between the ancient democratic traditions of the Mediterranean world, the political economy of immigrant life in Rochester, and the world of blackness that the author finds in his parents' hometown during the celebration of Saint Calogero, a black saint whose blackness Mangione connects to the racial otherness of the Italian Americans and to the jazz music that he and his siblings and friends play at home, with parental approval. Such an encounter allows Mangione to show the incompatibility between whiteness and the political economy of immigrant life in the United States, which is based on the Southern Italian notion of *rispetto* that prioritizes cooperation, mutuality, the primacy of the public space, the recognition of the other, and inclusive social relations over the logic of monetary profit.

Next comes a group of African American male writers that includes James Weldon Johnson, Richard Bruce Nugent, Sterling Brown, William Attaway, Willard Motley, and James Baldwin who use representations of Italian immigrants and Italian Americans to (re)negotiate difference and social normativity during Jim Crow. I argue in chapter 3 that these writers invest in Italian American men to reinvent blackness as a non-solely color-based issue and reposition the class racial struggle of their time. Italian American men allowed these writers to enact representational strategies of appropriation and subversion to build a version of the black male self during Jim Crow that would have been otherwise unavailable to them. The Italian American presence helped these novelists and poets to address and challenge the (stereo)typical formulaic representation of black Americans. For these six black intellectuals, Italian Americans serve to represent the complexity of the human condition, including homosexuality, for African American men in the context of and as a part of the modern American scene.

Chapter 4 traces the rise and fall of the Italian American gangster in Francis Ford Coppola's *The Godfather* and *The Godfather Part II*, Don DeLillo's *Underworld*, and Frank Lentricchia's *The Music of the Inferno*. I see Don Corleone as the signifier of the transformation and the contradictions of the gangster from the racial, working-class "other" refusing to play by the capitalist rules that the gangster embodied in the first few decades of the past century to white power broker in the last part of it. Partly as an answer to Coppola's development of the Godfather trope, DeLillo's and Lentricchia's novels reinvent the Italian American gangster to decompose the historical unfolding of modernity in the United States and its ideological corollary, the success story of assimilation.

Chapter 5 focuses on a number of female characters named Maria in John Fante's *Wait until Spring, Bandini*, Mary Tomasi's *Like Lesser Gods*, Michael DeCapite's *Maria*, a selection of Bruce Springsteen's songs, and Carol Maso's *Ghost Dance*. Maria represents the trajectory girl-woman-mother. She characterizes the Italian American novel by way of representing the (re)construction of a set of causal relations that recalls the personal and collective history of twentieth-century immigrant struggles. Her repeated manifestations recuperate and adapt the Mediterranean, nondoctrinal Catholic sense of the communal reality of men and women, their shared destiny, and their mutual responsibility and reciprocity. In symbolic terms, I view the Maria characters of these writings as the multifaceted literary development of Fortunata Mancuso.

I close this study with a consideration of the ways body language as a translator of historical memory in biracial performing partnerships triggers a process of mutual imaginative engagement that subverts the established symbolic domains of American racial politics. Specifically, I focus on Frank Sinatra's and Sammy Davis Jr.'s 1958 televised performance of "Me and My Shadow" and the photo of Bruce Springsteen and Clarence Clemons on the celebrated cover of Springsteen's *Born to Run* record, as well as their so-called soul kiss during their live performances.

In the Name of the Mother looks backward in order to look forward. In a very concrete sense, the world that made this book possible no longer exists. And yet it is precisely its disappearance that makes it available and tangible to us, a presence of the past and its unfulfilled possibilities, as well as of the promise of the present to be achieved. This temporal interplay reflects the book's basic assumption that people's humanity is always shared, especially when they might think that they have little, perhaps even nothing in common. Indeed, my belief is that there is no such a thing as absolute independence. After all, the reason why the stories of *In the Name of the Mother* overlap, often by way of juxtaposition, is that life is meant to be shared in order to acquire its full meaning, whatever that meaning is. In the end, the value of studying how different people choose to represent each other and what defines them as human beings is to help us to better understand ourselves and, consequently, gain a deeper understanding of the country we inhabit and the world around us.

1

NEW WORLD, OLD WOMAN:
OR, MODERNITY UPSIDE DOWN

THE ENCOUNTER BETWEEN Italian Americans and African Americans is an unacknowledged story of modernity, whose twentieth-century development it helped to define. A comparative mapping and assessment of how these people's literary and popular cultures painted this encounter and the relationships that it produced is the chief function and the subject of this study. My map does not begin in the canonical way, with the arrival of the Italian immigrants this side of the Atlantic between the end of the nineteenth and the dawn of the twentieth century—the largest segment of the European and Mediterranean migration to the United States. Neither does this story in the version that I present here adhere to the mainstream, to me unsatisfactory, narrative of assimilation, which, stated cruelly, is how the dagos came to the United States and became white, essentially at the expense of African Americans, what Toni Morrison has called the ethnic "surrender to whiteness" (57). On the contrary, it starts by following Booker T. Washington's 1910 trip to Europe in search of what he called *The Man Farthest Down*, as the title of the 1912 book that chronicles that experience, subtitled "A Record of Observation and Study in Europe," reads. In prototypical inverted modern fashion, after two months in Europe Washington concluded that the "man farthest down" was not a man. It was woman. A determining factor of his conclusions was the socioeconomic and cultural state of Central and Southern Italy, especially the condition of poor Southern Italian women who were leaving their native land for America, to whom he dedicated a substantial part of his thick volume.

Both thematically and structurally speaking, then, Washington's focus on the relation between poor Southern Italian women and modernity sets the tone of the African American investment in Italian immigrants and their descendants, the Italian Americans. Among the latter are the male and female writers and artists who helped define the Italian American experience by responding to the impact that blackness and African Americans had on it. The conceptualization and critical evaluation of this response is another goal of this book. For this reason, I will begin by reading Washington's Italian ruminations in juxtaposition with Emanuele Crialese's 2006 filmic saga of Southern Italian emigration to America called *Nuovomondo*, which also devotes a central role to female figures. This contrast serves us to establish the perimeter of the geo-historical region of culture that I address in this work. In particular, I will be concerned with the interplay between the factors that I posit as the coordinates of such region, which are the following: the inextricability of the race question from the historical trajectory of labor in the United States, which after the Civil War essentially becomes an ethnic and racial question, one of the processes of modernization that is actually still ongoing; the transoceanic interconnections between African Americans and the Italian diaspora to the United States; the symbolic detachment of Southern Italy from Europe; the African American writers' simultaneous orientalizing and racialization of the Southern Italian immigrants and what this tells us about the realignment and the redefinition of African American identity during the twentieth century; the presence of the mother as the organizing trope of this region; and, finally, the triangulation between modernity, African Americans, and what I call the Mediterranean humanism of the Italian immigrants and their offspring, a non-fixed cluster of bodily centered spirituality, instinctual class consciousness, sensuality, earthiness, unrestricted love of the body, and dialectical engagement with nature and the divine, the latter being a mix of pagan practices and Mediterranean popular Catholicism. I consider the racial aspect of this region a part of this humanism's subversive, yet *not* antimodern, reaction to modernity, as embodied by one of *Nuovomondo*'s main characters, Fortunata Mancuso, a fictional representative of the Southern Italian women that in so many ways affected Booker T. Washington, with whom we start our journey.

I

On August 20, 1910, the Wizard of Tuskegee embarked for Europe. He had already visited England and parts of Northern Europe with his wife a few years earlier, a sort of traditional Grand Tour that he described in his celebrated autobiography *Up from Slavery*, published in book form in 1901. On that occasion, he had been introduced to some of the political and cultural elites of several of the northern countries of Europe that he visited to consolidate further his reputation and promote the image of the United States as a nation that had made significant strives in the sphere of race relations. This time, however, he intended to visit all of the Old World and with a very different goal. He wanted to observe how the poor and the working classes of Europe lived, including those of Southern Italy. From there, immensely poor people were leaving for the United States every day. They had been doing it since the early 1880s, not long after the Kingdom of Sardinia had conquered the rest of the Italian peninsula, formed the Italian nation, exploited the lower classes, especially the peasants, and exterminated those who attempted to rebel usually by forming bands of brigands. They continued to leave on a daily basis, increasingly by the thousands, a phenomenon that interested the powerful and astute principal of Tuskegee, the headquarters of his operations whose lifelong goal was the gradual but steady and definite improvement and integration of his fellow black Americans in the social fabric of life in the United States, especially in the segregated South. In place of his wife, this time he was accompanied by his assistant Dr. Robert E. Park, who later dissociated himself from the ideas presented in *The Man Farthest Down*, where he appears officially as Washington's collaborator.

What fueled Washington's interest was the fact that many of those immigrants, as he noted at the beginning of the volume, reached the South of the New World, where they were hired to replace the former slaves in the sugar plantations and the cotton fields. The replacement of black labor with immigrant labor represented for some a solution to the race question in the South, something that threatened Washington's lifelong project. Fifteen years earlier, in his (in)famous speech at the Atlanta Exposition, he had invited the white elites to give work opportunities to black Americans instead of new immigrants. To accomplish this goal, he had played the nativist card. He had called the immigrants "those of foreign birth and strange tongue and habits," people inclined by nature to "strikes and labour wars." These people lacked the "fidelity and love" of black southerners, whom in contrast he had described as "the most patient, faithful, law-abiding, and unresentful people that the world has seen," whose "devotion" to white people was such as to make them ready to sacrifice their "lives, if need be, in defence of yours" (*Up*, 129). In other words, he had posited his anti-immigrant racism as a question of different civilizations. Perhaps almost twenty years of daily arrivals of immigrants had convinced him otherwise. Perhaps he had realized that the vast majority of those immigrants in those twenty years had actually settled in the urban North, the Midwest and the West of the country. Perhaps he had also figured out that soon enough his fellow southern blacks would follow the immigrants to those same areas by the millions.

Regardless, now he wanted to focus on what immigration meant to the race question. In the Atlanta speech he had pitted southern blacks against the new immigrants as a question of civilization and linked this difference to the question of labor. After his new trip to the old continent, he concluded that coming to terms with the movement of the masses from the Old to the New World was necessary in reconsidering the racial question in the United States. In the final pages of the book, Washington states that he undertook the journey to Europe searching for the man farthest down in the interest of gaining "some insights, and, perhaps, be able to throw some new light upon the situation of my own people in America" (*Man*, 390). In this way, he establishes a link between immigrants and African Americans. As in the Atlanta speech, he maintains that immigration and the racial question are two sides of the same coin, in the sense that they revolve around and are part of the larger question of labor, which to Washington is the question of what in *Up from Slavery* he calls "the markets of the world" (131). In *The Man Farthest Down*, however, he aligns the immigrants and African Americans. The immigrants become a tool to learn something about "the situation of my own people in America," a sort of reflection of the issues that plague African American life. Consequently, by linking the modern European and Mediterranean diaspora to the United States and the condition of black Americans, especially in the South, Washington indicates how both issues need to be viewed in the perspective of world history, in this specific case in a transatlantic perspective.

Thus we can look at and think of *The Man Farthest Down* as an extension of *Up from Slavery*, where Washington situates the encounter between immigrants and African Americans as the central issue of twentieth-century modernity in the United States and how this encounter might affect black Americans. Put differently, at issue is the question of modernity in the Western world at the onset of the past century and its implications for the future development of the United States, especially in terms of the gradual integration of black Americans in American life, Washington's lifelong goal. Modernity is the all-including theme of the book's inquiries, the one that the African American leader uses to frame the issue of the European and Mediterranean diaspora to the United States in the early twentieth century, the immigrants' adaptation in the New World, and what this means especially for the descendants of the African slaves. In *Up from Slavery* he had defined modernity as "a new era of industrial progress" (128). He had approached the issue from the internal point of view and the perspective of racial binarism. He had written that after the Civil War the freedmen and freedwomen overnight had been forced to grapple with the "the great questions the Anglo-Saxon race had been grappling [with] for centuries [which] had been thrown upon these people to be solved. These were the questions of a home, a living, the rearing of children, education, citizenship, and the establishment and support of churches" (12). The European and Mediterranean diaspora to the Americas led him to refashion the question of modernity from a different, transoceanic perspective. At the very least, such perspective presented those same questions in an even more complex dimension, the one that paradoxically he had attacked in the Atlanta speech. In one way, Washington was the victim of his own modernity. That was what led him to sail for Liverpool, England, and from there to reach the rest of Europe. He wanted to visit the future newcomers "in their homes, talk with them at their work, and to find out everything I could, not only in regard to their present situation, but also in regard to their future prospects, opportunities, hopes, and ambitions" (*Man*, 4). For him the diaspora was a moment in the global restructuring and realignment of capitalist modernity. Accordingly, he wanted to relate the effects of this movement of people on the black population in the United States. Of course, it did not escape his mind that some of the shamefully rich northeasterners that funded Tuskegee and his operations were also the owners of the railroads, the coal mines, and the factories that prompted the arrivals of the Europeans and Mediterranean immigrants to the American shore.

His prime concern was the advancement of his people, but now his perspective was the result of taking a larger view of the possible outcomes of modernity in the century that had just begun, because he concluded that black Americans were bound to share their future along with the new immigrants from Europe and the Mediterranean. In what Wilson J. Moses has called Washington's typical "utilitarian attitude to American Protestantism," he saw the immigrants as a potential source of practical knowledge and improvement for the conditions of black Americans (109). In addition, he connected the new immigration to the South, thereby joining the agrarian and the urban environments in both a national and transnational perspective at a time of sweeping socioeconomic and cultural transformations for the United States and the rest of the Western world.

In this regard, *The Man Farthest Down* is an eloquent title for three main reasons. The first is the metaphorical verticality of the title that, in spite of its indefensible accommodationist stance, reflects Washington's belief about social development and change in race relations as transformations that can only be propelled from the bottom up, something he had already argued for in *Up from Slavery*, not coincidentally another title that evokes vertical motion from the bottom to the top. He believed that the gradual social and economic uplifting of black Americans would benefit the entire United States because he thought of the African American population as a universal class, whose particular interests, no matter the specific sphere, bore the general interest of the country. The second reason is Washington's itinerary. To understand the direction of twentieth-century modernity and its consequences for his native country, he undertook and presented in book form a journey that geographically—and geography here mirrors history and hegemony—goes in the opposite direction of the Middle Passage of the Atlantic slave trade that sustained the colonization of the Americas, the formation of the transatlantic merchant class, the American Revolution, and the early rise of modernity. In short, the unstoppable rise to power of the bourgeoisie that essentially transformed Europe and the rest of the world in historically unheard of ways. A former black slave, he travels across the Atlantic to Europe to try to understand who these immigrant people are and the significance of this unprecedented transfer of people from one continent to another. The third, unusual element speaks to the novelty of the times and the originality of the volume. Both the itinerary and the kind of "observation and study" that he undertakes subvert the canonical bourgeois, white Grand Tour of Europe that seemed to be a requirement for both Northern European and American intellectuals. Washington acknowledges this fact by way of rejection when he writes that he has no taste for "what is old" and "what is dead," by which he meant the usual destinations of the Grand Tour: museums, cathedrals, royal palaces, art galleries, and the like (13). This is neither cultural snobbism nor a variation of the pathological anti-European sentiment of American intellectualism, itself a form of the Europeans' pathological snobbism toward the association of the United States with culture. It is a political position that reflects Washington's belief that "the past is something that you cannot change. I like the new, the unfinished, the problematic" (13).

His statement about the past might sound problematic, especially given his own past and that of his people, which of course is a part of our country's past. Yet we should resist the reading of these words as a straightforward denial or refusal to deal with the past altogether. Here Washington attempts to connect black Americans to the laboring classes of Europe and the Mediterranean, who have hardly anything to share with the past that the Grand Tour embodies, in order to contextualize their shared future. His interest in the poor immigrants belongs to this vision, which explains his attempt to link those laboring classes to the condition of African Americans especially in the South, where most blacks still lived in 1910. Even his repeated claims in the book that in some measure the living conditions of the black population in the South are factually better than those of the European and Mediterranean laborers neither intend to align these two groups nor to erase their past. After all, he was a master politician. He had a profound knowledge of the minstrel show, which taught him to speak "*back and blank*," to put it as Houston Baker Jr. does with regard to *Up from Slavery* (24). Claiming the contrary, that is to say, that southern blacks were living in poorer conditions than the immigrants, would have amounted to telling his wealthy white readers and funders that those immigrants were better equipped to satisfy their needs, as they were doing in the northeastern part of the country, where the immigrants formed the bulk of the industrial working class. That admission would have meant the demise of his entire project, which in the first place was a project of modernity for African Americans. At the same time, he was pragmatic enough to recognize that in their different circumstances and contexts the situations of these two groups of people, while not identical, were equal. Because of it, they were both bound to confront new and problematic contexts.

This is nothing short of a vision of modernity as transformation and continuity at once, one, however, that tries to position black Americans ahead of the immigrants on the basis of the equation of the United States with the very idea of modernity. People, and especially downtrodden people, not churches and museums, were moving to America. The sweeping force of the changes that the new era was bringing about required a kind of mind-set that was strictly forward-looking, something that in his opinion many of the European laboring classes had yet to develop. For this reason his goal was to bring together the facts that he had observed about the various laboring classes of Europe "into a single point of view" (9). He was an ambitious fellow. He had always been. Given the goals he had set for himself early in his life and what he wanted to achieve for his people, he could not act differently. This was the value of his study, his way of adding to the past, which is to say, the way he did not deny or refuse to deal with the past. As a matter of fact, his information on the historical and socioeconomic backgrounds of the various places that he visited in Europe was correct. Clearly, prior to his departure for Europe Mr. Washington had done his homework.

What is of interest about Washington's view in the end is precisely his view. Whereas most writers and intellectuals in the Atlantic world began to register a fragmentation of the old nineteenth-century subject and grand narratives, the black leader proposes a unifying view of the laboring classes that are crossing the sea to reach the United States. He links these migrating laboring classes and the black population of the United States, a link that he presents as a way to read modernity. Washington identifies "the man farthest down" as the repository of the universality of the new modern era that such a man is actually about to contribute to ushering in and defining. That is why he believes that his observations on these laboring classes could benefit his people, black Americans. They too, like the European and Mediterranean immigrants, would be different subjects in the new era, just as the European and Mediterranean immigrants arriving to the United States were going to be. The processes of modernization that soon would be largely associated with modern America such as urbanization, mass culture, and mass consumption were ongoing as he was writing. These processes would make those laboring immigrant classes new Americans just as they would create a new modern black American. These new Americans would mirror each other. Of this much he was sure.

As eloquent as it is, however, the title of the book is just as misleading. Twenty pages into the book Washington confesses, "If I may put it that way, the man farthest down in Europe is woman" (20), a statement that he repeats and emphasizes toward the end of the book, almost four hundred pages later, in a sort of circular rhetorical strategy that seemingly envelops the argument of the study, as if it squeezed the argument between the statement and its repetition, a sort of ring composition, to use the parlance of the European philologists. And yet his assertion should come as no surprise. Whatever one might think of this unusual, unorthodox, and fascinating man, the fact is that he never failed to understand and acknowledge the centrality of women in his life. Even recent commentators of his autobiography concede this much. In *The Man Farthest Down*, his argument amounts to a modern social program for women. "Women have the narrowest outlook, do the hardest work, stand in greatest need of education, and are farthest removed from influences which are everywhere raising the level of life among the masses of the European people" (20). Exclusion and discrimination are female, and so is the erasure of a subject: the woman.

Why, then, would Washington finally opt for the title that the book carries? One possible and plausible answer is that he refers to woman as a category of interpretation, a way of reading the various realities he encounters in his travel. His is a patriarchal way of categorizing that pairs his essentially instrumental and Protestant view of modernity. Nevertheless, it is a category grounded in the realities he observes. Washington deems it possible to establish a unifying synthesis of the differences that distinguished the European and Mediterranean laboring classes that were migrating to America. For this synthesis to be feasible, the starting point had to be the recognition that in Europe the woman was at the bottom of the human scale, just as the blacks were at the bottom of the human scale in the United States. As a result, Washington intertwined African Americans and the women of the laboring classes on the other side of the Atlantic, a connection whose defining moment occurs when he reaches Southern Italy and the connection becomes the beginning of a discursive and historical investment of black American writers in Italian Americans.

In Southern Italy, the miserable conditions of the women touched him so deeply that they brought back the past that he said he was not interested in revisiting. In the Naples area, the human scene he witnessed of the great number of women working in the fields brought back the abominable memories of slavery. Their hoes reminded him of "the heavy tools I had seen the slaves use on the plantations before the Civil War" (107). The past could not be factually changed, as he said. Nonetheless it found a distinctive way to reappear, as a sort of Southern Italian proletarian female return of the historically black repressed. Not only did Southern Italian women at work in the fields bring the past back. They brought back a specific kind of past, pre–Civil War slavery, in the form of an exhausting kind of human labor and the related forced displacement of its subjects. "Some of the women," the passage continues, "were merely leaning wearily upon their tools, as if they were over-tired with exertion. . . . I inquired why it was that I saw so many women in the fields in this part of the country. . . . I learned that it was because so many of the men who formerly did this work had emigrated to America" (107–8). America—and here America stands for white America—had enslaved black Africans in the past. Now America continued to haunt him, a former slave, with the memories of slavery that the Neapolitan women working in the fields brought back. The chronology still responds to his attempt to position black Americans ahead of the immigrants by situating the latter back in time, a time that his wealthy readers and funders had no interest whatsoever in bringing back, as the present was way more profitable for them. That is one reason why Washington was equating slavery and the Neapolitan women at work in the fields. But it is no coincidence that the two get naturally paired in his mind, that he cannot suppress his memory (even though he uses it to his advantage), just as it is no coincidence that it is only when he is in Southern Italy that the comparison and the association between women and slavery occurs. Likewise, it is no coincidence that the absence of men in the field generates his curiosity that results in the memories of slavery.

The parallels continue with the description of "a sad and desolate region" characterized by "earthquakes, malaria, antiquated methods of farming, and the general neglect of the agricultural population," which "have all contributed to the miseries of the people" (109). Like the previous description, this one too serves him to condemn as premodern the neglecting of hygiene and contemporary approaches to agriculture, and even the subjectivity of the peasants, their potential as modern subject. It is not difficult to point out that along with industrial education, these are the pillars of Washington's vision for the improvement of the conditions of the African Americans and the achievement of racial equality in modern America, as he had put them forth in *Up from Slavery* and in his work at Tuskegee. It might not be entirely irrelevant, then, to point out that in the association between the Neapolitan women and the black slaves in the South of the United States there is no mention of skin color. Washington does not say that those women remind him of black slaves in spite of their color.

Tellingly, the comparison between slavery in the United States and women occurs only when Washington talks about women in Southern Italy. Indeed, it also returns a second time when Washington arrives in Sicily, where he establishes a link connecting the land, the culture of the Sicilian society, and the condition of the women. This time the comparison is even more forceful than the one he made in Naples, if this is at all possible. To begin with, he notices how the harsh labor conditions as well as the social customs in Sicily seem to be germane to the desolate lands. On the train that takes him from Palermo to Catania, he traverses the areas from where most people immigrate to the United States. He notes how in Sicily the poor seem to be even poorer because of the landscape: "It [the country] was a wild, bare, mountainous region through which we passed. . . . Now and then I saw, winding up a rocky footpath, a donkey or pack mule carrying water to the sulfur mines or provisions to some little inland mountain village" (136). Secondly, Washington underscores the distance between the people in Sicily and modern life, a distance that he seems to posit as what separates him from these people, as an anthropological and epistemological difference. The Sicilians are "so saturated with antiquity, so out of touch, except on the surface, with modern life, so imbedded in ancient habits and customs, that it would take a very long time, perhaps years, to get any real understanding of their ways of thinking and living" (126). It is a description that would discourage anybody hoping to assimilate these people into modern America. Finally, he points out the special condition of women, which, once again, he is able to describe only by way of going back to the analogy with slavery. This time, however, it is in connection to these women's status as property devoid of freedom. They are "a species of property, live like prisoners in their own villages . . . live in a sort of mental and moral slavery under the control of their husbands and of the ignorant, and possibly vicious, village priests" (164).

In the Naples area, the farming tools that the women used in the field led his memory back to slavery in the pre–Civil War South. In Sicily, instead, what propels the connection between slavery and women are two sociocultural factors that make the typical Sicilian village a spatial entity that, given the author's biography and identity as well as the context of this description and the vocabulary employed, along with the overall goal of the book, seems to evoke a plantation in the South before the Civil War, where in place of the husband and the priest one would find the "master" and the "slave breaker." Social and cultural forms rooted in the ancient past and "a wall of ignorance" cut women off from the "outer world," a kind of internal contradiction as history worked as a sort of estrangement from its own development, since the past fuels the material living conditions that cage the mind of Sicilian women, as if these women remained timelessly undeveloped subjects because frozen not in but out of time, as if they did not even exist, as if they were invisible (164). The solution to this estrangement is emigrating to the United States, the forward movement of history, for Sicilian women even more so than for Sicilian men, because going to America is a regenerating experience. For Washington, the New World improves these women's existence because it emancipates them. The "journey to America is for the woman of Sicily a real emancipation," because America brings "liberty of thought to the women of Southern Italy" (165). The emphasis here is on the mental attitude, the labor of the mind, not the material circumstances of the Sicilian women who go to America. The journey unchains the mind, regardless of the material circumstances that surround these women, from which Washington detaches them.

Washington establishes a dialectical association that the slavery metaphor sustains rhetorically. The result is a male-authored narrative of female liberation that gradually becomes a narrative of modern subject formation that leaves behind the past "saturated with antiquity," only superficially modern, and with equally ancient social customs. This association is also racially inflected. It whitens the Sicilian women because it projects onto them the core principles that the director of Tuskegee championed as the road to freedom for black Americans that he had learned from upper-class white men and, especially, women, what David Leverentz calls "his culture incorporative whiteness" at the service of "black agency" (170). This "liberty of thought" was Washington's code term for self-reliance, another core principle to achieve the road to equality with whites for black Americans. In other words, this is nothing new or surprising. It is vintage Booker T. Washington. What is new and surprising, as the use of the slavery metaphor and analogy suggests, is that Washington's investment in Southern Italy and women is a way to talk about the race question and modern development of black life in the United States. After all, as he stated at the beginning of the book, his goal with this study was to improve the conditions of black people, especially in the South of the country. Washington does not equate Southern Italian women with black slaves. He aligns the working and mental conditions of Southern Italian women to those of the slaves in the pre–Civil War plantations and relates them to the question of modernity as he did in *Up from Slavery* when he recalled the freedmen and freedwomen immediately after the Emancipation Proclamation. As a result, he also projects a racial condition onto Southern Italian women. He explicitly says that he covered at length the condition of the farm laborers in Italy to show that "the Negro is not the man farthest down." His condition, even "in the most backwards parts of the Southern States in America, even where he has the least education and the least encouragement, is incomparably better than the condition and opportunities of the agricultural population of Sicily" (144). The same line of thought he applies to family life, religion, and women: "The Negro seems to me to be incomparably better off in his family life than is true of the agricultural classes in Sicily" (160); the Negro, he continues, "has a purer type of religion and a better and more earnest class of ministers. . . . the Negro woman, has some advantages which are so far beyond the reach of the peasant girl in Sicily. . . . Every Negro girl in America has the same opportunities for education that are given to Negro boys" (161).

Again, these observations could appear entirely fraudulent, not because they might be factually wrong, but especially because there is no mention at all of segregation. The little Sicilian village did not have different schools for different kinds of skin. If anything, it did not have schools at all. From a strictly pragmatic, *modern* standpoint, this might be worse than not having any sort of school, which is precisely Washington's point here. This is a calculated move to position African Americans within the new American racial mosaic in formation in the early twentieth century. It reflects Washington's instrumental, rationalized view of modernity that pairs with his "incorporative whiteness." Washington's investment in the Southern Italian women and the category of woman in the first place is functional to his vision of the new modern black subject, his lifelong project. The Southern Italian immigrant woman needs to change entirely, just as Southern blacks must. Her condition becomes a kind of point of reference for the black subject in America, which explains the detailed description of life in Southern Italy.

For instance, Washington describes how Southern Italians relate to their animals as equals, which prevents them from understanding the importance of hygiene and cleanliness that he considered essential to achieve modernity. In Naples, he is struck by the lack of sterilization of milk. He sees a man who stands on the sidewalk at the corner of a street with a cow. "It seemed to me that the natural thing would have been to let the cow stand in the street and not obstruct the sidewalk. But these people evidently look upon the cow as having the same rights as other members of the population" (115). The reason for this unusual scene, he explains, is that the man is actually milking the cow while some women in the neighborhood gossip waiting for their turn to do the same. He reports that families of six or seven live in a single, dirty and windowless room in a basement. In one of them, he sees "a blacksmith shop in one part of the room, while the family ate and slept in the other part" (119). He also notices that people even share their home with their animals, especially in urban environments. His observations on the conditions in the sulfur mines of Sicily are compelling, and again the analogy with slavery returns. He describes how in the mines the children are beaten and pinched "in order to wring from their overburdened bodies the last drop of strength they had. When beatings did not suffice, it was the custom to singe the calves of their legs with lanterns to put them again on their feet." He tells how the owners of the mines sexually abuse these children and concludes that these cruelties are "as bad as anything that was ever reported of the cruelties of Negro slavery" (203). The former slave who worked in a West Virginia mine as a young man concludes that "a sulfur mine in Sicily is about the nearest thing to hell that I expect to see in this life" (214).

Unusual or hellish views are not the only scenes that grab his attention. Something else strikes him, something that sets Southern Italy apart from the rest of Europe: the respect that Southern Italian culture pays to the guest in the tradition of the ancient Mediterranean civilization. Despite (or because of?) their poverty, people refuse to be paid when they offer a service: "Campofranco was the only place in Europe where I met men who refused to accept money for a service rendered me" (216). The observation on the locals' refusal to place a gesture of hospitality above the instrumentality of the logic of exchange value is a crucial point in *The Man Farthest Down* because here Washington begins to set Southern Italy apart from Europe. Symbolically, he cuts off Southern Italy from Europe, a detachment that he needs in order to orientalize the Southern Italians. This gesture—the dismissal of both the logic of use and exchange value—appears to him so powerful because it transcends his instrumental view of modernity. It sets Southern Italy apart from Europe. This is culture as consciousness, impervious to the instrumental and monetary practices that dictate modern life as regulators and arbiters of social relations. No less significant, this moment demarks Southern Italy's unproblematic relationship with racial diversity. The unpaid service is rendered to a black man by other men, whose color Washington does not bother to mention, as his obviously did not bother them.

What Washington does mention, instead, is the ubiquitous image of the Virgin Mary, his prime tool to orientalize Southern Italians as people who live outside modernity, cut off from it. He notes how this icon of the Mediterranean is "everywhere, built into the buildings, on street corners, and in every possible public space," often with a burning lamp before it to make it visible at all times (170). The Virgin is in the homes, where, in typical noninstitutional, pagan fashion women build small altars. The reverence that she commands spills from the private into the public sphere. The Virgin, in fact, is also to be seen in the fields "to protect the crops from the evil spirits," as the locals tell Washington (170). To him this is a sign of the influence of the Catholic Church rather than a sign of the superstition of Southern Italians, an observation that seems to signal, on the one hand, the Protestant anti-Catholicism typical of the time, and, on the other, his attempt to orientalize the Southern Italians, which is to say, to make both a complex female-centered Catholicism and the Southern Italians, especially the women, the "other" that lives outside of modernity. The use of the Virgin statues "is in fact merely the natural expression of the reverence and piety of a simple-minded and, perhaps, an ignorant people," which is to say, a people that needs to be educated, just as African Americans do, one might add (170).

Further proof of their simplemindedness is that they do not assign to the image of the Virgin in the field the power to "protect them also from thieves, or banish from the community the evil spirits that inspired men to rob and steal," which would do away with the need "to guard the fields night and day during the harvest season, by men armed with shotguns" (171). Washington concludes that these people's Christianity is "saturated with pagan superstition," an attitude that turned religion into fetishism: "It seems as if the image of the Virgin has become, among the lower class of people, little more than a fetish, a thing to conjure with." The example that he offers is the peasant who prays to the image of the Virgin when he attempts to exact revenge upon his landlord "for what he believes has been taken from him by fraud or extortion" (173). Depending on the outcome of his attempt, the peasant makes offers or curses or even spits upon the same image accordingly. One wonders who is the superstitious person here, the Sicilian peasant or Booker T. Washington, who refuses to see the realities of "the simple-minded and perhaps ignorant people" from their point of view as a result of his process of orientalizing Southern Italy, which precludes him from presenting and seeing these people in all their complexity, beginning with the centrality that they assign to a female figure. Their invisibility is the outcome of his utilitarian, patriarchal, modern vision whose goal is the education of his own people in the South of the United States. Such invisibility is even more puzzling because while Washington insists on and indeed invests his discourse in the ubiquitous presence of the Virgin in Sicily and among the lower classes, he makes no mention whatsoever of the presence of the many black Madonnas on the Mediterranean island, as well as in many other parts of Italy and Southern Italy especially. This presence, according to historian Lucia Chiavola Birnbaum, is evidence of the divinity of the woman in the pre-Christian Mediterranean area and, no less important in the economy of our discourse, of the figurative empowerment of that icon, which Chiavola Birnbaum describes as "a metaphor for the subaltern similarity of women, the persecuted, the marginal, outcasts, the poor, and those far from home" (120).

The Sicilian woman might be living in a sort of mental and moral slavery, yet the Virgin, a woman and a mother, is literally inscribed onto every building, in the homes where women build small altars, and even in the fields. The peasants appeal to her for protection and success in their effort to get from those for whom they work what they think their labor is worth. That is to say, the Virgin, a woman, the mother of all mothers, is the symbolic conductor of what Washington himself cannot help but present as these Southern Italians' instinctual class consciousness and proletarian revolt. The elevation of the Virgin to the role of protector of the poor, the peasants who revolt against the landowners, speaks of a proletarianization of the Virgin, the mother par excellence, which in turn makes her a very concrete figure, stripping away from her that symbolic aura that the Mediterranean aristocratic culture bestowed upon her. What Washington presents us with here is the subversion of a traditional symbolic domain typical of the modern era, precisely that representative icon of the otherness of the subaltern classes that Chiavola Birnbaum indicates. The Virgin is not the locus classicus of institutional, doctrinal, Catholic, aristocratic love celebrated in countless sonnets and *romanze*. From a class standpoint, her ubiquity equals her social and cultural demotion to proletarian figure, a process that makes her inherently a subversive figure. The peasants refuse to make her a protector of the field. They refuse to make her the protector of private property. Instead, they use her to claim what they think they are due as workers, subverting the instrumentality of the logic of exchange value. The fields are the private property of the landowners, the harvest their capital, which they accumulate thanks to the labor of the peasants. Yet these "simple-minded and perhaps ignorant" peasants believe that the landowners do not properly compensate their labor. It is all the more noteworthy that in another passage Washington writes that in Sicily he saw "hundreds of miles of high stone walls [that] have been erected in different parts of the island to protect private property from vandalism and thieves" (176). He does not question what motivates people to steal, whether the problem is the thieves and the vandals, or private landholding in feudal amounts instead. Likewise, he does not question whether the proletarianization of the Virgin might be the reason as to why "the simple-minded and perhaps ignorant people" refuse to believe that the Virgin in the fields can protect the harvest from "the thieves" or from "the evil spirits that inspired men to rob and steal."

To Washington the fact that the peasants may reward or spit upon the image of the Virgin certifies their primitive fetishism. In reality, these behaviors testify to a concept of the Virgin as both a symbol of devotion and a nondoctrinal, nonreligious figure. She embodies earthly expectations and given realities. The peasants consider her one of them and above them at once. No Christian person would spit on a symbol of Christianity, which speaks of both the pre-Christian origins of Southern Italians' religious view of life and the approach to spiritualism of the lower classes. The Virgin represents a vision according to which the peasants feel and regard the spiritual dimension neither as a purely abstract doctrinal notion nor as the aristocratic cultural moment whose controlling power is frozen and reified in images on the walls. On the contrary, she is regarded as a corporeal force that participates in their everyday life. This is the reason why the peasants do not make her protect the private property from evil spirits or thieves. They enact a social construction of the Virgin. They use her to bring an objective reality, the reality of the division between the rich and the poor, into their subjective reality as human beings and laborers, which the ever-present image of the Virgin reifies, turning internalization into externalization.

This symbolic transformation of the Virgin seems to be the reason for what Washington perceives and describes as the clash between poor Southern Italians who eventually immigrate to the United States and modernity, or at least modernity as Washington envisions it. The Virgin icon allows these Italians to combine, even harmonize their centuries-old spiritualism and a form of unmediated subversive class consciousness that is the result of their historically determined social relationships. In other words, at issue here is the clash between a utilitarian, patriarchal view of modernity and these Southern Italians' woman-centered cosmic view of life, one that does not separate the materiality of life from the symbolic and spiritual dimensions grounded in their history and cultural traditions that date back to the pre-Christian time. We might think of this cosmic view of life as a type of "from-the-bottom-up universalism." And it would seem that this is precisely what distances the Southern Italians from Washington's view of modernity. Accordingly, he describes the people who live "in the little villages" (123) as "people saturated with antiquity." Because of this, they are "out of touch, except on the surface, with modern life." Their "ancient habits and customs" are like a foreign language that prevents him from getting "any real understanding of their ways of thinking and living" (126). In the light of this inability to garner a "real understanding" of these people's "ways of living and thinking," we may wonder if the symbolic metamorphosis of the Virgin might signal the presence in Southern Italy and in Sicily of women who did not live in "mental and moral slavery," of women who already had that "liberty of thought" that according to Washington the journey to America had granted them. Likewise, we should consider the possibility that the presence of women who already had such "liberty of thought" might be somehow related to the omission of any consideration or note of actual Italian immigrant life in America. Throughout his description of Italy and observation of the Italians, Washington insists on enumerating data and historical facts about the peninsula. Yet he makes no mention of the late nineteenth and early twentieth centuries' social and economic struggles that Sicilian women participated in and often promoted. One such example is the so-called Fasci Siciliani, the popular revolt that a mix of spiritualism and leftist ideologies helped trigger at the end of the nineteenth century in which initially women played a significant and at times leading role and whose defeat further propelled Sicilian emigration to America.

It may not be a coincidence that women from Southern Italy were a significant presence in the labor movement of New York City's textile industry in the early twentieth century. Or that they led the protest for better sanitary conditions in New York City's East Harlem in the 1930s. Historians have been unearthing this history, but fiction and the arts offer just as much evidence, past and present. In Giovanni Verga's classic novel *The House by the Medlar Tree*, published in 1881, we hear Comare Zuppidda showing a spirit of defiance when she protests, "They ought to burn those tax collectors alive, all of them!"[1] where the tax collectors are the northerners who conquered the south of Italy to the Kingdom of Sardinia in order to complete the formation of the renamed Kingdom of Italy (44). Lucia Santa, in Mario Puzo's immigrant novel *The Fortunate Pilgrim*, is hardly a mental and moral slave. No wonder, then, that at the beginning of Coppola's *The Godfather Part II*, whose script Puzo coauthored, we see young Vito's mother holding a knife to the throat of the landowner who is responsible for the killing of both her husband and her older son, Paolo. "Rebellion," comments Thomas J. Ferraro, "is the secret tradition of Italian immigrant women" (*Feeling*, 77). One wonders if Washington's view of a new, immigrant, emancipated female subject only after women have crossed the Atlantic aims at creating a new, docile subject at a time of increasing social turmoil in the United States, which he decried in *Up from Slavery*. Such an emancipated female subject might elicit a similar attitude among its black American equivalent with whom it was coming into contact, in the urban North as well as in the rural South. It might be not coincidental that in *The Man Farthest Down* Washington describes Sicily as a bridge between Africa and Europe, further detaching Southern Italy from the continent. It might also not be coincidental that he links the fetishism of the Virgin to Africa to distinguish southern blacks from the Southern Italians: "I have heard that the savages in Africa will sometimes believe in the same way toward the object of which they have made a fetish, but I never heard of anything like that among my own people in the South. The Negro is frequently superstitious, as most other ignorant people are, but he is not cynical, and never scoffs at anything which has a religious significance" (174).

To raise these questions is not to indict Washington's ideas on the moral level or, worse, his morality altogether. After all, there is a whole line of African American culture that expresses similar positions even in later times. Richard Wright, hardly a fan of Washington's positions, expressed similar thoughts about colonialism in the 1960s. The point is to insert these questions in the larger framework of modernity as Washington thinks of it. His discourse about woman as a category of interpretation of modernity, as a liberating force, conflicts with the realities he describes. Washington may present the transformation as liberating, even emancipatory, but what actually this transformation liberates is the instrumentality of modernity itself, not the lower classes, and certainly not the women of the lower classes. Even the images of the Virgin seem to be the repository of past and present forms of being and acting in the world that clash with the black leader's view of the past. It would seem as if the past itself refuses to be forgotten, as happened when the principal of Tuskegee could not help recalling the slaves' working conditions after seeing the women working in the fields outside Naples. Washington himself seems to acknowledge this possibility when he remarks, "The Sicilian never forgets the past until he leaves Sicily, and frequently not even then" (146). The Italian diaspora, as Washington describes it, seems incompatible with an instrumentally utilitarian and basically Protestant view of modernity. Or, perhaps, modernity is incompatible with certain aspects of the Italian diaspora that these poor Southern Italian women embody.

We may go even further and suggest the possibility that twentieth-century modernity is incompatible with this kind of woman altogether. In spite of its transformative power, modernity seems unable to perform that act that supposedly propels it: to eradicate completely the past, a past that signifies a view of life that equals a way of life. Washington wants to eradicate a past that to him appears in female guise, that women represent. It would seem that what he wants to eradicate is women altogether. And yet, he cannot help but invest in such a past and the women who represent it, even though his investment has the goal of orientalizing its subjects. The contradiction, then, might as well be the idea of twentieth-century modernity as a liberating and emancipating force. The idea that the journey to America is an emancipatory moment only testifies to the fact that the man farthest down, which is woman, is already equipped to become a different subject, one that supposedly is no longer property of somebody else, whether the priest or the husband. This position, however, amounts to saying that the new female subject that emigration produces is created by negation. It is the result of what Sicily and Southern Italy have, which according to Booker T. Washington is precisely what America, the New World, modernity lacks. And what Sicily and Southern Italy have is class and sociocultural oppression that take the form of an anthropological condition, ways of being and views of the world that the reverence for the past and antiquated modes of production mirrors.

Washington writes that the future is his only interest. Regardless of his intent, he cannot stop his mind from bringing back to his present, modern self, memories of slavery in connection to the working conditions of Neapolitan women, as if his own modernity could not overcome his historical memory. He insists that immigration is a regenerative moment especially for Southern Italian women, but he acknowledges that Sicilians cannot forget the past even after they have left Sicily. He argues that America provides newcomers with liberating social and cultural codes that will emancipate and transform their oppressed selves, but he notes how the social architecture in Sicily recalls collective moments of social protest against private property and labor exploitation. He asserts that Southern Italians need to get rid of their age-old superstitions and biases, but he finishes his book confessing that he had left America mistakenly thinking of Sicilians as a "race of brigands," his own racism (214). Time and again, the materiality of what he sees contradicts the nature of his observations. What exactly is it, then, about these Mediterranean people that gets in the way of modernity? What is it in this past that Washington refers to as he confronts the Italian diaspora that theoretically prevents modernity from completely unfolding, something that will happen in the United States, the embodiment of modernity? How is it that certain historical formations of Italian immigrant life refuse to disappear? Where does such stubborn resistance to a new form of life that supposedly should liberate and emancipate people, especially women, originate from? Why does woman, this "man farthest down," embody this resistance? Why is Washington, a man who never refused to acknowledge the presence and the decisive role of racially diverse women, struck and even annoyed by the recurrence of the image of the Virgin and the power she holds among the lower classes? Why do Southern Italians not make an issue of Washington's color and reject the logic of use and exchange value when they render him services for free? In short, what does Washington's investment in Southern Italians begin to tell us about their relationship to African Americans and modernity?

II

One way to start answering these questions is by turning to Emanuele Crialese's 2006 motion picture *Nuovomondo*, which the American distributor retitled *Golden Door*. The movie presents the story of a plebeian Sicilian family, the Mancusos, who decide to leave for America, the new world of the original title, and rejoin one of the family members who is there already, the unnamed brother of the head of the family, Salvatore Mancuso. Salvatore is the son of Fortunata, a healer, as well as the widowed father of Pietro and Angelo. The movie is particularly apt at capturing the dimensions and the significance of these people's lives in their relation to modernity, because Crialese presents such relationship as a way to be subversively modern. The film portrays the same dichotomy between the Old and the New World as *The Man Farthest Down* and deals with many, if not all, of the motifs that captured the attention of Booker T. Washington. Curiously, even the narrative structure of the movie is similar to Washington's essay. Crialese hides America from his picture as Washington does in his book. In *Nuovomondo* we never get to see the New York City of the early twentieth century where the Italians and other emigrants land. The director leaves it up to the viewers to imagine America. Supposedly, the sea of milk where Salvatore, Pietro, Angelo, and Miss Lucy (the young, mysterious British woman who joins them in what appears to be the port of Naples)[2] swim before the departure for New York City symbolizes the emigrants' mythic fantasy of the New World. The only America we see is not properly America. It is the face of modernity as Crialese paints it, the brutal eugenic practices that the emigrants must undergo at Ellis Island in order to be admitted to the United States. Of course, the main difference between Crialese's film and Washington's book is that the Sicilian filmmaker confronts the same issues that the black leader dealt with, but from the vantage point of the early twenty-first century, after the (hi)story he narrates with and in his movie has happened. But this is exactly what makes the comparison instructive. It allows us to put Washington's reflections about Southern Italy and its poorest inhabitants in the after-the-fact perspective, so to speak, especially with regard to the position and the interpretative category of "woman" that the black leader puts at the center of his study of Southern Italy.

Unlike *The Man Farthest Down*, *Nuovomondo* does not present the Italian diaspora to the United States as a moment of female liberation. Neither, however, does the film describe the diaspora as a rejection of life in America or as a new beginning, which is what makes *Nuovomondo* an achieved movie. Crialese uses the journey across the Atlantic to portray the detachment, both mental and material, from the old ways of life that the emigrants experience during the voyage across the ocean and at Ellis Island. This detachment serves him to question the mainstream narrative of modernity as a narrative of human liberation, especially from a female perspective. The Italian director keeps together under the umbrella of modernity the idea of human, especially female, emancipation, the subversive potential of Mediterranean humanism, and, above all, the dialectics of twentieth-century modernity and the Italian diaspora to America. He accomplishes this task by looking at modernity from the standpoint of the emigrants, which is what makes the movie such a beautiful and insightful work of art for our purpose.

In his presentation to the American edition of the film, Martin Scorsese makes precisely this point. Scorsese points out how the viewers are offered a "journey seen from the point of view of the immigrants." This point of view, Scorsese continues, allows the Italian filmmaker to bring back to life "the connections to the Old World that were being broken and disappearing" during Scorsese's childhood in the 1950s, which in turn indicates the prolonged life and the strength of such connections. Crialese uses the camera the way a good oral historian uses his or her recording device. He lets his characters speak and tell their story collectively. He uses the photography and the music to interlock the various parts of the story and give cohesiveness to the film. Because of this narrative approach, the story of emigration itself is the speaking subject of the film. This is the novelty that distinguishes *Nuovomondo* and makes irrelevant the chronological distance from the historical time of *The Man Farthest Down*. As a result, the movie does not have a starring character. Rather, it has a group of characters. Fortunata (her first name, like all first names in the movie, is no coincidence, as we shall see) gives us the opportunity to see the journey to America through the female eyes of an old and poor Sicilian woman, one of those women upon whom, if we were to believe Booker T. Washington, America would bestow the "liberty of thought" that they lacked in native Sicily. By the end of the movie, her point of view becomes the point of view of all emigrants, not because she speaks for everybody else, but in the sense that everyone speaks through her. She lends them her voice, conjuring up her individual "I" with the collective emigrant "we" in the typical storytelling tradition of poor people, including—if not especially, given the economy of our discourse—African Americans.

The formal device also highlights the dimension of Fortunata's subversive humanism. A woman and a mother, as well as a grandmother, she is rooted in the old traditions, at once pagan and Christian, that define her culture, her system of thought, and her life because they provide her with the references to make sense of the world around her. We see the materiality of her humanism right at the beginning of the movie when Salvatore and Angelo climb a rocky mountain barefoot to reach a small shrine dedicated to the Virgin Mary in order to ask her to give them a sign as to whether they should leave for America. Crialese presents the opening climbing as an integral element of a stunningly desolate landscape where time appears to be nonexistent, as if it were suspended or frozen as in Dante's *Inferno*, one of the subtexts of the movie along with John Ford's *The Grapes of Wrath*, Luchino Visconti's *Rocco and His Brothers*, Francis Ford Coppola's *The Godfather*

Part II, and Steven Spielberg's *Schindler's List*. In his review of the movie Lorenzo Rinelli noted how this is a moment in a life "marked by natural and supernatural events that, before industrialization, used to be indissoluble." The two men are searching for a sign that would dissolve Salvatore's hesitations and validate his intention to go to America as his older brother did. In the next scene, we view Donna Fortunata using her healing skills upon Rita, one of the two girls (the other is named Rosa) who will join the Mancuso family in their trip across the Atlantic because of their arranged marriages with men whom they have never seen before.

In a typical moment of meta-cinema, Crialese sets the stage for what will follow in the rest of the movie, associating two different ways of acting and being in the world according to gender and inner condition. Donna Fortunata executes that control over life that her son seems to lack. On the one hand there is a man, a widowed father with his older son waiting for a supernatural sign to justify the decision to embark for New York City, which his mother disapproves. On the other hand, with her exorcism Fortunata asserts control over that primordial faith that guides these people's daily actions. Salvatore tries to communicate with the supernatural entity in typical premodern, pagan-inflected fashion. As they get to the top of the mountain, Salvatore and Angelo deposit the rocks that they have been carrying in their now bleeding mouths to pay respect to the Virgin in the hope that she will give them the sign they are waiting for. However, a modern object mediates this communicative act. Salvatore's younger son, Pietro, who is seemingly mute, reaches his father and his brother on top of the mountain. He carries with him several postcards that Salvatore's brother sent from America that depict scenes of life in America. Salvatore interprets the arrival of the postcards as the long-awaited sign, which is one of the main symbols of modernity, a printed visual image sent by mail across continents. Some of these postcards, which we should think of as the early twentieth century's equivalent of today's TV commercials, portray peasants with giant onions and carrots as well as equally gigantic farming animals. Some others portray springs of milk and dollar coins growing on trees. Pietro has already shown the postcards to his grandmother Fortunata, who has told him to burn them, obviously to no avail. Her request to burn the postcards, however, is not a form of primitivism that rejects modernity. We shall see how Fortunata relates to modernity when she confronts it face to face. Fortunata refuses to believe in a mythic overabundance that the *terra nuova*—and the word *terra* here needs to be intended first and foremost as the soil to till rather than the land to live in—would bestow upon the immigrants. Neither, I would contend, is her request to burn the postcards a sign of the incompatibility of the New World in the Old World, which is the thesis that Anthony J. Tamburri advances to interpret *Nuovomondo*.[3] Her refusal signifies a way of seeing and living life that foreshadows a gender and generational split between men and women, a division that at once identifies the human desire of the poor peasants to overcome the material struggles in the Old World and the conditions of their poverty.

We may think of this deeply mental process as the inner geography of the emigrants, which entails the juxtaposition of, on the one hand, poverty-originated hopes that foster a sense of illusion and a self-propelled dream of possibilities, and, on the other, an experience-generated keen sense of life as it is, which sets in motion the interplay between Mediterranean humanism and gender. Such interplay produces the mediation between human faith as a part of daily life and the latter's concrete actuality, reminding us of the materiality of life. However abundant and gigantic, milk and onions are not dreams. They are concrete objects that may be gained, but at the price of a radical transformation of the ways of living and the mental habits of the peasants. Fortunata does not object to milk, onions, and coins as the embodiment of the possibilities of modernity, the opportunity to overcome their poverty. She objects to the postcards as the embodiment of modernity. She objects to modernity as an image.

Her objection foregrounds the primordial and material dimension of her humanism. Her cosmic view of life is her humanism. By the turn of the twentieth century, neither Saint Paul nor Jean-Jacques Rousseau had made it to the Sicily presented in *Nuovomondo*, so to speak. The lack of churches in the first of the movie's three sections—peasant life in Sicily, the journey, and the immigration process at Ellis Island—is especially striking in a Southern Italian environment, even more so in the face of the symbolism of the first names of the characters, which are indicative of the gendered juxtaposition. Salvatore, Angelo, and Pietro—the savior, the announcer, and the founder of the Catholic Church—evoke the Christian mythology. The three men mirror the Christian Trinity *and* its concomitant lack of a woman and a mother, which is instrumentally elevated to a position of deference properly devoid of her corporality in order to neutralize her, which is to say, to erase her. "In the name of the father, the son, and the Holy Ghost" goes the prayer that Salvatore will encourage his fellow male emigrants to say in Ellis Island while they are waiting to learn if they can enter the United States. Equally telling is the name Fortunata, which evokes a belief in the divine, in supernatural entities that ancient practices, not theological doctrines, regulate. The name recalls the Mediterranean, pagan origins of Southern Italian Catholicism. It is Crialese's way to make Fortunata a repository of the complex history and culture of her native land that in different guises fuels her resistance to go to the United States. Also, the name indicates the role of destiny in the sense of the Latin *fortuna*, the impossibility for human beings to have complete control over their life, which, interestingly, we have come to categorize as a typical postmodern trait.

Fortunata's resistance to leave her native island is neither fear of the new nor a sentimental attachment to the miserable conditions of her life. She knows that the premises of the modernity that the postcards show require her to divorce her inner self from the lived experience that informs her reality and her sense of the universe around her. Her point is not that there is nothing real about the gigantic vegetables and money growing on a tree. Her point is that such an image cannot be real. Fortunata does not refuse the manufactured reality of the postcard. She rejects the possibility to manufacture reality because it demands her to get rid of her identity, her conscious sense of being human that includes being a woman and a mother. Such an identity includes the complex social and cultural references that Fortunata enacts and lives by to make sense of the world she inhabits, of being of and in the world, including a millenarian culture that her healing skills recall. One corollary of this female, Mediterranean subjectivity is her opposition to the idea of disposal typical of the logic and the process of the rationalizing instrumentality of self-interested exchange that guided Booker T. Washington's vision of modernity and his investment in Southern Italy. That is her defining trait throughout the movie, from the beginning in Sicily to the very end at Ellis Island, where she goes through the various stages of the immigration process.

Her conduct seems to be intentionally oppositional because in the first place her identity is incompatible with the logic of instrumentality. At one point we see Salvatore and his sons give away everything they own, their capital, which consists of a couple of animals, in exchange for clothes and shoes to make the trip across the Atlantic. The moment is significant for two interwoven reasons. One is economic, the other is aesthetic, and the two are intertwined. We see the three Mancuso men sell their collective capital to acquire used clothes and shoes, but we do not see Fortunata doing the same thing. Emigration to America, the initial moment to enter modernity, begins with a transaction of capital that results in a mutation in the look of the three men, their external appearance, as if modernity required that (ex)change, or, which is the same, as if modernity was an exchange that produces a different appearance covering one's original identity. The Mancusos lose their productive capital, their animals, what they possess, which is their means of production, in order to acquire the status of being presentable upon disembarking in the new, supposedly modern world. Whatever the value of their capital, such capital is collectively owned because it belongs to the Mancuso family. It is not divided. On the contrary, the clothes and the shoes that each single individual wears are, and they are not even interchangeable. Moreover, their animals, their capital, are for the Mancusos their means of production. They are not commodities or simply food to consume, let alone a way to secure a temporary social status. Their new appearance instead is a projection, an image of an expectation that reflects that of the previously mentioned postcards. It does not reflect their physical or mental health, which the immigration process will measure with a series of medical exams and attitudinal tests once they reach Ellis Island. The aesthetic of emigration requires a momentary step up in status and a definite economic step back, the loss of capital. Additionally, all the characters involved in this exchange are male, the three Mancusos and Zapparelli, the man who sells them the clothes and the shoes.

This aesthetics reveals an equally crucial aspect of the Italian diaspora to the United States as *Nuovomondo* presents it. The Mancuso men begin to experience modernity as the physical separation typical of any migration. Equally important is that this (ex)change exposes how such separation starts at the mental level, in order to connect the mind to the body. It invests their mental world and attitude, thus showing how concrete the mental world is, how initially the physical and the mental world are not separated, the previously mentioned cosmic view of life. The economic exchange causes a loss of capital that triggers a mental separation that begins in the native land of the emigrants. The clothes and the shoes the Mancuso men acquire may confer status and project an appearance of cleanliness and order, Booker T. Washington's cardinal principles of his project of modernity. The clothes and the shoes do not signify any tradition, any native aesthetics or sense of belonging. The three men are actually told that the clothes used to belong to brigands. Therefore, "the dead travel with you," as Zapparelli admonishes them. The men's clothes do not reflect a past that belongs to them. If anything, it belonged to "brigands," a past that historically and at the medial level will haunt the Italian emigrants once they become Italian Americans. More to the point here, the clothes indicate the beginning of their uprooting and the future Italian American man's divided self.

Unlike her son and grandsons, Fortunata does not sell anything. This difference helps us read her character within the economy of the movie. One way to do this is by comparing Fortunata Mancuso to another significant woman and mother figure of our culture from one of the previously mentioned subtexts of *Nuovomondo*, *The Grapes of Wrath*'s Mother Joad. Fortunata is to *Nuovomondo* what Mother Joad is to *The Grapes of Wrath*, another story of uprooting in the modern times, albeit an internal one from the strict geographical and cultural standpoint. Like Mother Joad, Fortunata leaves her home reluctantly. As with Mother Joad, once the journey to

Rita D'Agostini, Fortunata, Pietro, Angelo, and Salvatore Mancuso opposite to Miss Lucy Reed before embarking for the United States in *Nuovomondo* (directed by Emanuele Crialese).

the new land begins, Fortunata's main concern becomes what she already knows is going to be an impossible task to achieve: to keep the family together. The effort translates into the protection of the family from external elements that do not reflect the world that the family has inhabited thus far. The obvious example of this assertive territoriality is Fortunata's hostile reaction toward the presence of Lucy, the classy, educated, and worldly Englishwoman who initially joins the Mancusos because, like Rita, Rosa, and any other single woman who wants to enter the United States, she needs a man—and Salvatore, in this case true to the etymology of his name, is that man.

Fortunata fears that Miss Lucy will use Salvatore for what intrinsically any single man becomes as he steps onto the boat—a passport to America for single women who are prohibited from entering America without a present or future husband. Men need new (used) clothes to enter modernity. Women, instead, need men. In different ways, the power relations of the instrumental logic of exchange that marks modernity turn both women and men into objects. Salvatore becomes an expendable commodity, just like Rosa and Rita. From the strict theoretical standpoint, that is what new used clothes can do *to* a Sicilian male peasant and *for* an emigrant single woman. Both are turned into an image of what they are not. No wonder that, like Mother Joad, Donna Fortunata is skeptical of the promises of what supposedly is ahead of her. She knows that the coins, the gigantic vegetables, and the animals of the postcards project not what America holds, but what Sicily lacks. What fuels in the first place the Italian diaspora, a code word for a collective socioeconomic desire, is not the promise of a better life in a place that the vast majority of these emigrants would have not been able to locate on a map, just as they would have not been able to locate their place of birth in Sicily. It is the lack of opportunities at home. Negation is at the heart of the Italian diaspora to the United States. That explains why in much of the early Italian American literature we find a counter-fantasy of the native land as an ideal place of abundance and beauty, a moment that the Italian American experience crystallized with the expression *Mannaggia l'America!* (damn America). Of course, the lack of and the promise of a better life stand in dialectical relationship, but the process serves us to remember the cold materiality of life, which in theoretical terms we can think of as concrete ideology, the ideology of reality that lies underneath imaginative processes that the Italian experience in the United States fostered.

In the light of this, one last element that makes Fortunata and Mother Joad similar acquires significant resonance for our purpose. Like the heroine of *The Grapes of Wrath* during the trip to California, Fortunata, too, cautiously opens herself up to people who did not start the trip with her small community of men and women, her family and Rosa and Rita. Fortunata opens up to Lucy, the supposed threat to the unity of her universe, something she already knows is going to be impossible to maintain. Initially, Lucy seems the exact opposite of Fortunata. The contrast between the two could not be any starker. Fortunata is older, unattractive, formally uneducated, and of olive skin. Lucy is young, attractive, and literate, probably well schooled. And she is white as one can be. The starkest difference, however, is neither generational nor educational nor racial. It is an aesthetic difference that the clothes of the two women underscore. Fortunata wears the typical clothes of a poor Sicilian woman. Lucy's clothes are those of a woman who prior to this trip has inhabited a world of a different class from Fortunata's. It is tempting to see in these two women the mirror of a larger issue and argue that they represent two different worlds. Fortunata would be the representative of the premodern world and Lucy of the modern one. Such a dichotomy does exist, but it does not tell the whole story, because in spite of their differences, these two women share an important trait besides their gender. Both women are independent and autonomous subjects. Indeed, I would contend that their social, racial, and aesthetic differences reinforce this similarity and highlight a defining hallmark of modernity.

Lucy does not retreat in the face of the difficulties that the journey to the United States entails for her. Lucy has no problem in joining a family of swarthy peasants and adjusting to the despicable circumstances of the voyage. For weeks, the emigrants are clustered in the bowels of the ocean liner in utterly unhealthy, dangerous, and degrading conditions. By the end of the trip, once their ordeal at Ellis Island is over, she does not seem entirely oblivious of the genuineness of Salvatore's feelings toward her. While it seems

Fortunata, Miss Lucy, and, in the background, Rosa and Rita, at Ellis Island in *Nuovomondo* (directed by Emanuele Crialese).

likely that she surrendered to the blackmailing advances of the Italian emigration officer in the port of departure to be able to embark for New York City, now she resists the advances of an older, successful Italian American businessman in search of a young and beautiful wife. More important, toward the end of the trip Lucy ends up joining Fortunata and all the other women who clean each other's hair and, led by Fortunata, sing traditional Southern Italian songs, a moment that reflects a tradition of communitarian female life in the South of Italy and another similarity that *Nuovomondo* shares with *The Grapes of Wrath*, where the women in the government camp in which the Joads stop to wash the clothes all together while singing old hymns. Lucy puts her agency at the service of a group of women that extends beyond the family unit.

Ultimately, however, it is her self-interest that fuels such agency and sustains her social desire to enter America. Her initial motivation to join the Mancusos is her need to have a male companion that will guarantee her entrance to the United States. In the first place, her agency is inner-directed because of the power relations that structure the immigration process. She is forced to engage in a process of exchange that transforms her female self into a commodity and subjugates her identity. This is what she must do if she wants to enter the United States. After completing their physical examination, the emigrants must undertake attitudinal tests to prove their fitness to enter the New World. Lucy witnesses the eugenic practices of the examiners who deny entrance to anybody who is mentally or physically atypical, who does not fit a preconceived human topology. An officer explains to her that the modalities of entry for the Italians respond to the need to keep America pure and noninfected with people of scientifically proven and contagious inferior intelligence, which spurs Lucy's comment, "What a modern vision!" She too questions modernity. In the end, however, she submits to the practices that regulate this vision, which is not a vision of the world without women. After all, women can enter the United States, modernity, as long as they have a husband and they fit the required physical, mental, and cognitive parameters. Rather, this is a vision of the world *against* women, especially women who may actually be carriers of what Lucy would call a "modern vision," one, however, that differs from the bio-politics of the immigration process at Ellis Island.

Unlike Lucy, Fortunata's agency entails mutuality. She reaches out of her individual self to relate to the others as well as to the external environment. Fortunata puts her agency at the service of both her family and the people who are with her, beginning with Rita and Rosa, a process that culminates during the immigration process at Ellis Island. Her relationality brings forth and de-structures the bio-politics of the immigration process.

As soon as they arrive on the little island in front of New York City, Fortunata begins to disrupt the organizational framework of the process, challenging the gender dimension of the power structure. Right off the boat, the passengers are lined up in front of the building where they are going to undertake physical and attitudinal tests, the latter administered by male officers. One of them asks Fortunata what day it is, a tricky attempt to evaluate whether she has maintained a sense of time that would indicate a stable mental presence. Fortunata replies with a firm and crude tone of voice that she wishes she knew the answer, at once addressing the hardship of the trip and questioning male authority. Then she tries to dust off the mark that the officer has put on her coat with a piece of chalk, thus provoking the officer's ire, an image that for post-Holocaust generations should serve to de-mythicize the fable of immigration to the United States and look at the diaspora as for what it essentially was, a violent moment of uprooting in the global development of capitalist modernity. Inside the building, she protests another male officer's forceful attempt to check her eyes, as well as the female nurse who examines the physical condition of the female emigrants. What prompts her reactions is a cultural difference that she reckons disrespectful. When the nurse begins her physical examination, Lucy, who is next to Fortunata, tells the nurse that Fortunata is not used to being touched by other women. However, Fortunata's objection to the nurse is not related to the physical contact per se. After all, this is the woman who put her hands inside another woman when she practiced her exorcism, and on the way to America let other women wash and comb her hair.

Simply put, Fortunata is not willing to renounce her identity. She refuses to submit to the rationalizing instrumentality that connects the bio-politics of immigration and the new modern self, regardless of gender. In the end, Fortunata is not denied entrance to the United States. She refuses to enter the United States because she knows that the price to pay would be too great for her. Her refusal stems from her awareness that there is complete incompatibility between her way of being human and a woman and the universality of the demands that the immigration officer proclaims to be necessary to keep the New World racially pure. But her subversive refusal does not equate with an antimodern stance. Fortunata is not unwilling to accept transformation. She does not refuse novelties or innovation, what traditionally we associate with modernity and processes of modernization. After the physical examination, she takes a shower together with other women, including Lucy. Slowly, her initial diffidence toward the mechanical novelty disappears. Her diffidence toward something entirely foreign to her vanishes. Increasingly, she enjoys the warm water of the shower.

Her disposition changes during the attitudinal tests. The Italian men try to make sense of the unusual tasks that they are asked to accomplish according to their way of experiencing and thinking of the world. When the psychologist gives Salvatore the wooden objects he uses to test the immigrants' intelligence, instinctively he tries to re-create a small farm with a home and animals. Instincts, however, are the result of history and one's environment, not of biology, let alone of myth. Home is what Salvatore left, the animals is what he sold to get the clothes to be accepted in the New World. In other words, the person who theoretically would embrace change and modernity, the one who did want to leave his home, tries to re-create it exactly as it would be in his native Sicily, another moment of the return of the repressed that historically will take the form of the Little Italys of America.

Unlike her son, Fortunata questions the validity of the test itself, in a dispute that reverses the narrative of the fable of immigration to the United States, unmasks the nature of the universality of modernity, and suggests a different way of being modern. When her turn comes to take the test, Fortunata refuses to leave the bench where she sits next to other men and women and sit alone in front of the male examiner. In figurative terms especially proper for a movie where dialogue is minimal and which has more silent than spoken scenes, Fortunata's refusal turns her relationality into universal singularity. She remains seated among the other emigrants, thus embodying them when she questions the validity of the test by asking the officer what are the objects that he is using to test them. Here, the incompatibility between the two is irreconcilable. The examiner asks the male translator sitting next to him if "Mrs. Mancuso" fears that they are going to harm her, obviously ignoring the fact that Mrs. Mancuso has already been harmed, since the immigration process tries to strip away from her and the other emigrants the way they think about themselves, the social and cultural codes they live their life by, and the cognitive parameters that they use to interpret the world that surrounds them. This is what Fortunata refuses to give up. She questions the test itself and says no three times. She says no to having another person, a male, evaluate her intelligence; she says no to an equivalence that factually is a degradation of her essential humanity, the equivalence between objects and a human being implicit in the use of such objects as tools to measure someone's intelligence; and by doing this, she says no to the instrumental logic of rationalization that demands the renunciation of one's own self.

Her refusal is subversively affirmative. It disarticulates the gendered power relations of the immigration process necessary to enter the new, modern world and states her way of being modern. Right after refusing to sit in front of the officer, Fortunata asks the deeply annoyed man what he wants "from us who came from the Old World," thus switching subject and gender positions, turning herself into the examiner. In one sentence she reverses the New World's claim inscribed in the Statue of Liberty from which the American title of the movie is taken, which we now remember was also Booker T. Washington's contention, especially with regard to women: to give the immigrants a new life, a new self, to regenerate them, by being the giver rather than the taker. Fortunata's words unmask the story of the diaspora, which is not about what the New World gives, but what the New World wants. As she reverses the subject positions of the narrative of the New versus the Old World, the narrative of modernity, she also demolishes the authority of the male examiner who tells her that it is his duty to certify that these human beings are physically and mentally fit to enter the New World. She tells him, "Who are you, God, to decide if we're good to go?"

Fortunata's answer sets in irreconcilable contrast the supreme religious entity to the normative code. What makes her statement utterly subversive, however, is not the invocation of the Almighty. What does the trick is Fortunata's use of the personal plural pronoun "we" in opposition to the predicative and singular "you" in her question "who are you," which she associates figuratively with God, the symbol of universality par excellence. First, she resists the authority's attempt to categorize and interpret her according to a system that turns human beings from singular subjects into plural objects. Then, she questions the officer's jurisdiction to select who is fit and who is unfit to enter the New World, lending her voice to all the immigrants, "us immigrants." Finally, she replaces the universality of the normative power with the singular universality of a collective subject, the dispossessed, the poor, those who have nothing but themselves, each other, and their humanism, as indicated by the switch from the plural objective pronoun "us" to the personal plural pronoun "we" that contains the historical multiplicity of the diaspora. By so doing, she claims the equality of "the liberty of thought" of all men and women to whom she, a woman and a mother, the one without whom life simply is not, lends her voice, and, therefore, her self. The world that the Southern Italian women were entering might have been new, but "the liberty of thought" that according to Booker T. Washington such a world would provide them with was actually rather old. The implications of this seeming contradiction and some of its main ramifications are the subject of what is ahead.

2

ROCHESTER, SICILY: THE POLITICAL ECONOMY
OF ITALIAN AMERICAN LIFE AND THE ENCOUNTER
WITH BLACKNESS

After all, you know, I'm white, ethnic, working class. I'm mostly Sicilian, actually.
—Mario Savio, "Beyond the Cold War," October 2, 1984

NO SINGLE BOOK CHARTS the political economy of the early stage of the
Italian American experience better and more comprehensively than Jerre
Mangione's 1942 *Mount Allegro*. His "Memoir of Italian American Life," as
the subtitle of the last authorized reprint of the book reads, depicts the grid
of purposes, socioeconomic contexts, and the cultural forms and contradictions of this life in a multiethnic, working-class neighborhood of Rochester,
New York, one of the cities where Italian immigrants settled at the turn of
the twentieth century, lured by the prospect of a steady, well-paying job that
all too often did not materialize. One of the achievements of *Mount Allegro*
is the subtle ways in which the author documents the importance of the racial diversity of the Italian Americans by linking such diversity to the history
of their land of origins. By so doing, Mangione politicizes this issue in a
transoceanic, working-class perspective, proves the degree to which racial
identity and history are inextricable from the political economy of "Italian
American life," and in turn shows how the latter is structurally incompatible
with the political economy of whiteness in the United States. The geographical stretching of the conceptual boundaries and the experiences narrated in
the last section of *Mount Allegro* in a reversed transoceanic direction allows
us to go beyond the book's insights about American ethnic writing in the
first part of the past century and question *Mount Allegro*'s supposed preference for culture over civilization.

Werner Sollors's reading of *Mount Allegro* in *Ethnic Modernism* privileges this option. According to the German American critic, Mangione presents the Sicily of his Rochester relatives as the island of banquet and tale, a
sort of Italian American platonic dialogue that D. H. Lawrence's admiration
for the Sicilians mediates. Banquet and tale do take center stage in *Mount
Allegro*. The typical Italian conviviality around the kitchen table in conjunction with magisterial storytelling defines the book's light tone as well as the

splendid fluidity of the language, whose fusion of English parataxis and Mediterranean images depicted with the voices of the people who populate the memoir makes for one of the text's most significant formal achievements and mirrors the duality of the inner and outer America that these people experience. Yet Mangione also links this twoness to Italian American life to underscore its entanglement with blackness in America, an entanglement that Mangione uses to question the Italian Americans' assimilation to whiteness, which is what I am interested in pursuing here.

The beginning of the memoir, and the dialogue between the characters that follows it, makes clear that this duality is what the book is all about:

> "When I grow up I want to be an American," Giustina said. We looked at our sister; it was something none of us had ever said.
>
> "Me too," Maria echoed.
>
> "Aw, you don't even know what an American is," Joe scoffed.
>
> "I do so," Giustina said.
>
> It was more than the rest of us knew.
>
> "We're Americans right now," I said. "Miss Zimmerman says if you're born here you're an American."
>
> "Aw, she's nuts," Joe said. He had no use for most teachers. "We're Italians. If y'don't believe me ask Pop."
>
> But my father wasn't very helpful. "Your children will be *Americani*. But you, my son, are half-and-half." (1)

This intergenerational, bilingual, and dialogical opening crosses gender, starts out by giving voice to two female subjects, and closes with the dismissal by patriarchal authority, setting in context and in contrast both generational and gender positions. The father is not helpful with the issue of American identity that his daughters raised. When in 1981, almost four decades after the original publication of the book, Mangione added a chapter called "Finale," he reiterated the primacy of the duality of the identity theme. He wrote that his relatives "engendered problems of identity among their offspring who, reared in a bicultural situation—Sicilian at home, American on the street and in the classroom—were seldom sure who they were. Psychologically, at least, the immigrants were better off than their children. *They* had no identity problem" (*Mount Allegro*, 307).

The generational dichotomy could not be any starker. Home is Sicily—and home is the immigrant parents' unquestioned kingdom. America is the street and the classroom—and both places are battlefields for the children of the immigrants. At home, with a Sicilian-speaking environment strictly enforced, the kids of *Mount Allegro* must listen to their parents and their relatives, especially the women who rule inside the homes. In school, where the language of instruction is obviously English, they must listen to their teacher who tells them they are Americans (never mind that the teacher is a German Jew); in the streets they confront local Americans. The inner, private sphere is Italian; the outer, public sphere is white. The spatial focus of the book is the private sphere: home, Italy, Sicily, the banquet and the tale, or, in short, culture. Yet those tales and banquets execute a psychological and social function that responds dialectically to the outer conditions. They are not solely inner propelled with the help of nostalgia for a land that for the immigrants never was the place they like to mythicize. The tales work as a shelter that the immigrants build around themselves—their children notwithstanding. Nonetheless, these tales, often told around the table, also bridge the private and the public sphere, perhaps to preserve, if not to protect, the production of values and social ties that they document from assimilation into whiteness. I want to suggest exactly this and read the book accordingly. In this perspective, the crossing of the private into the public sphere presents itself as simultaneously the cipher of immigrant life's incompatibility with whiteness and a form of crossover into blackness, as an American novelty and a self-realization of the political economy of the immigrants' Mediterranean heritage. Mangione presents their way of seeing, perceiving, and acting in the world based on the practice of forms of communal action, starting with storytelling as a collective, polyphonic action; their preference for mutuality; their search for consensus; their sense of community that transcends the strict definition of the nuclear family and is symbolic of the value of cooperation that their way of being human enacts; and, finally, their lack of self-interest and the concomitant primacy of what Mangione defines as the characters' "gregariousness," their need to inhabit the same physical space and communal contexts, to share their experiences and mutually recognize each other, certify the value of each other's existence (23). We can think of *Mount Allegro* as an extension of the politics of sharing that Fortunata Mancuso refuses to give up at Ellis Island.

Such a reading of *Mount Allegro* requires us to focus on the four major interconnected layers that compose the book and represent modernity to the eyes of the immigrants: the working-class identity of their environments, broadly conceived; the social negotiations that whiteness imposes on them and their children out of their home; theirs and their children's racial diversity, which begins to fashion a non-solely color-based notion of race that defines the Italian American experience under consideration in this study; and, finally, the historical moment that marks the book, which surprisingly but fittingly for a book about Italian American life published in 1942 and that essentially is the byproduct of the author's experience in the Federal Writers' Project is not the Great Depression. It is, as we shall see, fascism. The minimal reference to the Great Depression in *Mount Allegro* is indeed re-markable, if not altogether stunning, considering both Mangione's involve-ment and lifelong fondness for the FWP,[1] of which later on in his life he would write the history titled *The Dream and the Deal*.[2]

Yet the lack of representation of the Great Depression is not the only notable absence in *Mount Allegro*. In strict terms of history and politics, what is most puzzling in a "Memoir of Italian American Life" centered on the 1920s is the lack of any reference to the Sacco and Vanzetti case. There is no hint, let alone mention of this defining moment in modern American history, not even in the "Finale" chapter of 1981, a chapter that has a more direct political tone than the rest of the book. In "Finale," Mangione writes that one of the goals of *Mount Allegro* was to produce "a work that might help dispel some of the more spurious clichés pinned to the image of Italian Americans by an uninformed American public" (302). In light of this goal, one would think that the Sacco and Vanzetti case should have resonated greatly with a first-rank Italian American leftist intellectual of Mangione's caliber. The fact that *Mount Allegro*, for the most part, describes Italian American life at home is not a satisfying answer to explain this absence. On the contrary, it was especially in the intimacy of the home, often in ethnically homogeneous neighborhoods, that Italian Americans did not have to hide and felt actually free to express their political opinions in their native lan-guage. Frank Sinatra, a man six years older than Mangione with a sense of immigrant life and the Italian American experience just as deep as that of the Rochester native, told Pete Hamill that as a teenager growing up in Hobo-ken, New Jersey, in the 1920s, at night from his second-floor room he could hear his parents sitting at the table talking about Sacco and Vanzetti.[3]

The lack of any reference to the two Italian anarchists is even more strik-ing because of Mangione's work for the American Guide Series. When in 1937 the Federal Writers' Project published the Massachusetts guide, a polit-ical furor invested the director of the project Henry G. Alsberg and his crew over the account and the number of lines accorded to the Sacco and Vanzetti case in the "Labor" essay of the guide. The then governor of Massachusetts, who had signed a laudable introductory page to the book without bothering to read it first, in typical American white fashion called for the burning of all the published copies of the guide. The polemic was so fierce and the political pressure on Alsberg so strong that they crossed state lines and reached Wash-ington, D.C. In *The Dream and the Deal*, Mangione recalls how one day in the aftermath of the diatribe that followed the publication of the Massachu-setts guide, President Franklin D. Roosevelt visited the WPA's headquarters and joked about the furor that the guide had caused. Eventually, the WPA had to surrender and publish a revised edition of the guide with an expurgated version of the "Labor" essay that limited the story of the Sacco and Vanzetti case to one innocuous paragraph. More than half a century later, on March 20, 1990, on the occasion of a lecture at Harvard, Mangione made a point to recall the hysteria that the original Sacco and Vanzetti description in that guide had occasioned.

In that same lecture Mangione identified the prejudice that at the time surrounded ethnic groups, especially Italians. In the most classic stereotypical fashion, such groups were considered prone to crime and therefore were a societal problem. In other words, Italian Americans materialized the fear of the other that characterizes and reifies whiteness. As Mangione told the Harvard students in the audience, in the 1930s ethnics "were considered a problem; there was a great deal of misunderstanding about them. The Italians for one, I can speak from experience. There was a great deal of prejudice against them. They were all considered Mafiosi for one thing" ("Federal Writers' Project"). Albeit in a soft and cheerful tone, *Mount Allegro* conveys a deep sense of the white anti-Italianism of the period and how it touched the lives of the immigrants and their children. In the first chapter, Mangione describes his father reading the newspapers' accounts of murder stories carefully to see if Italians, especially Sicilians, were involved in them. "'It is bad enough for an Italian to commit a murder, but it is far worse when a Sicilian does,'" Mangione recalls him saying, thus pointing out how the external social clime produced the psychological internalization of the possible consequences of prejudice (5).[4]

This brief excursion on the lack of investment in historical immediacy—whether national (the Great Depression), or more directly Italian American (the Sacco and Vanzetti case)—serves to underscore the book's focus on the political economy of modernity that working-class Italian Americans experienced in the United States. A brief, unpublished summary of the book that the author penned and is now preserved in his archives at the University of Rochester points exactly in this direction. "Essentially [*Mount Allegro*] is the spectacle of the Sicilian temper clashing with the American tempo. . . . In essence the story of the Sicilians in *Mount Allegro* is the story of every large immigrant group that came to this country early in the [twentieth] century" ("Brief Summary"). By describing the ways in which Italian Americans lived and clashed with the "American tempo," Mangione portrays a way of being modern, one with ancient ramifications in the history and culture of his Mediterranean people that transcend the historical immediacy of the time, no matter how relevant such immediacy might be. By so doing, he disarticulates the political economy of whiteness in urban America in the early twentieth century, which might as well be Mangione's way to explain the lack of focus on historical immediacy. It is on this turf that Mangione connects

Italian American life to blackness in order to expose its incompatibility with the world of whiteness. First, Mangione shows how the various aspects of Italian immigrant life at home are not reconcilable with the logic of exchange value and self-interested individualism that sustains the political economy of whiteness in the United States; then, toward the end of his memoir, he links the immigrants *historically* to blackness. He achieves this through the examples of specific cultural and religious manifestations pertaining both to the private and the public sphere that the reproduction of communal social ties characterizes. These manifestations define the Mediterranean identity of the Italian Americans of *Mount Allegro*. In this way, Mangione aligns the identity of the Italian immigrants to the symbolic domain of blackness that traditionally identifies the exploited and excluded subject of America. Mangione historicizes blackness in a transnational perspective to conceptualize Italian American life and identity. He does not equate Italian American identity with blackness, let alone with African American subjectivity altogether. At issue here, I argue, is the historical otherness of Italian American life and identity as a marker of its incompatibility with the economic and cultural logic that attends to and sustains whiteness, what Mangione calls the clash with the "American tempo."

In many respects *Mount Allegro* resembles and follows the formula of a bildungsroman. By the time we get to the pages that precede the narrator's voyage to Italy, the childish narrative voice(s) of the beginning, the polyphony of the many characters that gradually enter the stage of the Italian American life that Mangione paints, and the multilayered storytelling that goes back and forth between western New York and Sicily to create the micro-stories that constitute the macro-pattern of the text have given way to the author's voice and his ruminations about the lives his relatives lived and how that way of living is a vital part of his self, of his historical subjectivity, as well as a tool necessary for him to be and to live in the historical present. Mangione explains that once he left Mount Allegro to go to college in Syracuse and eventually to New York City to work in the publishing industry, he started recognizing the significance of his relatives' ways to appreciate life in the face of economic poverty and social exclusion. He describes the experience of the memory of his life in Rochester as "a *root* feeling, a sense of the past which I seemed to need to make the present more bearable" (238).

The root feeling and the sense of the past lead him to search for his Sicilian origins, a quest that he presents as a threefold epiphany. To begin with, he discovers that Sicily's history dates back to "the foundations of time, even down to the region of mythology" of ancient Greek culture that the temples near the native area of his ancestors materialize (238). The discovery of Sicily's Greek past results in a second discovery, the varied identity of his ances-

tral land. Sicily's past includes the presence of "the Phoenicians, the Saracens, the Romans, the Normans, the Spaniards," all of whom, in different
ways and times, "left their marks" on the Mediterranean island (239). The
diversity of the Sicilian past, which the faces and the bodies of his Sicilian
relatives in Rochester translate, makes him question the idea of the American melting pot that supposedly would turn the poor Italian immigrants
into new people who "spoke English with almost no accent and developed
a marked preference for potatoes to spaghetti." Mangione disputes what he
calls "the apparent goal of the melting pot theorists," a word, this last one,
that clearly signals Mangione's interest in the conceptualization of modernity
within the political economy of the narrative about early twentieth-century
America. The goal is for the newcomers to become Anglo-Saxonized, an obvious code term for becoming white. "Was it in the chemistry of human life
for my relatives to become Anglo-Saxonized—the apparent goal of the melting pot theorists?" (239). If the word "theorists" is calibrated, so is "chemistry," which by definition is a combination of elements, a differentiated
plurality. Mangione posits such differentiation as the foundation of the condition of human life, which inherently has a political dimension, as the rest
of the paragraph indicates. As long as his relatives "believed in freedom and
democracy—*and their long history showed those ideals to be as ingrained in
them as their religion*—was it necessary that they try to change themselves?
Didn't America need their wisdom and their warmth, just as they and their
children needed America's youth and vigor?" (239; my italics).

Written with the haunting specter of fascism in the back of the mind,
these lines are nothing short of both an appeal for social integration and
an elegant but firm political statement about Italian Americans living in the
American scene of the first few decades of the twentieth century. Mangione
stresses how the Italian immigrants have a past, a history, at once ancient
and of extreme cultural significance for present-day America, for the development of modern America. Additionally, he uses the immigrants' past to
demolish the melting pot theory according to which in the United States
immigrants gradually lose their heritage in order to adjust to Anglo-Saxon
codes of conduct and ways of life, which is Mangione's way to say that they
become white. This is how Mangione defines whiteness as a political economy, something that also includes language and social customs such as eating habits. Mangione highlights the monolithic aesthetic dimension of the
American melting pot. Moreover, as he demolishes the whitewashing of the
Italians, he adds that if there is such a thing as a melting pot, it is actually to
be found in Sicily. The Italian island's inhabitants include almost the entire
spectrum of Mediterranean populations and the one Northern European
group, the Normans, who by the year 1130 had extended their presence in

England, Scotland, and Wales, as well as areas of northern Africa and the current Middle East. Unlike the American melting pot as its theorists conceived it, the Sicilian one includes different color gradations. It is valuable to point out that within an American context, and even more so in the first half of the twentieth century, Phoenicians and Saracens are code names for dark-skinned, often black people, as well as (in the case of the Saracens) Muslims—that is to say, non-Christian and non-Western people and cultures. Likewise, here Romans stand for pre-Christian, pagan people. In other words, Mangione does not erase color from his idea of a melting pot, from his vision of social integration and political economy. He complements it with different gradations. He stands the very notion of the American melting pot on its head by identifying people who embody different monotheistic and pagan religions. As if this was not enough in 1942 America, Mangione also rejects the pillar of American exceptionalism, the idea that America gives immigrants unconditioned freedom and teaches them democracy. On the contrary, freedom and democracy are already part of the immigrants' history, just as their religion is—and religion or the lack thereof is one of the elements that define people's identity, their ways of living and looking at the world.

Mangione refuses to erase the immigrants' past while at the same time advancing a specific, inclusive idea of modern America. He does not pose the Mediterranean world of his relatives in binary opposition to the Anglo-Saxon universe. Neither does he identify the Anglo-Saxon universe with America. He contends that America needs the "warmth and wisdom" of his relatives just as much as their children need America's "youth and vigor" (239). Such a fusion eliminates the possibility of, on the one hand, identifying whiteness with democracy and freedom, and, on the other, America with the Anglo-Saxons and with white people solely, therefore opening up the question of an all-inclusive idea of modernity. As a result, in the middle of the most destructive war in human history that his native country was fighting also against the native country of his parents and relatives in the name of freedom and democracy, Mangione eliminates the possibility of identifying the United States as the natural and only homeland of said freedom and democracy. In this way, Mangione disarticulates American exceptionalism while he positions democracy and freedom against a transnational and trans-cultural horizon. The identity of these Mediterranean immigrants already includes freedom and democracy. The immigrants do not need to learn freedom and democracy. Better yet, they do not need to be taught freedom and democracy. Not only do they know what freedom and democracy are; they also have something their new country needs, their wisdom and warmth, their "high spirits, their easy naturalness, and their extraverted love of life" (221). America needs them in the first place because the multitude of Italian immigrants and their children are now an integral, however discriminated against, part of America; they live in America; they are an essential component of the country's social fabric; they *are* Americans. Additionally, America needs them in order to learn and appreciate the complex diversity of the human condition that whiteness and capitalist modernity tend to erase. Finally, America needs them because democracy and freedom are a shared and communal experience that must include everyone to be such. Mangione's memoir describes *for* his readers a way of being modern that is democratic and free because of its needed sense of the past that fosters the mutuality, cooperation, common purpose, and shared interest in the present.

The center of this discourse in *Mount Allegro* is the home, which is here to be intended as the combination of the physical site and the family members that inhabit it and surround it, what Robert Orsi, borrowing the term and the definition from Emmanuel Le Roy Ladurie, calls the *domus*, "the unifying principle that linked man and possession," the shelter from "the external powers surrounding it" for a people who were "not yet possessed, like their modern counterparts, with the problem of land," which in our modern, poor, working-class urban context needs to be viewed as the problem of private property. Likewise, the family here is to be understood in Ladurie's terms as "the chief unit of social relationships and cultural transmission" (*Madonna*, xlvi). It is all the more noteworthy that rarely, if ever, does Mangione employ the word "family," preferring the word "relatives," which on the one hand allows him to keep together on equal terms the focus on single individuals within the larger community, playing out the dialectics of individual and community without erasing either from the economy of his discourse, and on the other makes it possible for him to extend the family boundaries beyond the nuclear family, along the lines of Ladurie's definition, virtually reconceptualizing the idea of the family itself through the actions of the people. Mangione situates the home as the center of the life of the people in the book because the world that those people confront outside is a world of exclusion and coercion, concrete as well as mental, which here materializes in the guise of class division and racial prejudice. Mangione does not intentionally juxtapose the home and the outside world that embody two different ways of being modern. The two spaces naturally collide because the political economy of the home produces a consciousness that is incompatible with the world outside it. Mangione pictures the outside as a signifier of conflict because it rejects and exploits the poor, diverse, socially neglected, culturally isolated, and rebellious working-class America that the neighborhood where his relatives live represents.

The spatial division that Mangione portrays throughout the memoir, beginning with the vivid description of his neighborhood, mirrors the ideological one that he and his relatives experience in school, at work, or in the local media. The ideology of reality is the reality of the ideology, and it invests the racial identity of the young protagonist who is already caught in between two worlds, the Sicilian at home and the white world that he encounters outside his neighborhood. Mount Allegro, as the narrator's relatives nicknamed the few blocks where they live, is hardly *allegro* (cheerful) on the outside. It is a wasteland. In the street where the protagonists of the book, the Amorosos, and their relatives and friends live "there are no commercial establishments." Half a block down the road there is "a large and roaring laundry." Farther down, "the biggest optical company in the world" pollutes the Genesee River that provides it with the energy it needs to operate, an inversion that signifies the inherent lack of harmony and conflictual nature of capitalist modernity. Of course, the ones who pay the price of this modernity are the poor and the ones who are literally, in the sense of urban topography, at the margins of society, which is both a topography of exclusion and indifference toward the Italian Americans, the concrete manifestations of their *invisibility* in the eyes of white America. When the wind blows in the direction of the Amorosos' home, "you breathed the stench of the river and the smoke of the factory." Around Mount Allegro there are tailor factories where the narrator collects "half-finished coats and suits" that his mother has to sew at home because the doctor told her that she is not strong enough to work in one of the factories, as many of the other women do to help support their families. Because the railroad track is five minutes away from the house, the blackest smoke is a constant presence, and at night the whistle of the "sad locomotives" sounds even closer (39).

The poverty described in these passages is an economic as well as a spatial condition. And it is organic to the life of these people. Their natural environment reflects their material one, which is a collective, mutual dimension; "we were as poor as the others" (4). Poverty *is* these immigrants' environment, the materiality that they inhabit. It is not, however, the result of chronic lack of work, let alone a supposedly racially inflected laziness that white America typically bestows upon foreigners and nonwhite people, or even lack of initiative, as we shall see shortly. It is the face of modernity that confronts the immigrants in the forms of two of the biggest symbols of their America. One is the factories that pollute and affect the health of the people who live nearby; the other is the locomotives whose sound announces sadness rather than the traditional promise of progress as it does in much of the nineteenth-century mythology of America, for example in Walt Whitman's "To a Locomotive in Winter" in *Leaves of Grass*.[5]

In addition to ecology, health, and economic security, modernity denies these people even the vicinity of basic consumption, as the lack of any com-

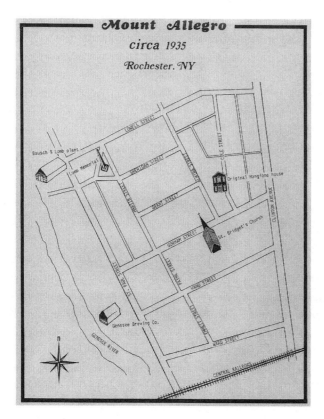

Map of the Mount Allegro neighborhood, circa 1935. Mangione Papers, Department of Rare Books, Special Collections and Preservation, University of Rochester, River Campus Libraries.

mercial establishment in the area attests. The absence of any possibility of consumption is an even more notable inversion because it gives us a real sense of the depth of the exclusion that these Italian Americans experienced at the very moment when consumption becomes the engine of the American economy and the shaping factor of the modern way of life in the United States, not only through commercial establishments but also with the mail catalog, the cipher of the irruption of the advertising industry in modern America. The consequences of the expansion of consumption were at once economic, social, and cultural. In *Making Whiteness*, Grace Elizabeth Hale has pointed out how both the corner store and the mail catalog fueled the crossing of racial boundaries. Paradoxically, this is precisely one of the issues that afflict the life of the Italian immigrants of Mount Allegro. In addition to the lack of a safe and healthy environment and economic security, the exclusion from the possibility of consumption is what connects the self-realization of their working-class consciousness and of racial and ethnic identity to their outsiderness. Along with the Italians, the young narrator-protagonist of the first section of the book plays out in the street with Jewish and Polish friends, which Mangione uses as examples of the psychological coercion America exerts on the immigrants, but also as carriers of traditions as well as indicators of the contradictions of assimilation into whiteness. Tony Long is the Polish friend whose family changed their name upon arriving to the United States in order to avoid dealing with the natives' incapacity to spell correctly the last name. Yet his mother cannot communicate in English with him, something that Tony is ashamed of. Abe Rappaport goes to the synagogue every Saturday and in spite of his age exhibits quite an advanced level of education. Although he is from Russia, physically he resembles the narrator more than blond, Polish Tony, as Mangione makes sure to point out. The only two people who live on the same street as the narrator and dislike the multiethnic group of kids who play there are a Canadian woman and an American (read white) man, the remnants of the neighborhood's demographics prior to the arrival of the Eastern European and Mediterranean immigrants. Naturally, both these people distance themselves from their new neighbors. The Canadian woman keeps her window's shutters always closed except when she spies on the kids who play near her yard to make sure they do not trespass on her property. The man is a factory boss "who would never hire anyone with an Italian name" (47).

The tone of the book may be light, as the kids playing in the street evoke innocence and provoke a smile on the reader's lips, but the message is no joke. Private property, racial prejudice, and social exclusion go hand in hand. The coupling of private property and social exclusion conveyed in the image of a Canadian woman horrified by the idea that the immigrants' children may trespass on her property and an American factory boss who discriminates against Italians is Mangione's nuanced way of indicating that social dimension and cultural consciousness are the white walls erected against the immigrants and their children. That is modern America for the American-born children of the immigrants who struggle to understand why they are not who they think they are, as the beginning of the book tells us. Exclusion and discrimination define their social life outside their homes because of who they are and where they come from. When young Gerlando, the narrator, asks his relatives the difference between Italy and Sicily, his uncle Nino starts a tirade against the American school system that in his view does not educate the children as it should. Afterward, he explains that Sicily is beautiful but immensely poor because "some government clique in Rome is always kicking it [Sicily] around. That, Gerlando, is the chief reason most of us are in this *maliditta terra*, where we spend our strength in factories and ditches and think of nothing but money. All that journeying and all that work just so that we might live and die with our bellies full" (19). In between the scorning of the American school system and the self-realization of the trans-national class dimension of the immigrant experience, Uncle Nino tells us that the experience of immigrants like him and his relatives is one of alien-ation. The ultimate meaning of the journey and the work is mere physical sustenance, nutrition. It bears no other meaning. As such, it is the cipher of the dry consciousness of the country that excludes the immigrants it needs to help it grow, develop, and prosper, which, again, might as well be one of the main reasons why this country needs the "high spirits," the "easy natural-ness" and the "extraverted love of life" of those immigrants. From subject to object seems to be the trajectory of the immigrants in America as Uncle Nino describes it. One wonders, then, if Mangione's assertion that psycho-logically his relatives had no identity problem relates in the first place to their racial identity.

Uncle Nino may give us a first hint in this direction when, in the middle of his tirade against the school system, he interjects in it the racial dimension of his nephew, which he frames in the context of Sicilian history, and of course here Uncle Nino speaks for Mangione. As he tells his nephew, the Greeks, the Romans, the Saracens, the Normans, and the Arabs are among the people who in different periods inhabited the Mediterranean island that gave birth to Gerlando's parents. Of this history, Gerlando's physical ap-pearance and character are the manifestation, which is to say, a non-solely color-based notion of race is the cipher of his history. "One has only to look at your Roman nose, your Arab complexion, and your Saracen disposition to realize the truth of what I'm saying. You, Gerlando Amoroso, are merely a transplanted seed" (18–19). We might translate this description in this way: a pagan nose, a dark complexion, and a Muslim disposition define Gerlando. These are hardly the traditional connotations that, in the national psyche, define an American, because obviously they are not the connotations of the prototypical white American. We might consider, then, if Mangione is historicizing the hybridization of the Italian Americans' racial identity as a way to reconceptualize the interplay between such identity and the politi-cal economy of modern America.

This interplay pervades the book from beginning to end and, in the final section, provides a link to blackness. As we shall see shortly, it serves Man-gione to illustrate how his relatives' identity is their way of life and vice versa. The alienation that Uncle Nino describes seems the outcome of the incompatibility between, on the one hand, the immigrants' identity that pri-oritizes communal social relationships, shared values, and mutual recogni-tion that trigger their constant "gregariousness," and, on the other, the polit-ical economy of self-interested individualism, exchanged value, and social exclusion that identifies whiteness and that forces the immigrants to spend their "strength in factories and ditches and think of nothing but money." Their subject position within the racial mosaic of the United States is the cipher of a system of social relations forged by the actualization of the principle of exchange value that divorces the economy from social relations.

For Mangione's relatives America is the land of king dollar, which they blame for disrupting their established social and cultural norms. "They blamed America, and they said it was a land where money was put above respect and honor" (159). It is tempting to read the contrasts between values and money in the typical context of the strict dichotomy of *la via vecchia*, the familiar, safe, even convenient way of conducting life, the ancient habits and traditional values, against *la via nuova*, the new, perhaps exciting, but uncertain and unknown way, habits, and values. To an extent, this is part of the story. Mangione himself invites the reader to look at the Italian American life he narrates from this angle. He goes back and forth between Rochester and Sicily, both geographically and historically, the two poles that he connects with the web of micro-stories that constitute that macro-pattern of his memoir. His cheerful tone furthers the possibility to read the book according to such binarism. His use of the micro-stories is a way to discuss social norms and conduct such as gender roles that do highlight the discrepancies between life in the Old and the New Worlds.

However, it seems to me possible to read the Old World not in opposition to, but rather as a world operating within the new one. I want to propose not a cultural reading of the overdeterminations of the Italian American life that Mangione paints, but one where the Old World functions as a critique of the political economy of capitalist modernity and whiteness, as a narrative that describes a way of being modern that is inclusive and democratic; a way that affirms the primacy of being human that entails dialogue, cooperation, mutuality, and inclusive social relations over individual self-interest and monetary profit; a way to be subjects of modernity rather than objects of it, one where the individual is a member of a shared *destino* (fate) and therefore deserves dignity. To paraphrase Robert Orsi, this is the Mediterranean way of being human in the modern world, what Mangione calls his relatives' "gregariousness," their need to be together that distinguishes them from other ethnic group in the neighborhood, including the "clannishness" of his playmates: "whereas my Jewish friends were content to see their relatives occasionally, my relatives were constantly seeking each other out to celebrate the existence of one another" (24). They seek each other constantly in the first place because, in the tradition of Mediterranean spirituality, as Mangione's choice of the verb "celebrate" indicates, they believe that mutual recognition engenders the sacred value that they assign to life. At the same time, this constant search for one another is a way to prevent individual isolation, a way to find a psychological shelter in what clearly is a hostile external environment, a hostility that they constantly perceive, even internalize. Thus, in this bodily social dimension of togetherness there might be partially reflected the effects of the psychological fear of the anti-Italian prejudice and discrimination encountered in the public sphere.

In the beginning of the memoir Mangione describes his father's anxiety when he reads to the rest of the family the newspapers' account of deadly crimes involving Italians or when he prohibited his sons from carrying knifes "because of the unpleasant association they had in the public mind with Sicilians" (7). The Mediterranean way of being human therefore functions also as a support system, a protection from the invasion of the racist public sphere into the personal one, which tells us how the personal sphere does not equal an individual or isolated, private sphere. Rather, it indicates a practical and practiced belief in a shared, communal dimension of life, one to be distinguished from both the idea of the nuclear family and the private sphere. Being together *is* their life. One significant moment of this way of living is when Mangione reports how any of the mothers of related children playing together "felt she had the prerogative of delivering stinging slaps with the back of her hand, regardless of whether the target was her own child or not" (15). We will have time to detail the centrality of the mother's role in the overall development of Italian American life. It is enough here to point out how this episode of seemingly customary discipline denotes how in the home power and respect are not prerogatives of single individuals. The mothers partake of power and respect because they guarantee the reproduction of the notion of respect that guarantees the primacy of the person.

This is not solely a matter of the behavioral sphere or intergenerational relationships. It is the Mediterranean way of being human in a modern context, which revolves around the notion of *rispetto*. In *The Madonna of 115th Street* Orsi has studied the various, complex ways in which *rispetto* manifested itself and regulated the life of a rather homogeneous urban community from the standpoint of what he defines as "lived religion . . . ideas, gestures, imaginings, all as media of engagement with the world" (xxvi). Orsi is quite adamant in stating that this is a form of interplay rather than an identity form, an interplay that occurs against the background of the material world of the Italian immigrants of East Harlem that he studied, the world that contributed to shaping them and their daily existence. Unlike Orsi's East Harlem, in the strict theoretical sense, the world Mangione describes is secular. Yet this same world is equally as sacred as Orsi's Italian Harlem because *rispetto* governs the lives of the people he narrates and makes these lives sacred in each other's eyes. That is what explains the fierce family feud between Uncle Nino and Gerlando's father. In essence, the two men fight over values, not money or property. For these people *rispetto* affirms what Orsi defines as "the dignity of the person respected as well as the person respecting" (228). It entails the inescapability of the concreteness of reality and people, including the other, whose presence is therefore recognized, made visible—the exact opposite of white America's denial of the Italians. It implies "connotation of reciprocity, an insistence on shared responsibilities and mutually recognized dignity" (228). It testifies to the commonality of their daily realities, the latter's communal dimensions, as well as the belief that destiny is shared as a fact of human life. It is no coincidence that the immigrants of *Mount Allegro* value property in community, labor for the benefit of all, and share their resources.

Mangione does not present the political economy of his relatives' life as something that belongs to a distant past that has no value. We shall see momentarily how little by little he fashions it in a forward-looking frame to make it relevant, actual to his historical present, a present that by way of the incremental growth of the tales he interjects in the memoir brings the past that his relatives' stories embody into the present of his experience. All the stories that Mangione recalls from the Sicilian past of his relatives serve to advance the chronology of the memoir, which always moves forward. It is, of course, a narrative strategy of oral historians that most likely he learned during his time with the Federal Writers' Project. Mangione employs it to extend the boundaries of his narrative, connect the Mediterranean world to the United States, and include class consciousness and racial outreach as recognition of the self-realization of one's own historically grounded diversity. The examples abound and, aptly, concern communal moments of life that intertwine the personal and the public sphere and inherently transcend the profit motif, the very idea of *making* money, a contradiction in terms revealing of the repressed social desire of capitalist modernity that is expressed by way of negation in the practice of consumerism, the public manifestation of private self-interest.

When Gerlando's father, Peppino, makes peace with one of the cousins with whom he had a family argument, as a sign of reconciliation he offers his service as plumber, carpenter, paperhanger, cook, and pastry maker without asking any monetary compensation. He acknowledges that what unites the two is not some mythological blood, but the fact that they belong to the same reality that conveys a shared sense of being equal. One of the consequences of this reciprocity entails the self-recognition of the use-value of the various skills that the factory system (where most of the immigrants work) erases, which is to say that are wasted in the system of accumulation of capital by way of reification that the assembly line, the free market, and the consumer society embody. A second, even more telling example concerns

Peppino's skills as pastry maker, which he acquired in Sicily when he worked as a young man with a famous pastry cook. As Mangione recounts, his father had become extremely skilled in this art, something Mangione reiterates more than once in the space of a few paragraphs. Because of his skills, Baron Michele, the richest man in the province of Girgenti (Agrigento), took Peppino with him during the baron's honeymoon to Palermo. Had he remained in Sicily, Mangione comments, Peppino "might have become a celebrated pastry maker," an example of the self-made-man trope that is precisely what America supposedly promotes and celebrates, unless one's name is Peppino Amoroso (128). In other words, Sicily, not America, might have turned out to be Peppino's land of milk and honey, a complete inversion of the mainstream narrative of America as the land where hard work, observance of the established rules, and self-drive guarantee individual achievement, both financial and in status. In Rochester, instead, the lack of social integration resulted in the lack of a market for Sicilian pastries, particularly Peppino's favorite specialty, cannoli, and forced him to become a factory worker like so many other immigrants. Peppino saves his art for special occasions, when friends and relatives are his guests. Because of their financial circumstances, these events occur less and less frequently. In the end, only the immediate family and friends end up being occasionally graced with boxes containing the right number of cannoli for each person. The prize of the cannoli, however, is not a monetary one. It is Peppino's request to the relatives and guests not to let anybody know about them because he does not want to hurt those with whom he cannot share his cannoli. Mangione comments, "He never took money for his *cannoli* and would be hurt if anyone tried to pay him" (130). Mangione adds that at one time his father did open a pastry shop, but despite the many clients, he made no money. As he realized after closing the shop, he was not charging enough to cover the expenses for the ingredients.

Obviously, the values of *rispetto* and recognition of the other that Peppino lives by are not reconcilable with the profit motif that the so-called free market requires. Yet the passage is revealing for other reasons as well. Like the previous example of family reconciliation through the offer of free services to a relative, this recollection suggests that one of the seldom acknowledged stories of immigration to America, of twentieth-century modernity, is that of a de-skilling of the immigrants, whose devaluation inevitably has an impact in the personal sphere, at the inner level, and to an extent leads to a degree of desocialization. Equally important is these people's refusal to take money in exchange for a service, which we remember is exactly what amazed (or maybe scared?) Booker T. Washington in Sicily. The refusal to take money is not the cipher of a mythological primitivism of the immigrants in a modern society where money is king. On the contrary, these are extremely modern people. After all, they are able to survive in a foreign land, to work on the assembly line and as plumbers, carpenters, paperhangers, and cooks as well. Moreover, they can prepare very sophisticated pastries, a process that Mangione carefully details. And they read the local newspaper, especially because they are aware of the criminal reputation that the media so willingly bestow upon them. In other words, they fully grasp the power of the media. Likewise, they understand the power of whiteness, or, better yet, they understand that whiteness is power in America. So much for the illiterate and inferior peasants of Ellis Island! These people do not see money as an arbiter of the value of fellow human beings. Perhaps that is exactly the reason why the melting pot theorists want to erase their past, assimilate them. When Mangione's father refuses money for his famed cannoli, he is not refusing money because he is not in need of it or because he fails to understand the importance of money in American life, especially for poor immigrants like himself. He is valuing his relatives' and friends' recognition of his culinary artistry, which makes him achieve personal, inner satisfaction as an individual. This is the kind of self-interest the immigrants' political economy entails, one aspect of what they referred to as *rispetto*. Their politics of sharing as Mangione describes it gives primacy to people over money because in the first place it acknowledges the presence of people, their tangible humanity, which, as such, needs to be respected. This practice results in mutual recognition, equality of identity as fellow human beings who inhabit the same realities, which is their concrete equality, and does not erase the subjectivity of the single person. On the contrary, as Peppino's example demonstrates, it can also foster individual self-fulfillment.

The political economy of *rispetto* that Mangione's memoir describes is not an isolated example. On the contrary, it would seem to identify an essential trait of the immigrants' way of being and living, one that crosses genders and historical periods and is not necessarily restricted to the private sphere either. We find the same idea outside the Amorosos' household in the public arena. One such example is available in the civil poetry of sculptor Onorio Ruotolo. In the poem "In Union Square Park," he writes

Perhaps because that oasis, an island
Ill known and ill famed,
Lost and forgotten
In the heart of the boundless city
Swarming with greedy and grasping beings,
Is a true, integral democracy:
So that the wandering pilgrims
Of all ages and all races,

All faiths and all ideals,
Like its hundred varicolored doves,
Find a place of refuge, outlet, and peace
In Union Square.

Little park, with no other laws
Than free and brotherly tolerance
And mutual respect
For the civil liberties of all! (231)

Likewise, Diane di Prima, who in "Ode to Keats" claims poverty as her Italian background—"the children of the poor/of whom I am one" (57)— shows us the wholeness of respect in "April Fool Birthday Poem for Grandpa," a poem whose political context recalls the epistemology of Fortunata Mancuso and the immigrants of *Nuovomondo*, where nature and human beings are part of the same cosmos and where production is not at the service of consumption. She writes

No punches, back there in that scrubbed Bronx parlor . . .
Pulling my hair when I
Pulled the leaves off the trees so I'd
Know how it feels. (69)

In *Mount Allegro* the code of *rispetto* by which the immigrants live defines the dimension of money as well. From a medium of exchange, money becomes a tool to share and generate social ties. In the middle of the Great Depression, Uncle Luigi decides to gamble five cents on the lotto, a racket very popular in Italy, also known as the numbers game. Unlike most of the relatives, Uncle Luigi has never played lotto before. The three numbers he plays are the winning numbers. Uncle Luigi cashes in two hundred and fifty dollars, truly a significant amount of money in the 1930s, even more so for poor people. Immediately, he shares part of the money. He gives each of his children and his sisters ten dollars. "Like most Sicilians," Mangione explains, "he was superstitious about good luck and felt that unless you shared it with others it would surely turn into bad luck" (237). Again, we need to go beyond the surface of what appears to be a primitive superstitious habit and realize that Uncle Luigi's action responds to the logic of these people's communal attitude toward human existence. Uncle Luigi *feels* that positive events demand to be shared with others because this is how individual self-fulfillment is achieved. This is not lack of reason, in the common sense of the modern philosophical tradition from Vico and the Enlightenment to Marx and Gramsci. Common sense here needs to be understood as a feeling that identifies the *right* thing to do because the wholeness of life implies the recognition that reality is communal. Consequently, it can also be personal and intimate. It does not erase the individual self. Rather, the individual self is celebrated just as much and in the most proper way. It is celebrated in aesthetic terms.

It is no coincidence that the second thing that Uncle Luigi does with his money is buy himself "a complete outfit of clothes, enough to wear until he was ninety" (237). This purchase is a form of *rispetto* for reality that acknowledges one's mortality and one's dignity in front of it. The need to literally embody dignity before death is how these people transcend the materiality of death and give primacy to human life. Ultimately, the very idea of dignity is the fruit of the recognition of people's common destiny, because people are first and foremost different and differentiated selves. That is why Uncle Luigi saves a few dollars for a game of poker and uses the rest of the two hundred and fifty dollars for food and wine to throw a huge party for his family and his relatives. The people to include are so many, Mangione recalls, that Uncle Luigi has to organize two parties. At noon, his sons and daughters and their families celebrate him. The rest of "the family circle" attends the supper, eating pizza and other Southern Italian food and drinking wine (237). The table becomes once again the place where existence is celebrated because it is universal, turning a private moment into a public one and, by so doing, pairing culture and consciousness. Nutrition is turned into a form of reproduction of values within the home, which in turn becomes a site that produces social ties and values whose reification reaffirms for the immigrants their shared destiny and the universality of such destiny that each individual self inhabits.

It is poignant, perhaps even revealing that at this point in the narrative Mangione introduces American blackness into his memoir of Italian American life. As he finishes recalling Uncle Luigi's memorable party that both family members and the larger Italian American community of the neighborhood attended, he informs the reader that after the food and the wine, the celebration continues in different forms. The adults share memories of their life in Sicily, of their past. Mangione's father, Uncle Nino, and Uncle Luigi play the card game of *briscola* for almost the entire evening. The youngsters, instead, "danced and listened to jazz" (237). How is it that the children of the Italian immigrants, the first generation of American-born Italian Americans, listen and dance to jazz, the music par excellence of modern black and urban America? Where does jazz come from? How did it enter this Italian fortress where the English language, what the immigrants call the American language, is forbidden to the children? Are not the dagos supposed to listen to opera and play the mandolin? What kind of game is Mangione playing here? Thus far, he has traced a strictly dual world. The Italian inside the home; the American, white world outside it. Both worlds as Mangione depicts them are rigidly governed by the norms that reflect this dichotomy of identities. The Jewish and Polish kids who play out in the street with the Italian kids are the only variation to this almost Manichean division, a difference that only reinforces the division between the outer world and the ethnic homes. At home, the kids are forced to speak Italian, or what their parents think of as Italian but is a Sicilian dialect. They follow the Italian traditions, pay homage to Dante instead of Lincoln, hear the constant sanctification of Sicily, observe the parents playing Italian cards games and, more to the point, listening to opera religiously. Until this point in the book, Mangione referenced racial diversity especially with regard to the bodies, which he presented as custodians of a Mediterranean history of colonization and migratory movements that produced the racial difference previously mentioned in Uncle Nino's physical description of young Gerlando. There is no sign whatsoever of American blackness in the outside world that Mangione describes. How, then, did this black music enter their Italian American home? What do we make of it? Equally important, what is the point of this recollection, and why does blackness enter the book through jazz right here in the memoir, after more than two hundred pages that Mangione used to describe what we might call the world of Rochester, Sicily?

Originally, without the added "Finale" chapter, *Mount Allegro* consists of 285 pages. On page 237, we are told that the youngsters listen and dance, obviously with parental approval, to a modern musical genre that historically identifies black America and the outset of twentieth-century modernity. Of course, by the 1920s the contribution of Italian Americans to jazz had been already relevant, which speaks of an achieved, factual, ethnic and racial working-class form of crossover and hybridization that takes us precisely to the core of the question. The point here is that the outer America that enters the Italian American *home* where Italian American life happens, we might even say is performed, is black America. The America the Italian American children embrace or are attracted to is intertwined with black America. Whether Italian Americans or black Americans perform the jazz being played in the Amorosos' household is irrelevant. If anything, the fact that Mangione identifies the musical genre instead of the performers indicates that the American-born children of the Italian-born parents dance to the same music that black Americans perform and dance to. The preference for the genre over the performers reiterates the association of the Italian Americans with black America and the hybridization that it generates.

To make things even more complex, and interesting, this moment occurs after Mangione has spent the previous 236 pages describing in detail a way of living that projects a world completely detached from and with hardly anything in common with what he identifies as America—and America here means invariably Anglo-Saxon America, again Mangione's code term for whiteness. Furthermore, anytime the Italian Americans and their way of living come in contact with white America, the end result is some sort of conflict. Whiteness identifies economic stability and power relations. It becomes a way of life. Mangione writes how his relatives were both suspicious of and admired white Americans because they signified "getting on in the world. The bosses were Americans. The police were Americans. In fact nearly everyone who had plenty of money or a good steady job was either an American or *was living like one*" (223; my italics). Money and the economic stability that a steady job provides are the signs of class and social status that define America for the immigrants who are left out of this world, out of the privileges of whiteness. And the color of this status is white. Because of this, white disappears as a color that identifies a race and becomes the norm to follow to be financially safe and socially respected, or at least accepted.

The cipher of this normativity is the Italians who have become professionals, the doctors and lawyers. They did not waste much time in marrying "blonde American girls" and moving far from the neighborhood. Some even "dropped the vowels from the end of their names, so that people would think they had always been American." Not only did they attempt to erase their past. They even broke family relations and customs as they "stopped associating with their relatives" (223). Their wives walk little dogs that are synonyms of elite status and replace children. The only time they deal with Italians is to get "money in their pocket" (224). These Italians, Mangione is telling us, marry blond girls and pass as white, a color that identifies money and the social status that money guarantees in a society divided in classes. Conversely, these Italians testify to the original otherness of the Italians within the taxonomy of the racial mosaic of modern America. If leaving Little Italy is the passport to whiteness and its privileges, staying Italian, so to speak, means being nonwhite. And so, what is Mangione after when he associates the first generations of Italian Americans with blackness, an association that color signifies but does not exhaust?

To begin with, Mangione presents the structural dimension of the Italian Americans' encounter with blackness because blackness is an integral part of the immigrants' identity and history. It belongs to Southern Italians. It is part of who they are, as a people and historically. When the narrator of *Mount Allegro*, now an adult, arrives in Sicily in search of his roots with the goal to understand who he is and who his people are, two things strike him as complete novelty: the poverty and the scenery of the island, which reflect each other. Gone is the fabulous Sicily of Rochester, the product of his relatives' longing for a land that never was what they desperately wanted it to be. What does *not* strike him, instead, is the way people look and their diversity:

> Everywhere I saw replicas of my Rochester relatives. There was the same variety of types. Some had the coloring and features of Arabs; others looked like models for El Greco. Sometimes you would see a Moorish head on a Spartan body; or the raven hair and lustrous black eyes of a Saracen set off by a Roman nose. There were redheads like my Uncle Nino; soft brunettes, like my mother; and a scattering of blue-eyed blonds. (265)

What is missing here is plain white people. The "scattering" exception confirms the rule that is inscribed in the essence of these people's identity, their religion. Back in his mother's native Girgenti, from Porto Empedocle where he is supposed to meet Rosario Alfano, an old Rochester friend who returned to the native island, Gerlando asks his great-uncle Stefano to take him to see the famous temples. His great-uncle turns down Gerlando's request because he has no use for the glory of "pagan gods" (280). Mangione points out how "like many other Sicilian Catholics I knew, my great-uncle would have denied that the religious customs he observed had any connection with his non-Catholic ancestors." And yet, Mangione continues, "the evidence was all around, particularly on the days when the saints were feasted," when the connection to blackness unfolds entirely, and with it the political reasons that prompt Stefano's refusal of Gerlando's request to visit the temple of the "pagan gods" as well as Mangione's motivations in recollecting how "the saints were feasted" (281).

The description that follows of the *festa* that celebrates Saint Calogero, the patron of Girgenti, begins with a reference to Harlem, which by the time of the publication of *Mount Allegro* was already the black mecca of the world. Mangione writes, "One morning I woke to the beating of drum rhythms *that took me back to the Harlem night clubs*. Wandering around the streets were peasants with long, narrow drums hanging from their neck. They were pounding them all over the city to announce the annual four-day celebration for Saint Calogero, the patron saint of Girgenti" (281; my italics). There is here a fascinating return to the roots, one that, among other things, informs Mangione's previous comments on the racial mosaic of Sicily and of the Italian Americans of Rochester; the note on the youngsters listening and dancing to jazz at Uncle Nino's big party; and the America outside of and after life in Mount Allegro. In Sicily, Mangione realizes that the racial diversity of the Sicilians, which includes the sound that the peasants bring to the city and that takes Mangione back to black Harlem, reflects their civilization. It is part of the Sicilians' most deeply felt, respected, and carefully observed traditions. It is an essential part of their life. It is "ingrained in them," as he said when he compared his parents' ideals of democracy and freedom to their religion. It is a component of who they and their replicas in Rochester are. What this racial diversity tells Mangione is that blackness is an inherent component of Italian American identity. It identifies a way of being in and seeing the world that is not reconcilable with the political economy of whiteness, the cause of the exclusion and the racism that the Italians of Rochester experienced, unless they abandoned their neighborhoods and their ways of living, married blond girls, and passed as white.

That is why the sound of the drums, the African instrument par excellence that evokes the rhythm of pagan life, human interdependence, and a dialectical communion to nature, as well as the instrument that sustains jazz music, brings Mangione back to the Harlem of the 1920s and its clubs, to black America. For the same reason, this essential moment of life in Sicily does *not* take him back to white America. African music Sicilian style—we might say a premodern form of association not unlike the previously encountered one between the Italian Americans of Mount Allegro and black America through jazz—is the sound of the past of Mangione's ancestors, what, in fact, leads Mangione to the sound of *his* recent, (Italian) American past, to his dancing to jazz in Rochester and the Harlem nights, connecting the two across lands, oceans, and histories, overlapping continents and civilizations. Just as Booker T. Washington could not repress the images of slavery when he saw the Neapolitan women working in the fields, Mangione's inner self, its unmediated consciousness, reacts to the sound of his past by associating it with the most iconic place of the African American experience in modern times. The association invites us to reconsider how rigid the color boundaries might have been and, more important, how such a porous border, however briefly hinted at in *Mount Allegro*, at some level might have been the indicator of a more consistent and complex, we might argue even structural, interaction between African Americans and Italian Americans. At the same time, we will do well to be mindful that both Washington's and Mangione's self-realizations occur when the two are outside their native country, when they think about life in the United States from the outside.

However, Mangione does not stop at the sound of Mediterranean blackness. He continues to use the story of Saint Calogero to dig into and give a political twist to the ancient history and the civilization he sees displayed in front of him, in action. To begin with, he informs the reader that Saint Calogero was a missionary doctor from Ethiopia whose fame resulted from "his miracles in curing the sick and the maimed" that prompted the locals to revere him and the Catholic Church to canonize him soon after his death. Then, he adds, "No one had ever disputed his Ethiopian ancestry—you had only to look at the features and coloring of his statue to be convinced of it"

(281). Again, Mangione, who writes for an American audience with the intent to give a non-distorted image of Italian Americans, establishes the connection between his Southern Italian past and blackness. He achieves this by way of recalling the most sacred of the tradition, which, accordingly and tellingly, evokes a politics of sharing and mutual respect between an African man and the people of Girgenti, especially the poor, the peasants, and the mothers of sick children. In the evening the peasants carry to the church "crude but very graphic crayon drawings illustrating the numerous ways that Saint Calogero had interceded to save their relatives from some horrible disease or accident," further proof of skills and an aesthetic sense rarely accorded to them by the mythography of the ignorant peasants that the self-appointed guardians of official history codified (281). During the procession, Mangione continues, "anxious mothers with sick children waited for the parade to pass their houses" and ask for the saint's help (282). The mothers hand the child to the priest, who blesses and returns the child to the mother. In turn, she kisses the feet of the black saint. History, aesthetics, social relations, a sense of common purpose, and religious traditions—we might as well call this a civilization. This is what unites blackness and Southern Italians, especially the mothers. Better yet, the mothers function as the connector between blackness and Southern Italians. There is no sign of racial tension involved in this picture and in this passage that, incidentally, and perhaps not altogether fortuitously, recalls Frederick Douglass's observation of the statue of Jesus in Rome in *Life and Times of Frederick Douglass*: "I had some curiosity in seeing devout people going up to the black statue of St. Peter—I was glad to find him black, I have no prejudice against his color—and kissing the old fellow's big toe, one side of which has been nearly worn away by these devout and tender salutes of which it has been the cold subject" (577).

What fuels racial tension is politics, and a specific kind of politics—fascism. Mangione points out how on the year of his visit to Sicily some particularly enthusiastic fascists "carried away by the conquest of Ethiopia, were insisting that Saint Calogero had been a Sicilian who acquired a heavy coat of tan" (281). Mangione was too keen of a writer and an intellectual to disregard the symbolic and historical importance of Ethiopia for African Americans. At the same time, as somebody who lived in New York City until he received his appointment as coordinating editor of the Federal Writers' Project in Washington, D.C., he knew that if the drums of the feast of Saint Calogero brought back sweet memories of the Harlem nights, the drums of the Italian aggression in Ethiopia signified the Harlem riots between Italian Americans and African Americans and, eventually, the Roosevelt administration's sanctions against fascist Italy. No less relevant is the fact that *Mount Allegro* was published right in the middle of World War II, which explains why Mangione ends the recollection of the feast with the description of an episode that ridicules Il Duce and pays homage to the black saint.

The *festa* closes with fireworks that portray Saint Calogero and Mussolini, an improbable association that speaks volumes about how ingrained the blackness and the values that the saint em*bodies* are in the identity of the people that honor him. Whereas the former "blazed his full glory," Mangione reports, "Mussolini glowed doubtfully for two or three seconds; then a pinwheel of green fire jumped out of place and went whirling over the expanse of Il Duce's jaw. The next moment the whole portrait burst into flames and collapsed" (283). The symbolic irony of the episode and of the entire description of the feast of the black saint is easy to detect. Mangione elevates the blackness of an original outsider like Saint Calogero above fascism, elevates a religious tradition that is part of the Sicilians' identity and Mediterranean civilization over the figure of Mussolini. If anybody has conquered a people and a land, it is certainly not Mussolini. It is the African doctor who, instead of weapons and chemical gases, used his medical skills and his empathy for the local people. Love, not death, won over the Sicilians, earned their *rispetto*, and became part of their identity and civilization. That is why the Sicilians, and the mothers especially, revere him.

And yet this is not the entire story. We can go further and gain an even keener sense of this complex net of historically determined racial relationships and of how transatlantic modernity impacted these relationships by looking at another moment of Mangione's visit to Sicily. When the writer tells the conductor of the train that takes him to Girgenti that he is from New York, the conductor comments that he does not "*look* like an American" (247). In Girgenti, first he is welcomed by a rally of relatives; then he is inundated with various forms of hospitality, "particularly at meal times" (253). His attempt to contribute financially to the meals fails miserably. His relatives forgive his attempted contribution, which naturally would be an act of disrespect and violation of the unwritten law of Mediterranean hospitality, because he is an American, precisely what the train's conductor questioned about Mangione's physical appearance. We could read this contradiction between appearance and facts as a form of reversed passing, Italian American style, so to speak. What makes the whole episode even more intriguing, however, is how Mangione's relatives rationalize their forgiveness. They conclude that, because he is an American, he "must have been brought up among a lot of Indians" (253).

His relatives consider Mangione's attempt to contribute to the meals an act of somebody who does not know how to behave appropriately, which they identify with the native tribes of North America. One way to read this passage is through the lens of Eurocentrism. Yet these are the same people who venerate a black saint from Ethiopia whose history dates back to God knows when. What is at stake here is a way of viewing the world that equals a way of feeling modern. To Mangione's relatives, America is the symbol of industrial modernity, of technological progress. That is the reason why, when Mangione arrives in Girgenti, as a way to honor him and take him around town they rent a car, the ultimate symbol of the technological advancement that they associate with America, as the former consulting editor of the American Guide Series knew all too well. When they accuse him of breaking the hospitality code, however, they associate his behavior with primitivism by way of associating him with the Indians. Yet this primitivism is paired with his offer *to buy* some of the provisions, which goes against the Mediterranean tradition of welcoming the guest, the other, the one who comes from outside, and showing respect by providing for such a guest. It is the same tradition and conduct that Mangione's father follows when he does not charge his guests and relatives any money for his cannoli. Again, *rispetto* does not include self-interest and exchange value that money represents through its purchasing power. Paradoxically—and paradoxes are an indication of history—to Mangione's relatives the Indians are an analogy of modern America, of a modernity that is considered primitive because it breaks the unwritten law of providing for the guest, for the outsider. It is telling that Mangione's relatives do not tease him by saying that he must have grown up among black people, or, as Booker T. Washington has it in *The Man Farthest Down*, among "the savages in Africa" (173).

Mangione's relatives think of themselves as modern people precisely because they maintain their tradition of hospitality that the principle of *rispetto* regulates, in spite of their extreme poverty that "made their hospitality seem all the more painful" to Mangione (253). They accuse the *americano* of acting like an American, which is to say acting white or, which is the same, as we have seen, "not Italian." And how could Mangione's relatives and friends in Sicily accuse him of anything else, given their racial variety and history? How could this not be the case when they revered, kissed, and asked for help from a black saint from Ethiopia? We may find an explanation in the recurrent investment of pivotal African American writers in Italian Americans during the age of Jim Crow.

[3]

STRUCTURES OF INVISIBLE BLACKNESS: RACIAL
DIFFERENCE, (HOMO)SEXUALITY, AND ITALIAN
AMERICAN IDENTITY IN AFRICAN AMERICAN
LITERATURE DURING JIM CROW

IN 1912 BOOKER T. WASHINGTON was not the only African American writer to invest in Italian Americans in order to make an argument about race and modernity in America. That same year, James Weldon Johnson published *The Autobiography of an Ex-Colored Man*, arguably the founding text of African American literature, as well as the first of a series of literary texts by black male writers during Jim Crow that include a central Italian American presence. These texts are Richard Bruce Nugent's *Gentleman Jigger*, written between 1928 and 1932 but published posthumously in 2008; Sterling Brown's poem "Harlem Happiness," from his second collection of poetry titled *No Hiding Place*, which Brown wrote in the mid-1930s but published only in 1980; William Attaway's *Blood on the Forge*, which appeared in 1941; Willard Motley's 1947 best seller *Knock on Any Door*; and, last, James Baldwin's *Giovanni's Room*, which reached the bookstores in 1956. In different ways, these works represent important moments in the development and the trajectory of African American literature. They are an integral part of the African American literary canon. The centrality of the Italian American presence that they share, however, is yet to be accounted for, which is the prime goal of what follows. What are we to make of these writers' investment in Italian Americans as a way to address the relationship between race and processes of modernization in the twentieth century? How do we explain the gendering of this investment and the insistence on Italian American working-class homoeroticism and homosexuality in Attaway, Nugent, and Baldwin? Does this shared presence help us understand the lack of an equally significant Italian American literary investment in African Americans during the same historical period that these books delimit? Consequently, how is it that the centrality of the Italian American presence greatly diminishes after the demise of legal segregation? How do we extricate ourselves from this entanglement of processes of modernization, historical periodization, literary canon, and the class-based racial and sexual politics of these diverse texts?

My premise is that the Italian American presence in these texts needs to be related to the rise and the identity of African American literature as the result of segregation. This syncretic presence and its termination amplify Kenneth Warren's conceptualization of African American literature as "a postemancipation phenomenon that gained its coherence as an undertaking in the social world defined by the system of Jim Crow segregation, which ensued after the nation's retreat from Reconstruction" (1). The Italian Americans in the writings that I consider in these pages allows us to move from Warren's critique of the elites and widen the perimeter and the depth of Erich Auerbach's insights that inspire the African American literary critic's thesis, according to which certain "contextual forces shape a set of assumptions *about what ought to be represented* and that as these contexts themselves undergo change, those representational and rhetorical strategies that at their peak served to enable authors and critics to disclose various 'truths' about their society can begin to atrophy and become conventionalized so that they no longer enable literary texts to come to terms with social change" (9; my italics).

Because of the parallel advent of and collision between Jim Crow and the European, Mediterranean, and Caribbean immigration between the end of the nineteenth and the beginning of the twentieth century, the established black-and-white dichotomy reflected in the normative realm, the racial discourse, the economic structure, and the national psyche changed dramatically. New skin colors and gradation of skin colors arrived to the American shore by the thousands on a daily basis. With them also arrived thus far atypical, if not entirely new religious faiths and ways of practicing them, cultural traditions, social norms, languages, and everyday life habits. As always in our country's history, a massive new wave of immigration equaled labor exploitation, which in turn drove down workers' wages. Often this endemic structure of a capitalist system triggered conflicts between race and ethnic groups, old and new. Sometimes it created interracial and interethnic unity. Either way, however, these old and new groups came in contact, dramatically impacting established racial formations and sociocultural parameters.

My view is that as the American mosaic underwent these drastic changes, African American male writers invested in Italian Americans as a way to recalibrate and reconsider the role of race in twentieth-century America in conjunction with larger processes of modernizations that took effect in the nation and the entire Atlantic world. The presence of Italian American men allowed the African American writers here in question to enact representational strategies of appropriation and subversion in order to build a version of the black male self during Jim Crow that would have been otherwise un-available to them—one in which color, or the lack thereof, was not the only unit of measure of African American male identity in the eyes of white and, to an extent, black people alike. The Italian American presence helped these writers to address and challenge the formulaic representation of black Americans that Alan Locke lamented in *The New Negro*: "In the mind of America the negro has been more of a formula than a human being" (quoted in Sollors, *Neither*, 229). Italian Americans served these writers to represent the complexity of what it meant to be human for African American men in the context of and as part of the American scene during Jim Crow. Italian American men helped to make their black counterparts and their diversity visible under a different light. The subversive consequences of these representations might have even exceeded these writers' expectations. All of a sudden, the subject that historically represented the other in the supposedly most advanced modern nation and a threat to whiteness had the potential, albeit a fictional one, to be everyone's self. As this reciprocal singular universality intersected working-class and homosexual identity, it questioned the patriarchal and classist heteronormativity of Western civilization. It also made visible how the concomitant establishment of segregation and the Mediterranean and Eastern European immigration to the United States reified a social order of collective division and flexible group exclusion.

It is no coincidence that the site of representation of this Italian American presence is the city and the industrial factory. As it is no coincidence that a recurrent trope of these works is the ethnic gangster, the figure that David Ruth considers a great contributor to "the replacement of complex, progressive-era racial taxonomies with the conception of a monolithic white race" (73). No wonder that these writings share a high degree of violence, however differently visualized. We will see in the next chapter how the gangster became the cultural trope of choice for the representation of the Italian American man's attempt to enter whiteness after the end of Jim Crow. In these pages, the focal point will be on the African American writers' insistence on what I call the "invisible blackness" of the Italian Americans, their composite, fuzzed, and unstable mixture of racial status, ways of being and acting both publicly and in the private sphere, and cultural variety that at once baffled, repulsed, and attracted white and black Americans alike. The invisible blackness of the Italians has this chief function: it provides African American writers with an opportunity to question the all-inclusive notion of white ethnicity and Eurocentrism as the influence of segregation in the life of Americans increased. The highlighting of the invisible blackness as the structural mark of Italian American identity leads to the black detachment of Italian Americans from a Eurocentric view of modern epistemology.

Paradoxically—and paradoxes exposes essential truths of modernity—these writers stand on its head the racist definition of Southern Italians as Euro-Africans that (in)famous Italian anthropologists and criminologists Cesare Lombroso, Alfredo Niceforo, and Giuseppe Sergi had advanced in the early twentieth century to classify their fellow citizens, including women and children, as natural-born killers, that is to say, as subhumans. Gradually, the African American literary investment in the invisible blackness of the Italian Americans allows the credible dilution and the seeming hiding of color from the black subject and reorients the discourse about race from a color-dominated issue to questions pertaining to twentieth-century America that include, these writers say, the question of who is white and what is whiteness. Whiteness, not blackness, tied together a political system and a social order. The *narrative strategy* of decentering blackness as color and reinscribing it in the invisible blackness of the Italian Americans made blackness invisible and yet present by way of showing it in an Italian American body, one that could represent whiteness as well as blackness, which is to say, a hybrid body. In the hands of the aforementioned black American writers, the invisible blackness of this body tells us the Italian American man's position within the complex racial taxonomy of the United States during Jim Crow and reveals itself as a structural aspect of the way these writers confront racial difference.

Johnson's *The Autobiography of an Ex-Colored Man* inaugurates the series of encounters between African Americans and Italian American identity as a question of and about modernity. The book is the fictional account of the life of a biracial man born in Georgia who grows up in Connecticut. During his entire adult life, he keeps secret the black part of his identity that he discovers traumatically early in school. This shocking experience is followed by six more micro-stories that shape the structure of the novel: the death of the narrator's mother and his failed attempt to attend Atlanta University owing to the inadvertent loss of his inheritance; his experience as a cigar roller in Jacksonville, Florida; his bohemian life in the black clubs of New York City; his travels in Europe with a white patron; his return to the Deep South, which he flees right after witnessing the lynching and burning of a black man, something that persuades him to pass as a white man for the rest of his existence; and lastly, his encounter with his future wife and mother of his two children, a white woman. It is in the last of these sections, the one where the narrative and purpose of the novel completely unfold, that the literary engagement of African American writers with Italian Americans starts.

The novel is narrated in the first person, but Johnson never mentions the ex-colored man's first name, a formal strategy to indicate that potentially any reader could be the ex-colored man. When he meets his future wife, whose

name also we are not told for the same reasons, the ex-colored man confesses the nature of his physical appearance, his Italian complexion. His
confession is probably the only moment in the book where Johnson speaks
in place of the narrator, as if the historical voice of the author replaced the
fictional first person of the narrative. In the last chapter of the book, the
ex-colored man is in New York City. He attends "a musical which was given
at a house to which I was frequently invited" because of his musical abilities
as a pianist. There, he notices the woman who will become his wife. She is
dressed all in white, another narrative strategy to underscore what we are
about to learn. He intends to approach this woman at the end of the program, but unexpectedly he experiences an emotional retreat that turns him
into "the bashful boy of fourteen," the boy who had discovered his true
racial makeup (119). Nonetheless, he manages to find himself near her and
hear her praising his execution of a Chopin composition. A friend of his
seizes the moment and introduces the woman to the ex-colored man. At this
point the narrator intervenes to alert the reader about the perils of a subjective recollection, how the use of memory can be slippery. The ex-colored
man admits that he cannot recollect the conversation he and his future wife
had. He is intentionally very detailed about this confusion. He remembers
that despite his attempt to be clever he felt increasingly uncomfortable about
himself, that he felt completely inadequate, to the point that this inward
inversion made him look like a person that he is not, a form of ontological
passing, we may say. His attempt to look smart produces the exact opposite:
"I don't know what she said to me or what I said to her. I can remember that
I tried to be clever, and experienced a growing conviction that I was making
myself appear more and more idiotic" (127).

His experience is a true modern inversion. It is conveyed as a somehow
vague, fuzzy recollection, especially in stark contrast to the very dense and
detailed description of all the people and the environments throughout the
entire book. The ex-colored man remembers the inadequacy of his attempt
to engage the woman, to interest her, but he does not remember his or her
words or, for that matter, much else, except that she was dressed entirely in
white. There is one other thing that the ex-colored man remembers besides
the color of the woman's dress, something that he has absolutely no doubt
he is recollecting correctly. This extremely detailed and fine writer who pays
close attention to the execution of the language from the beginning to the
end makes a point to convey to the reader the certainty of this remembrance,
its factuality, as the position of the adverb "too" to reinforce the adjective
"certain" underscores: "I am certain, too, that, in spite of my Italian-like
complexion, I was as red as a beet" (120). This line is how we learn that the
ex-colored man is an Italian-looking guy in early twentieth-century New York

City. It is a stunning confession to begin with, one that comes literally three pages before the end of the novel when the ex-colored man laments that he has sold "his birthright for a mess of pottage" (127). He has quit on both his color and the possibility of doing something for the betterment of black Americans—his "mother's people," as he calls them (126)—because he switched his racial identity to make "a little money," an exchange whose outcome is the production of whiteness and money on the one hand and the erasure of otherness and the female gender that his "mother's people" represent on the other (127).

There are several reasons why this is a stunning confession. First of all because nowhere else in the course of the narration are we informed of this kind of complexion. Not even during the ex-colored man's time in the clubs of New York City or his extended period in various capitals of Europe, where one could reasonably expect that the ex-colored man's Italian bodily semblance would be mentioned. More important, in 1912 the dark complexion of Italians in New York City was hardly a passport to white privilege. If anything, the dark complexion that the immigration officers of Ellis Island registered on the immigrants' papers after they disembarked positioned these Italians closer to blacks in the white-designed racial taxonomy and hierarchy of the day. The popular literature of the time offers plenty of examples of this coupling. One such example is a drawing of an Italian shoe shiner titled *Homo Italicus: Original Wop*, published in the popular magazine *Life* in 1911, a year before the publication of Johnson's novel.

The utterly racist language of the drawing's caption needs no comment, one should hope. Obviously, being Italian is not the same as being white, this drawing tells its (white) readers. Likewise, the class position of the two men is self-evident in the verticality of the image depicting the Italian shoe shiner below the white customer and in the clothes that the two wear. What is more relevant for the economy of our discourse is the root of this racist anti-Italianism, which the physical appearance of the Italian man reveals to be his blackness or the potential of the Italian man for being represented as a black-looking man. His nose, lips, and arms, as well as his apelike pose, leave no doubt about his Italian blackness, his racial association, and what such blackness and racial association meant in terms of social position in the public mind of mainstream white America.[1]

In the light of this, Johnson's description of the ex-colored man as an Italian-looking male seems to be out of place, if not a contradiction altogether. His Italian-like complexion would seem to highlight the ambiguity, even the fakeness of his whiteness rather than to allow him to pass as a white man, let alone to court, or even approach, a white woman of good social status. No less worthy of note is the fact that according to Johnson such

Homo Italicus

Original Wop

One pound o' spaghetti, kerchief 'round da neck
stiletto in the fustian pants
a buncha garlic gulped down like animals do
and talent for shinin' shoes

Cartoon published in *Life* magazine, 1911.

invisible blackness defines Italian American identity. The ex-colored man does not associate *looking* Italian with *being* white. Neither does *looking* Italian evoke the association with em*bodying* whiteness. The one thing the Italian complexion can embody, the drawing and Johnson tell us, is its potential to represent blackness. What makes possible the ex-colored man's Italian-like complexion is his, as well as the Italian's, invisible blackness. Appearance is disjoined from white identity. The ex-colored man turns red as a beet—something that can happen only to white people—*in spite* of his Italian-like complexion. It is as if this man was now tricolor.

The disarticulation of racial appearance from one's identity and one's self would seem to indicate that color is one of the terms of the racial equation of American modernity rather than the whole equation. The African American and Italian American identities share their invisibility in front of white people, albeit one of different degrees, historically speaking. At the same time, the Italian American invisible blackness is capable of performing a mediating function that can be used to cross or move from one racial sphere to another and from one geo-social and cultural context to another. It is profitable to remember that in the chapter that precedes this passage, the ex-colored man found himself in Georgia, where he witnessed the lynching and burning of a black man. The crime worked as a counter-epiphany for him. It led him to move back to the North and pass as white. But it is equally profitable to note that in the "*j'accuse*" of the lynching and burning of a black man by a "crowd of men, all white . . . blond, tall and lean" (the detailed description is not optional), the narrator condemns and decries America, her civilization and democracy, because a human being is a subject of this unspeakable violence (113). The narrator repeats the definition "human being" in place of "black man" two times with regard to the meaning of the lynching and burning of the victim: "and shame for my country, that it, the great example of democracy to the world, should be the only civilized, if not the only state on earth, where a human being would be burned alive. . . . I do not see how a people that can find in its conscience any excuse whatever for slowly burning to death a human being, or tolerate such an act, can be entrusted with the salvation of a race" (113–14). Race is a question of civilization and democracy, a question of the human condition and, at this point in history, an eminently modern question. The function and meaning of the Italian-like complexion are a part of this question.

We begin to see here a pattern in the African American investment in Italian Americans that entails one's visibility, ways of being, even the significance of the bodily presence as part of larger processes of modernization that raise the question of the essence of a civilization. We gain a better sense of this distinction if we contrast the Italian-like complexion of the ex-colored man with a subsequent second Italian reference. The occasion is the ex-colored man's quick summary of his married life. He informs the reader that his wife gave birth first to "a little girl, with hair and eyes dark like mine," dark like his Italian-like complexion, we might say, or at least eyes that well fit such a complexion; two years later, instead, he tells us, she gave birth to a boy, "a little golden-headed god, a face and a head that would have delighted the heart of an old Italian master" (126). The children literally embody a clear, almost Manichean distinction that replicates itself across generations and overlaps genders. The girl inherited the blackness of the Italian-looking father. The boy, who resembles his mother instead, is the epitome of one of the countless renditions of the baby Jesus with the Virgin Mary, the *Madonna con bambino* of the Italian artistic tradition generally related to the masters of the Italian Renaissance. The gender division reflects the racial one between the children as it reproduces the ex-colored man's racial lineage. The boy embodies the whiteness of the ex-colored man's father. The girl embodies the blackness of the ex-colored man's mother, this latter a pairing that goes beyond the strict biological makeup because blackness identifies his "mother's people." At the same time, the ex-colored man distinguishes between his Italian-like complexion, which he presents in racial guise, and the aesthetics of the artistic tradition of the old Italian masters, those male artists for the most part at the service of northern, white centers of power during the Renaissance that, by way of pictorial representation, contributed to create the individual as the subject of history in the early modern age, the age of the nascent merchant and banking class. But also, and equally important in our context, the masters who managed to turn what today we would categorize as a Middle Eastern child of a Middle Eastern woman into a white child, often with blond hair and sometimes even with blue eyes, as, for example, in Botticelli's *Madonna del libro* or Leonardo's *Vergine delle rocce*. The gender and racial distinction that the ex-colored man articulates is predicated upon an internal distinction that separates an Italian complexion that equals one's racial identity and visibility, and the Italian artistic culture that helped conceptualize the individual (upper-class) male white self as the subject of history.

Johnson's coupling of the Italian physical appearance with southern origins of the Italian Americans is obvious, but in one sense it is also beside the point. A more pressing matter with regard to Italian Americans is that Johnson, similarly to Booker T. Washington and Jerre Mangione, begins to detach Italian Americans from the Eurocentric view that aligns Central and Northern Europe with whiteness. The internal disarticulation of the Italian identity from the most eminent artistic tradition of Italy inserts race and the question of one's visibility, of one's identity, squarely within the larger issue of a civilization—and the Italian Old Masters do represent a civilization,

Sandro Botticelli, *Madonna del libro*, 1480–81.
Photo: Scala/Art Resource, New York.

Leonardo da Vinci, *Vergine delle rocce*, 1506.
© National Gallery, London / Art Resource, New York.

after all. Johnson's subtle distinctions toward the very end of the novel should come as no surprise. Already earlier in the novel he made somewhat similar considerations. Earlier in the book the ex-colored man overhears a conversation about race while he is riding a train in the South, a not-too-indirect reference to *Plessy v. Ferguson*, given the choice of the means of transportation. The narrator witnesses a white man from Texas claiming the superiority of the Anglo-Saxon race while his interlocutor, an old soldier from the North, responds that all "the great fundamental and original intellectual achievements" that elevated civilization belong to "what we now call inferior races" (98), and the word "races" here is notably in the plural. The list that this ex-soldier makes is a long and impressive one. It encompasses the arts and the sciences, nature and reason, emotions and the intellect, aesthetics and knowledge: "the art of letters, of poetry, of music, of sculpture, of painting, of the drama, of architecture; the science of mathematics, of astronomy, of philosophy, of logic, of physics, of chemistry, the use of the metals and the principles of mechanics" (98). The only "original contribution" the Anglo-Saxon race has made to civilization, this northerner continues, is what Anglo-Saxons "have done with steam and electricity and in making implements of war more deadly" (99).

Johnson presents us with an inverted narrative of the advancement of Western civilization already prefigured in the geographical identity of the interlocutors. A southern man claims the superiority of a northern race; whereas a northern man claims the achievements of races traditionally identified with the south, foregrounding a counter-narrative that at once decomposes and indicates the needs to reappropriate the narrative of modernity as the byproduct of a white civilization. Conversely, the old soldier subverts the historical construction of race as part of the white narrative of civilization. He replaces such a racial construction with a racially inclusive and diverse view of modernity that privileges the intellect, self-fulfillment, and humanistic and scientific advancements. Johnson aligns a monolithic, unicolor, instrumental view of modernity with the use of the two forms of energy, steam and electricity, that fueled industrialization and war, or, which is the same, modernity and the collective violence that capitalism generates, which the Anglo-Saxon race embodies. At the onset of the twentieth century, Johnson, the American diplomat, aligns the internal construction of the modern white American self and the rise of the American empire with a narrative of appropriation of Western modernity that excludes nonwhite races, including the Italian Americans of Southern Italian origins that he detached from a Eurocentric view of modernity. One wonders if this larger theme is what the ex-colored man has in mind when he closes the novel regretting the decision to pass as white, to opt for his "lesser part" and sell his "birthright for a mess of pottage," as the last line has it (127).

Foundational texts such as *The Autobiography of an Ex-Colored Man* rarely, if ever, provide answers to the questions they pose and the issues they raise, which is one of the reasons why they are foundational texts. By so doing, however, they lay out the context for subsequent works to answer those questions and articulate those issues, which those works usually do by posing further questions and issues. One such a case is Richard Bruce Nugent's Harlem Renaissance novel *Gentleman Jigger*. Arnold Rampersad has called Nugent's book "a landmark in our literature" because it displays "a degree of confidence and facility rare for writers of the Harlem Renaissance in dealing with its controversial, indeed forbidden, subject matter," which is the intertwining of race, ethnicity, class, and homosexuality (viii). Even more relevant might be the way Nugent went about this subject matter, the style of the novel, which Rampersad places squarely in the realist mode: "At its core it [the novel] is an example of realist fiction" (ix). What we read reflects the urban realities of the time of the novel, including the social and homosexual relationships that the protagonist of the book, Stuartt Brennan, the son of an elite, light-skin black family of Washington, D.C., entertains with various Italian American gangsters in New York City and Chicago in book 2 of the novel, "Greenwich Village to Chicago." This section of the novel explores life outside what Nugent calls the "Niggerati" circle, the fictional name of the Harlem Renaissance group of which Nugent was a part, here also called "the leaders of the New Order" (26).

By the beginning of book 2 Stuartt, initially described as "a muddy complexioned little boy with well-brushed hair" who "had never been allowed to play with dark children" (7), has already overcome his childhood racial prejudices toward black people, what the novel calls "his chauvinistic upbringing" (20). And so have other members of the Harlem group like Raymond Pelman, a character inspired by Nugent's fellow Harlem Renaissance member Wallace Thurman (the one responsible for coining the term "Niggerati"), who instead has overcome his prejudice toward "light-complected Negroes" (22). Now that Stuartt and his darker-skin friends are racially acquainted with each other—which means now that they are acquainted with themselves, now that they recognize color and its various gradations as what Thomas Wirth in the introduction to the book calls "the fluid, blurred boundaries that do not really separate the races" (xi)—Stuartt can venture and experience homosexuality, can fill the space between words and actual life, "for he was not, in fact, homosexually experienced as his witty conversation had implied" (172).

Spaces and their description are essential in this novel, and the places of Stuartt's homosexual education are no exception to the rule. This education begins in Washington Square, where Stuartt discovers his homosexual attraction to and predilection for Italian American gangsters, whose depiction is as important as that of the locations: "Lithe Italian hoodlums in exaggerated clothes creased to razor sharpness, with dark, sallow skins and oiled hair, strutting with clicking heels and a cocky grace which was almost vulgar, but which was strangely attractive nonetheless" (174). He looks at the hoodlums hoping to be reciprocated with "their bold eyes on him," a gaze that triggers his excitement, aptly expressed with a typical corporeal image when this happens: "He could feel his stomach quiver with excitement" (174). But it is also a gaze that causes his disappointment when the excitement does not translate into an actual meeting, "disappointment that confused him when they passed with the most casual glances, as though he were an empty bench or a tree"—an analogy, this last image, that underscores how the excitement may start with, and yet is not exhausted in, the "dark skin" of the Italian hoodlums (174). What fuels Stuartt's attraction is the combination of these Italians' dark skin and the aesthetics of their clothes, shoes, and hair. Stuartt observes the "various villagers and tourists pass" (174). Nonetheless his attention "always" tips "back to some group of swaggering Italians, so conscious of their own specific kind of allure" (174). Stuartt can even imagine them doing their dirty work, "going off to some dark room hallway—imagine the ugly, attractive happenings: the hoodlum pocketing money or terrorizing the boy because there was not enough money and taking whatever of value there was for him to take" (175). Still the attraction remains intact. Indeed, it seems to increase. "He allowed his imagination to wander over them, to conjure encounters with them—exciting and pleasing encounters of words, glances, and return glances" (175–76).

These scenes may as well be the literary baptism of what Rampersad calls "the realistic depiction of African American sexuality, and especially homosexuality. Almost three decades before James Baldwin, there was Bruce Nugent . . . the fearless pioneer" (vii). Rampersad's assessment is correct, but we should add that what makes such a new beginning possible, what liberates African American literary (homo)sexual identity, is the invisible blackness of the Italian American men that become Stuartt's object of desire, the locus of his homosexual investment that combines their physical appearance with their attire and poses. Already in book 1 Stuartt has a homosexual encounter at the Harlem headquarters of his group of artists and intellectuals, involving a young Italian bootlegger who provides the group with the booze for a party, this too a moment of realistic rendition of Prohibition and the 1920s. However, this first encounter is presented as the result of the disinhibiting power of alcohol. Its unfolding transmits a purposeful lack of agency. We witness an unfinished group scene, as if the group's collective presence were necessary to approve the homosexual desire of the black individual, even to justify it in front of the others. "'Come on good looking' Stuartt tells the young bootlegger. The young Italian grinned and took the glass Stuartt had handed him. 'Come on, take off your hat and let's have a party!' He took the Italian by the hand, led him off to a corner and sat down beside him. Bum looked at Rusty and Rusty looked at Bum. Then they laughed. It was to be a party" (129). On the contrary, in Washington Square Stuartt is spatially displaced. He is outside his territory that the color line delimits. This spatial crossover foregrounds his homosexual investment in the Italians as an intentional and deliberate choice. Stuartt crosses the lines because the invisible blackness of the Italians allows him to do so, just as it allowed the Italian American bootlegger to cross into the territory of Stuartt's Harlem group. The fact that the bootlegger has an economic motive to cross the spatial urban line only reinforces the strength of the mutual attraction and the willingness to literally embrace the blackness of the young Italian who accepts the invitation to the party. The Italian's crossing into black territory indicates how an actual economy of exchange technically does not concern itself with color, which in turn indicates the economic dimension of race as well as the endemic social self-insufficiency of an economy of exchange.

Some critics have raised the issue as to whether it is possible even to speak of a queer black identity when such identity is validated by white culture, if it is even possible to consider such identity as black. David Gerstner wonders if it is feasible "to articulate queer blackness by sidestepping the charge that this identity is nothing more than a perverse manufactured body of whiteness." Gerstner wonders why do black queers need an aesthetic of whiteness "to assert their identity" (5). One of the premises of this critique—even when the answer is that for Nugent aesthetics is the possibility to love freely, as Gerstner argues convincingly—is a tendency to view aesthetics as an overarching theme, if not as a totality at the expense of other questions. A second, interconnected premise is to discount the invisible blackness of the Italians as a determining role in Nugent's view of black homosexuality, something that in the novelist's eyes clearly detaches Italian Americans from whiteness.

We will see shortly how book 2 unfolds the aesthetic and racial dimension of this disarticulation. But already in book 1 Nugent conceptualizes this separation, this time in terms of the history of culture and the institutionalization of pedagogy in the United States. During a discussion about racial identity and the United States at the "Niggerati mansion," light-skinned Stuartt laments the exceptional position of black people in the United States, which is obviously the flip side of the coin of American exceptionalism. "Why is it you expect a French Negro to dance a juba up the Champs Elysees. Why only here in America, where every custom the African brought with him has been driven underground by the Ku Klux and intermarriage, are Negroes expected to be so goddam different?" (39). Dark-skinned Rusty replies by questioning the hegemonic tendency of whiteness, which he presents as a civilization that suppresses everything that is not white: "We go to your colleges, learn your lessons, and have Goya, Velasquez, and Rembrandt thrown at us. Scott, Keats, and Tennyson are poets we must know. We learn psychology from Nordics, sociology from Nordics, anthropology from Nordics—even take courses in the interpretation of spirituals from Nordics. Why then is it such a mystery that we should be like every . . . ?" (39). The merit of the discussion is here secondary, beginning with Stuartt's erasure of any trace of the African heritage. What concerns us is what is missing from this white and Nordic list that, geographically speaking, includes non-Nordic artists like Goya and Velázquez. How is it that the one interlocutor who objects to the hegemony of a Nordic civilization even with regard to the hermeneutics of the prime musical tradition of black American slaves, the spirituals, mentions neither Italy nor an Italian artist or poet in this exchange that includes two Spanish painters? How is it that a writer and an artist like Nugent, who according to Rampersad "saw his own life as his finest possible work of art," a man of "'Italianate' good looks," makes no reference to his favorite culture (viii)? Such absence is even more surprising because of the artistic debt that the painters here cited owed to the "Italian masters," as Johnson has it in *The Autobiography of an Ex-Colored Man*. No less symptomatic of the relevance of this absence is the debt the British romantics owe to the tradition of the Italian sonnet. We might even recall that both Byron and Shelley lived and worked in Italy, which certainly Nugent knew.

In Nugent's eyes what separates the Italian Americans from the civilization of whiteness is their invisible blackness. The chief function of that invisible blackness in *Gentleman Jigger* is to depict a modern civilization that does away with the Western universal racialization of beauty and the interconnected patriarchal heteronormativity of the established social order. Nugent's choice to create homosexual gangsters of ethnic, working-class origins is at the service of this artistic vision, which is a political vision to begin with. Certainly, there is an autobiographical dimension to it as well. In his introduction to *Gay Rebel of the Harlem Renaissance*, Wirth tells us that Nugent "became acquainted with the local mafia don" in Buffalo (15–17). Yet it is profitable to remember that in the period that registered the rise of mass media and mass culture, the ethnic gangster represented everything

that white America publicly hated and privately loved. At the same time—
and this might as well be the reason for white America's private attraction
to the ethnic gangster—the mobster guaranteed the reification of the political economy of capitalist modernity.

From strictly a cultural perspective, the gangster as the public face of organized crime functioned as the organic intellectual of the social environment of Prohibition, a word that we need here to read etymologically. The
gangster represented the opposite of what the mainstream culture wished
could be prohibited, which was much more than a shot or two of whiskey.
The ethnic otherness of the gangster, his working-class outsiderness, sexual
promiscuity, liberality of social customs and norms, his very high level of,
if not complete comfort with, other racial subjects when it came to money,
social mores, and sex, all of it undermined the puritanical and Victorian
roots that helped fuel Prohibition. It might sound blasphemous, but the fact
is that the world of the gangster integrated more people than any piece of
social legislation or any social movement ever did with the exception of popular music, especially jazz, whose development as a social and commercial
art form is tied with the rise and the power of the mob, and, later on, rock
and roll. At the same time—and this is the paradox of modernity that Nugent is after in *Gentleman Jigger*—the gangster became the epitome of the
modern businessman at the head of a company with international ramifications, whether cultural or economic or both, thus preceding the establishment of the figure of the head of a transnational corporation. His public
image, and the aesthetics of it that the clothes and the perennial cigar com-
municated, made him the ideal character, along with sportsmen, to represent
the transition from what Warren Susman has called the old culture of "character" of eighteenth- and nineteenth-century America to the early twentieth-
century modern culture that "insisted on 'personality'" (xxii). Finally, and
crucially with regard to *Gentleman Jigger*, in terms of representation, literary as well as cinematic, the ethnic gangster contributed to what David Ruth
has called "the replacement of complex, progressive-era racial taxonomies
with the *emerging conception* of a monolithic white race," of which the
godfather trope became the epitome, as we shall see (73; my italics). It is this
"emerging conception" and the civilization that expresses it that Nugent
intends to subvert in his novel, a novel written while movies such as *Little
Caesar* and *Scarface* contributed to the formation of the Italian American
gangster trope, as Stuartt somehow hints toward the end of the story.

Stuartt's encounters and description of his social and homosexual relationships with Italian American gangsters in book 2 and his conceptualization of the Italian American invisible blackness respond to this vision. His
first encounter with Renaldo, "Ray," one of the young hoodlums walking

the streets around Washington Square, is presented as a moment of initiation and liberation, the beginning of a new world and a new way of living. True to his gangster identity, Ray is the one who acts, as Stuartt admits. "You're the first—this is the first time I . . ." Elite-born Stuartt talks. Italian American gangsters of working-class extraction like Ray act. "Ray slipped an arrogant thumb under his suspenders and, as they fell, began to calmly take off his shirt. As Stuartt entered the room, he saw Ray in the bed, propped up on one elbow." Ray speaks only in order to act. "Well . . . put the light out and come on." (179). When the lights are back on, the new world is in front of the reader, and it is no longer a black-and-white world, because of Ray's racial complexion that Nugent underscores, as if to point out that whiteness did not liberate black homosexuality. The invisible blackness of the Italian American gangster did. The detailed description is not limited to skin color, the traditional preeminent factor of racial identity. It extends beyond color by way of pointing out color in the first place:

> He looked at Ray, noting his green-brown skin, darker than Stuartt's own. . . . Stuartt seemed unusually aware of detail—of the thin, sensual lips smiling slightly, of the long eyelashes, the hair, mussed and curly—and thought it strange that sleep could so change one and still leave one so the same. . . . He knew that when Ray wakened, his lashes would become artifices rather than the naïve complement they now were to the counter of his cheeks. He knew that the hair would be sleeked to a glossed highlight to outline the round head. That the lips would be slow and conscious. And Stuartt knew also that the metamorphosed Ray would be as attractive to him as the sleeping one. (180)

From this moment to the end of the novel, this and the subsequent homosexual relationships that Stuartt has with other gangsters first in New York City, then in Chicago, the setting of the largest section of book 2, articulate the Italian American invisible blackness as a model of modernity antithetical to the rationalizing universality of Western epistemology and its organic classist social order.

The relationship with Ray rejuvenates Stuartt, as if he had found his true self. Rusty notes this change, how all of a sudden "there's a sort of aura, almost, around him" (190). Stuartt himself admits as much. "Everything I am, I owe Ray," he tells Bum, another member of the "Niggerati" (193). Ray's invisible blackness forges Stuartt's newly expressed homosexual identity. This is not to say that color as a sign of otherness is erased from Stuartt's new self. There is no such a thing as a post-racial conceptualization of identity in *Gentleman Jigger*. There is, instead, an attempt to reformulate identity. Thus, Stuartt reiterates Ray's blackness when Bum asks him about his new companion: "He is Italian—short, slight, sallow, olive-complexioned—

with thin, well-shaped lips and brilliant black eyes. His hair is glued to a blue-black sheen" (194). But what distinguishes Ray, Stuartt continues, is that "he is Italian, and I like Italians" (194). Nonetheless, the reason for his choice extends beyond his partner's racial complexion. It encompasses a variety of factors, including "the bed fine manners instinctive to his race and kind" (196). Yet this is a trait, Stuartt agrees, that does not distinguish Italians only, one that "so have loads of other people, I suppose" (196). What makes Italian Americans appealing and different to Stuartt is that they do not conform to the normative model of social relationships that Rusty evokes when he challenges Stuartt to explain how a "guttersnipe" can have what Stuartt calls a "wholesome attitude," how Stuartt can present as a model "one who preys on queers and 'does' the baths in order to meet them," one "who steals and who complies with any sex arrangement that pays" (197). Stuartt's reply questions Rusty's normative categorization, which is rooted in the artificiality of a classist culture historically associated with whiteness: "But it *is* wholesome, damn it! It may not conform to your artificial definition of respectability, but it—oh, well—" (197).

Nugent further elaborates on Ray's non-normative way of being when Bum interjects in the conversation to observe, "I think he's comparing it to the simple way of acceptance that is peasant rather than tenement, and as such is wholesome and clean. Not cluttered up with a lot of do's and don'ts that creep in, in other classes—particularly the middle class." Bum's comment seems to suggest the traditional modernist recuperation of primitivism as a counter-modernity. The difference here is the centrality of the class-based analysis of this dichotomy. Stuartt envisions Ray's invisible blackness in place of middle-class assimilation, repressive cultural uniformity, and homogenization of social conducts, which even the criminals internalize mentally, according to Stuartt. "That's it! That's it, Bum! He has none of the conventional narrowness of the middle class, nor any of the vicious indulgence in sensation of the upper class—or its analogous neurosis found in the criminal class," says Stuartt—a brutal condemnation of the American way of life (197).

Stuart's elaboration begins a series of infringements of the normative public code of middle-class conduct that Nugent obviously enjoys describing, beginning with the breaking of ethnic and racial spatial social accommodations proper to urban life in America. This is how Nugent starts deconstructing the accepted sociality of the time that he wants to rearticulate. At the end of their conversation about Ray, Bum suggests that the entire "Niggerati" group drive to a restaurant in Prince Street, much to the delight of Stuartt, who immediately exclaims, "See me welcomed into Little Italy" (199). Bum's suggestion is Nugent's narrative strategy to de-personify the hybridization of the narrative and avoid making Stuartt the all-inclusive center of it. At the Italian restaurant, while Stuartt engages in conversation with the homosexual waiter proverbially named Tony, Rusty tells Bum that Stuartt never "*wanted*" to pass, "and you see he *could* if he liked" (202), an observation that indirectly exposes Ray's comfort with racial otherness and how willing Italian American men are to enter in a homosexual relation with Stuartt. At the table, the proper setting for a conversation involving Italians, the discussion veers toward what Kris, another member of the group, defines as Stuartt's not "unreasoning infatuation" for Italians (204). Pressed to explain his motives, Stuartt reiterates the racialized hybridization of the Italians that extends beyond color. It includes an aesthetic consideration. "They're a flattering race. Then, they're a dark race, and I like dark races—a purely artistic and personal preference. To me there is in them more warmth, more variety, more various pleasing and harmonious combinations" (204).

The invisible blackness of the Italians is a racial marker to which Stuartt is attracted because it rests on the harmonious combination of internal differentiation, which he goes so far as to pose as a racial model for black Americans, thereby associating the two groups: "I *prefer* Italians. As a group. As individuals of a group. Because they are so much more truthful, fundamentally, than other races and, I suppose, because they fulfill so many of the promises Negroes hold for me—promises never fulfilled by Negroes" (204). This is a stunning proclamation, which only an African American writer could afford to make. Naturally, Bum questions Stuartt's racial association. "Come now Stuartt. . . . You don't really mean that Italians are like Negroes, do you?" (205). The object of the question is not race as an auto-referential entity. It is an attempt to pose the racial question as a question of civilization. Stuartt's response first highlights the internal differentiation of African American identity in terms of color, which is Nugent's way of maintaining the geographical centrality of color while challenging the monolithic view of it. "Hell no, Bum. Only that they embrace a variety of colors as subtle as those embraced by Negroes. (By 'Negroes' I always mean the American product.) But with Italians the range of color is more subtle; it's not carried to the extremes" (205). Then, Nugent positions the invisible blackness of the Italian Americans outside the normative, rationalizing, and repressive realm of Western civilization, the target of his discourse. "And I like Italians because they are emotional, because they too feel like an ancient, healthy animal race. But in their case the civilizations they possess come from within the race itself and its past; these civilizations were not absorbed from, or injected into them by, some foreign and blonder race" (205).

The accuracy of the historical record of these Italian civilizations as free of white races is doubtful, to say the least, although it may give us an indication of the internal racial composition of the Italian immigration to the United States as white and black Americans alike observed it. It may also give us a sense of the depth of their epistemological outsiderness that we had occasion to witness in the previous chapters. But it seems rather self-evident that Stuartt's elaboration is Nugent's way to warn of the peril that the repression of the entirety of one's identity entails. Conversely, it is also an invitation not to forget one's past, let alone to submit to the logic of uniformity that the rationalizing universality of the West demands. There is nothing stereotypical in the description of the Italians as "emotional." Nor is the invocation of their ancient history or how salutary the full expression of one's identity can be a mythological interpretation.

Nugent's emphasis on the multiplicity of the Italians' civilizations is a way to rebut a flattening and shrinking modernity that detaches the racial as well as any other social sphere from the larger question of modernity's monolithic dimension. As Bum asks Stuartt if he is overplaying the influence of the past with regard to Italians, if he is "believing—or rather living—a little too much in the past? In the Roman rather than the Italian tradition," Stuartt's reply leaves no doubt about Nugent's politics and his belief in the pastness of the past, in the strength of a people's history and the possibilities it stores: "No Bum. But I do believe that the Roman tradition lives a little in the Italian. You should be the first to admit a thing like that. You who are always throwing in the tradition of my sorry African drop to color completely my others. As it, of course, does. And, as my others, conversely, do" (206).

Stuartt's subsequent descent into the criminal underworld responds to Nugent's political view and the subversive potential of what Gerstner calls Stuartt's "outsiderness within outsiders," what we might interpret as an extension of the perimeters of otherness that pairs with his repeated moving "*in and out of contained places*" (21, 26), a kind of floating that includes the disruption of fixed ethnic and linguistic territoriality as a strategy for racial intermingling. Figuratively speaking, such floating occurs horizontally, across lines, but also upward in the underworld's hierarchy. Stuartt quickly advances in the underworld ranks. Ray introduces him to "the biggest shot" he knows (210), Frank Andrenopopolis, a mobster who begins to see Stuartt regularly and supports him financially until on a trip to Chicago he introduces him to the real big shot, Mario Orini, the boss of organized crime, whom Nugent seemed to have modeled after New York City's (in)famous Lucky Luciano.

The spatial movement of the novel mirrors its politics. The form matches the content, because the form is content, and vice versa. Stuartt's trajectory began with the black elite of his native Washington, D.C.; continues in Harlem with a group of black and white writers and artists; reaches Italian and Greek homosexual gangsters in New York City's Little Italy and in the Village; and finally extends to Chicago at the top of the underworld before returning to New York City for one final scene. This geo-social and (homo)sexual urban topography signals the passage from one world to another and from one culture to another. It sets forth an expanding view of modernity at a time when the view of modernity began to flatten. Stuartt's encounter with the man at the top in the underworld, a spectacular oxymoron, is the perfect image of Nugent's vision of modernity because it manages to harmonize opposite extremities without setting them in binary opposition, which is what allows him to reformulate the conceptualization of race and avoid the trap of a post-racial discourse.

The description of the chief mobster during their first encounter in his Chicago home suits this vision. Orini is of "dark skin," a trait that Stuartt's selection of a "creamy white" pajama for him highlights (236). The color of the skin is not the only way that Orini's otherness manifests itself naturally. The language does it, too. When Stuartt repeats his first name, Mario, twice, Orini asks him "what is the matter?" lapsing into "the Italian English that ordinarily never showed in his speech, except to faintly color his 'Rs' or to stress slightly the penult of words, which in English are accented on the antepenult" (236). The linguistic slippage occurs a second time later on in the novel, when Orini tells him, "I don't never know what to think about you," as Stuartt tosses aside the envelope with the money that Orini has brought him because he wants him to stay in Chicago (288). Orini's invisible blackness embodies the dialectical process that results in an expansive vision of modernity. "Stuartt realized that Orini was unaware of any *incongruity* of attitude—those very characteristics in him that Stuartt insisted were racial and instinctive with Italians as a race having worked in their customary, *paradoxical* way in Stuartt's favor," writes Nugent, playing with words that constantly evoke the idea of a nonlinear dynamism of conduct that from the individual moves on to include the collective identity of a people, to their way of being (280; my italics). "Characteristics," continues Nugent, in describing the essence of this affirmative modern vision, "which included that strange ability to accept anything, no matter how disliked that thing *itself* was, if it was found in persons for whom they had a personal regard; that ability to form personal bonds *through* the very things they disliked" (280). This is the ultimate inversion. Its outcome is a modern vision that affirms difference by standing on its head one's acquired customs and accepted social practices. "So Orini, who disliked everything for which Stuartt stood, liked him now despite and even because of these very things, while still disliking those things anywhere else. He even *liked* them in Stuartt, because he liked Stuartt" (280).

This modern vision of antisocial social intercourse reaches its peak when Stuartt, in a verbal exchange with Orini, forces the gangster of all gangsters, the male trope that came to represent the heart of the heteronormative, patriarchal modern social order, to subvert such a conception. Aptly, Nugent's dismantling and reconceptualization of manliness occurs rhetorically, with the use of the most representative and democratic of the figures of speech: the dialogue.

Their dialogue unfolds in three moments. Initially, Orini refuses to engage Stuartt's argument about their mutual attraction and the gangster's inability to recognize how his patriarchal heteronormativity obstructs his ability to accept Stuartt's love, which in turn causes his inability to achieve personal fulfillment. Orini uses a stereotypical image of masculinity based on a negative connotation of women and homosexuals, the effeminate other of the bourgeois tradition. "Ain't nobody talking about love . . . That's a lot of crap. Women and, *I guess*, fags go sappy—but I ain't see you do that yet," Orini says, again using the incorrect English typical of working-class people in response to Stuartt's assertion that "if it wasn't an embarrassing thing—embarrassing to you—*for you to say*, you'd say I was in love with you" (289; the second italics is mine). Then, Stuartt explains the aesthetic and social terms of his own manliness, which he subtracts from any sort of rationalizing generalization by defining it as a relational idea at the service of the single individual.

Stuartt begins his argument by establishing their mutual attraction on the basis of a man-based gender equality between them, between the homosexual black man and the Italian American gangster with darker skin. "It, of course, flatters you to have anyone as crazy about you as you think I am—but it disconcerts you because *you* like me. *And I am a man and you are a man* and when men do that and mix it up with sex, it's all *too* complicated and mixed up for you" (289; the second italics mine). Tellingly, only after he has established these foundational parameters does he connote as consequential the physical attraction that replaces a hierarchical view of gender. "You don't like liking me when you know that I'm what you have always looked down on. Only this time you can't look down. We like each other—at least I like you as one man should like another. Then I also like you physically—I like to look at you—tease you" (289–90). Right after, Stuartt switches the subject position by subverting conventional characterizations of manliness in order to assert his higher degree of manliness. "I guess *I am* sappy. But then I've got more nerve than you have. I am not ashamed of any of the ways in which I like you. I am not afraid to, just because it is considered wrong and *not normal*" (289–90; my italics). The African American homosexual is more masculine than the Italian American gangster at the top of the underworld. Unlike the gangster, Stuartt is neither ashamed nor afraid. The final line closes the circle of Stuartt's argument. "I guess I am only interested in what's normal for me—" he says, an affirmation of the single individual's liberty to invert the conception of what is normal (290).

Stuartt affirms his homosexuality as one form of manliness, one way of being a man, which naturally is one way of being human. He affirms his masculinity against the mainstream attitude of the time. "You mean," he asks Orini rhetorically, "that no matter what my ability in masculine endeavor— no matter if I should happen to be superior in these things masculine—I can't be a man because—well, because I might want you to kiss me, maybe?" (290). His vision of manliness leaves open the space for the other, for Orini to assert his own. By negation he creates an open space that fulfills his own identity as a man and leaves room for another male subject to join him in, which Orini does as he accepts a gift that suddenly Stuartt tosses into his lap. The scene had started with Orini tossing the envelope with the money to Stuartt, who disregarded it, much to Orini's dismay. The same scene closes with its exact opposite, with an inversion, with Stuartt giving Orini a gift, a star sapphire ring, the same kind of ring that Orini already wears, this one, however, with engraved on the side the legend "Stuartt-Orini 1929" that prompts Orini to say, again in the incorrect English that discloses his Italian American invisible blackness, "I ain't never had a present before" (291). Stuartt's reconceptualization of manliness is a reformulation of the modern self that entails a switch from the politics of Victorian culture to the politics of mutual recognition that he envisions in the dialogue with Orini. It is a switch informed by an understanding of love as an other-directed form of action in place of what Nugent defines as the Victorian self-interested vision of it. Previous to the verbal head-to-head with Orini, Stuartt had told Wayne, a young woman he met after spending the night at Orini's mansion, that her idea that "love *is* giving" is an idea proper to a "Victorian female. But sometimes receiving *is* giving" (287).

In this sense, for Stuartt the invisible blackness of the Italians is a form of giving and mutual recognition. Stuartt reiterates this in theoretical terms in the letter to Bum that precedes his return to New York, where he addresses his preference for Italian hoodlums. Stuartt rationalizes his preference on the basis of the Italian Americans' invisible blackness that fosters equal recognition regardless of one's biology. "They are so fundamentally in tune with essential truths and values. It may only be that we are all anti-social, and so really instinctively recognize each other as *paisani*. They are each individuals.

So am I" (295). Their way of being is their identity, away from the "colorful other way" that makes "the popular belief as depicted in movies and gangster thrillers quite understandable," a line that confirms Nugent's acquaintance with the white-media-generated popular depiction of the Italian American man of the early 1930s (295). "The only thing binding us into a separate group, into a kind, is our anti-social tendencies, outlook, and behavior," writes Stuartt, once again asserting his vision of an antisocial sociability (295). The same factor explains Orini's attraction toward him. "What is the thing that makes a person like him," a gangster, a man that "has met and conquered the anti-social world, the corrupt and hard urban world that is his," find "enjoyment, sexual *as well as other*, with a person like me?" Stuartt wonders (297). His answer is his own antisocial way of being, something that he shares with "criminals, artists, homosexuals, the cripples, etc." (298). This form of otherness is shared because it affirms their relationality and mutual recognition, their belonging to each other as individuals. "Each of us bears such a mark that we are all kin and recognize each other as inhabitants of the same world?" (298). This vision is what finally explains also Stuartt's "interest in Italians per se" (301). Although Italians might pay lip service to "popular convention" (302), they are "more animal (though human in expressing it) than are most people of the sort I've always known before" (301). Nugent defines their animality not as a sign of a mythological primitivism that rejects modernity. Their animality expresses bodily and erotic practices that do not conform to the instrumental rationalization and the normative realm of a capitalist modernity; "they have their selective preferences that are tied up with voluptuous and sensuous physicalities—with the human body and contact and responsiveness vocal, emotional, and physical, and the satisfaction to be enjoyed through it" (302).

Once Stuartt achieves his homosexual liberation, he is also free to assert his blackness. He does this as he returns to New York City for a show together with Bebe, a girl who accompanies Orini in public appearances. By now, Stuartt is an achieved artist who forms a public "quartette" along with Bebe, Wayne, and Orini. His own "reputation," "remuneration," and "glamour" even increases after the death of Orini's homosexual Sicilian friend and bodyguard Tony, who is murdered by a competing gang nearby the proverbial floral shop of the gangsters' world. The increase in public recognition is a strategy to accentuate the moment when Stuartt reveals his black identity to a famous gossip columnist before the dance show he and Bebe are to perform in front of an audience that includes most of the novel's characters, including Stuartt's brother Rhythm, who introduces Stuartt as "Well-Known Artist," as Wayne's fiancé, but, more importantly, as a "Negro" to an audience of mostly "white tables" that turns suddenly silent. "There was a dead hush—an embarrassed quiet over the entire place" (325). The one person not to be embarrassed is Stuartt, who calmly waits for the next number to finish before escorting Bebe to the exit joined by his former partner Frank Andrenopopolis and his bodyguard. First Stuartt introduces the notorious gangster to the Hartrights, a white elite couple sitting at the table together with their hosting company, including Stuartt's mother Palma, the "pale" woman whom Stuartt's father had married "against all precedent, as it was the motto of the new race and social order to marry as near white as possible" (3). As they all start walking toward the exit, Orini joins the group. Undisturbed by the announcement of Stuartt's racial identity, the gangster salutes Stuartt with the look of someone who appears "pleased with this drama" (327). "Orini! This is also too much," replies Stuartt, successfully struggling to hide "his warm tearful feeling" before he introduces the Italian American gangster with "darker skin" than his to the white table. "Do you know Mr. and Mrs. Hartwright? Sweetheart Orini, patron of arts and dabbler in criminal activities. A tsar, I've heard tell. And my *friend*, Palma" (327).

II

Perhaps not surprisingly, we find another gendered encounter between African Americans and Italian Americans in another writer associated with the Harlem Renaissance, albeit less coherently than the group's founding members. Sterling Brown's poem "Harlem Happiness" opens *No Hiding Place*, the volume of poetry that Brown submitted unsuccessfully to his publisher in 1935 following the success of *Southern Road* in 1932. Harlem is the site where Brown locates the encounter between two young black lovers and an Italian couple, Pietro and his wife, who at three in the morning are out in the street with their portable family business, their "dago fruit stand," she knitting a garment and he "the wop asleep" (165). Of course, Brown's use of the typical derogatory words for Italian Americans is a rhetorical strategy of a superbly skilled African American poet who turns the meaning of these words into a laughing matter—and laughter for African Americans is historically a tool for surviving white oppression. The ex-colored man of Johnson's novel, for instance, learns that "to laugh heartily is, in part, the salvation of the American Negro; it does much to keep him from going the way of the Indian" (36). In the twentieth century, however, black humor aimed at segregation just as much as at integration, and no bigger integrationist ever existed in the African American literary tradition than Sterling A. Brown. Not surprisingly, in the second half the 1930s Brown became the editor of Negro affairs for the Federal Writers' Project.

Here the two derogatory words expose the racial status of the Italians in the eyes of white people. But they also sustain the tone of the language that serves to visualize laughter as a way to unmask the absurdity of racism as well as the tool of mutual understanding and recognition between the two couples, the black lovers and the Italian Americans. In this way, Brown projects onto the two Italian Americans a sense of equality and "dignity that respects itself," as one reviewer of the *New York Times* wrote of *Southern Road* (quoted in Brown, "Harlem," 7), which the feeling of reciprocity that pervades the entire poem supports. This is the reason why the opening line of a collection that is almost entirely about black people reads, "I think there is in this the stuff for many lyrics" (165). The dignity comes from the work, the equality from the class condition of all four characters, and the mutuality from the bodily description of the Italian woman, whose name, unlike that of her husband, Pietro, remains untold, as if this woman could be any woman.

The subtlety of the details reveals the poem's subversive power, beginning with the semantics of its parataxis. Here "dago" refers to the fruit stand at 3 a.m., underscoring the class dimension of the Italian American experience that forces a man and "his woman" to be up in the early hours of the morning while, as Brown implies, white America sleeps (165). The Italians may be dagos, but they are up working at three in the morning in Harlem, perhaps even in the cold winter of New York City. In the realism that infuses and layers Brown's poems there is no room for the trope of the Italian Americans that on the one hand portrays the man as the breadwinner of the family and on the other the woman as the guardian of the home and the children. There is room, however, for gender identification and difference. Brown calls the man "the wop" and "swarthy" (165), but he addresses his female companion as a "woman," theoretically elevating her above the man and positioning her at the same level as the black lovers. This characterization perhaps explains how in addition to the trope of the man as provider of the family, even that of his physical endurance, the pillar of masculinity, is subverted. The wop is asleep while his woman is knitting "a tiny garment" (165), likely for the child in her womb, which of course adds the family dimension and motherhood to the texturing of mutualism and recognition. It is the woman, "she," the female gender and the future mother, that welcomes the two black lovers who "approach her/Flashing a smile from white teeth" before weighing the large grapes and the plums that the black couple is about to buy (165). There is no color barrier between the woman soon to be mother and the two black lovers. In its place, there is a mutuality expressed with a smile flashed from white teeth. That the most prominent and achieved black poet in the United States, whom Jerre Mangione in an unpublished paper titled

"Sterling A. Brown and the Federal Writers' Project" described as "a prophet of his people with the vision of a universal poet . . . a national cultural hero to cherish forever" (4) uses the adjective "white" to describe the teeth of the wop's woman is no coincidence, especially because he continues to use colors to describe another part of her body, her lips, which he compares to the "purplish red" of the grapes and the plums, "quite as this lady's lips are" (165).

Of course, teeth are white by definition. Yet historically they also occupy a specific position within the representation of black people, especially the kind of representations that the minstrel show influenced, which is to say, literary as well as popular culture representations. To stick with one of the texts here under consideration, in *The Autobiography of an Ex-Colored Man* Johnson mentions the "glistening white teeth" of Shiny, the narrator's newfound friend in school, who had impressed the ex-colored man because his face "was as black as night, but shone as though it had been polished" (11). Moreover, here the phrasing is ambiguous. In light of our theme, we might say that it is appropriately dual, in an in-between position. The line "Flashing a smile from white teeth" refers to the Italian American woman, but it could also be describing the two black lovers. Regardless, not only does Brown omit the white color to describe the rest of the woman's body. He also uses it to highlight her "purplish red" and "firm" lips by way of contrast. On the one hand Brown seems to underscore a bodily mutuality that recalls the ex-colored man who turns "red as beet" in spite of his Italian complexion; on the other the colors bring to light the invisible blackness of this Italian American woman and future mother. Here the association of the woman with "Grapes as large as plums, and tart and sweet" does not recall a typical pastoral romanticism that white Americans projected onto sunny Italy (165). It recalls the southern Mediterranean identity of the woman. "Well we know the lady," continues Brown, making clear that this is not an occasional encounter *and* establishing the racial connection between blackness and Italian American womanhood and motherhood. Hence the communal laughing of the two lovers and the woman that follows when she wakes her snoring husband, the factual proof of their mutualism. "We laughed, all three when she awoke her swarthy, snoring Pietro/To make us change, which we, rich paupers, left to help the garment" (165).

The welcoming laugh of the woman has its counterpart in the two lovers leaving the change for the future child and *to* the future, to Italian Americans in concrete figurative terms, a disinterested act that transcends money, the money that in the words of the ex-colored man sums up "a white man's success," as if the two left a black legacy to Italian Americans, a future memory given to the child in the name of the mother (117). This is "the dignity that respects itself" as well as the other that also aligns the four different people along class line, where class is to be intended not solely in terms of economic status, but first and foremost as the commonality of the characters' human condition and in terms of identity, as the oxymoron "rich paupers," and especially the noun "paupers," make abundantly clear (165). "Harlem Happiness" embodies the politics of sharing of *Mount Allegro* out in the street, where different people meet and share what they have because they recognize that they have each other, that their differences make them equal. That is why as the lovers walk off, Pietro and his woman laughed "in understanding," together (165). At this point, the two Italian Americans thank the black lovers, a gesture of recognition, because they "brought back an old Etrurian springtide," which is not a climatic condition, but a spiritual one that the two black lovers also experience when "beyond their pearly smiling" they taste the grapes of the dago fruit stand and their own "lips, and laughed at sleepy Harlem," furthering the figurative commonality of the entire scene (165).

The happiness of Harlem is the commonality of the politics of sharing that integrates, the gospel that uplifts the blues of these poor people, so to speak. The African American tradition of laughter combined with the irony typical of a modernist writer would not suffice to make Harlem happy. As a matter of fact, this happiness is to be found nowhere in the rest of *No Hiding Place*. What changes the picture here, what makes the happiness possible is the Italian Americans' invisible blackness that especially the woman soon to be a mother represents. In this sense, "Harlem Happiness" is the beginning of a poetic trip that is also a historical one through folklore, dialects, as well as geography, the thread that unites all these dimensions as the narration brings the reader from the North to the South, from Harlem to "the Cotton South," Atlanta, and Washington, D.C.

III

William Attaway's *Blood on the Forge*, published on the eve of the United States' entry into World War II in 1941 but set in the turbulent year of 1919, also takes the reader on a historical trip that is at once a voyage in folklore, dialects, and the meaning of American geography. Unlike Brown's poem, the geographical direction of Attaway's second novel takes the main characters and the readers from the South to the North, from the fields of rural Kentucky of three African American sharecroppers, the Moss brothers, to the steel mills of a small town outside Pittsburgh, where Big Mat, Melody, and Chinatown, the three men, go to find work and a home. The geographical direction equals a switch of modes of production, from agrarian landownership of a feudal type to industrial capitalism in the early twentieth century that is also the brothers' entry into modernity. As such, their entry foreruns the problem of achieving a new black consciousness while adjusting to a new socioeconomic environment that includes an uncommon kind of white people, the immigrants from Eastern Europe and the Mediterranean area.

The brothers move northward because Big Mat believes he has killed his white riding boss when the latter referred with callous words to the ugly death of his mother. The white man denied Big Mat's mother her humanity when he compared the value of her life to the economic value of an animal that traditionally is associated with white exploitation of black labor. "Killin' a animal worth forty dollars, 'cause a nigger woman got dragged over the rocks," the riding boss tells Big Mat (47). To avoid the guaranteed lynching, Mat and his siblings accept the offer of a jackleg white man on a trip to re-cruit black men for northern steel companies in search of cheap labor (tradi-tionally employed to divide the rising union movement formed by predom-inantly white ethnics). For Mat, moving north also means leaving behind his wife, because the hiring company does not transport women.

Big Mat's reaction and the brothers' subsequent migration is not the har-binger of a future economic improvement. It is the byproduct of the anger of centuries of white oppression and exploitation that results in the cynical refusal to recognize the dignity of and respect a female human being who is black and a mother. Big Mat hits the riding boss in the name of his mother and "his mother's people," as Johnson would have it. His "familiar hatred of the white boss" is the flip side of the coin of the denial of the humanity of black people (33). Attaway inscribes this lack of recognition and its subver-sion into the body, which throughout the novel becomes the concrete and symbolic signifier of the conflict between blacks and whites that translates persistent social hierarchies. Thus, when Chinatown gets a new gold tooth, this tooth becomes his way to refuse the whites' denial of the value of black life and, conversely, to affirm his visibility as a black man. White bosses, he says, make him feel like he "ain't nothing, and a man got to have somethin' he kin grin a little to hisself about" (62). That something is the gold tooth, and gold, of course, is the material that determines the value of money, including the forty-dollar value of the mule that triggered Big Mat's violent reaction. "Without it I ain't nobody. Now everybody turn and see who it is when Chinatown smile" (62).

The centrality of the body in *Blood on the Forge* aligns the novel with the literature of the Great Depression. From Faulkner's *Sanctuary*, likely the first Great Depression novel, to *The Grapes of Wrath*, male and female bodies signify this tragic period of twentieth-century modernity. Attaway, however, writes after the beginning of the end of the economic depression and sets the story well before the actual beginning of the Great Depression. While the bodies of *Blood on the Forge* signify the crisis of the 1930s, they remind us that for black Americans the Great Depression was nothing new, because, as Sterling Brown pointed out in "The Negro" essay he penned for *Washington, D.C.*, in the American Guide Series, they had always lived in a depression. And that, Attaway might suggest, was part of the problem that led to the Great Depression, as well as part of the solution.

Accordingly, things do not get any better when the three brothers arrive in the Pennsylvania small town, but for reasons different from the old racial and economic hierarchies of the feudal South. In addition to the trauma of the new landscape made of red ore, yellow limestone, and black coke, which looks to the Moss brothers like snow in August, an obvious metaphor of a different mode of production, Big Mat, Melody, and Chinatown encounter "a hatred and contempt different from anything they had ever experienced in Kentucky" (69). The hatred emanates from the eyes of a group of Slavs who identify new black people in town as strikebreakers. When the Slavs throw rocks at the brothers, Chinatown comments that the rocks are the difference between the North and the South. As Melody says that the Slavs must have mistaken them for somebody else, Chinatown replies, "When white folks git mad all niggers look alike," words followed by the image of one of the Slavs looking at Chinatown with contempt as he spits on the ground (70). No matter the geography, at a first glance there seems to be no difference in terms of race relations and in the way the three black men experience racism. Yet the difference is there. In Kentucky the brothers are neither seen nor recognized and respected. Their humanity is not seen and is denied because they are black. In Pennsylvania, their visibility as blacks is what makes them all alike and the target of a never-before-experienced hatred. In the South their blackness is what makes them invisible and the cause of the denial of their humanity. In the North blackness is what bestows upon them a human condition and the cause of the hatred toward them. It is a different kind of negation of their humanity.

There is, however, another difference. White folks do not look all alike to the Moss brothers, who inside the factory, in the workplace, experience the respect that they never had in Kentucky or that is missing outside the mill. This respect comes in the guise of an Italian open-hearth worker who amicably approaches the brothers, an encounter with clear racial implications that bodily images underline. Whereas previously the black body serves as the signifier for white people's lack of recognition of African Americans, here the Italian American body is the tissue that connects Italian Americans to blacks.

The first day of work in the steel mill, an Italian American man whom everybody calls Mike, as if this man could be *any* Italian American man—

and clearly the choice of such a common name, especially among Italian American males, reinforces the idea of Mike as the embodiment of what being Italian American means and who an Italian American is—talks to the brothers to give them safety advice. Mike is the only person in the factory who dares to talk to the brothers while they are sitting on a bench, far from the other workers who give them "cold stares." The Italian shows a caring attitude toward the brothers. He shows them how "to tie the handkerchief around the neck. He made sure they had smoked glasses and heavy gloves. He warned them to wear two pairs of pants if they were put on a hot job," because hot-job men "always had a lot of holes burned in their clothes." His advice and warning indicate a caring behavior whose precondition is the recognition of one's self in the other. Mike warns the black men about something that he does not want to happen to himself, and that likely did happen to him already. The verbal exchange between the four men also sparks a moment of hilarity, as if the warning transcended the solidarity that shared working conditions have the potential to produce. When Mike tells the brothers how one time he fell asleep at the furnace and the sparks caused his pants to drop off his behind as he woke up, the three boys cannot help bursting into laughter. This is a moment of solidarity among workers, but it might be such because in the first place it is a moment of mutual understanding and recognition that the laugh signifies, as it does in Brown's "Harlem Happiness." Attaway describes Mike as a man with "a good heart," a predisposition that can be said of anybody, if somewhat stereotypically. Yet Mike is also the person with his locker "next to the Moss boys," the first indicator of his invisible blackness that seems to be visible to the Moss brothers (79).

The disposition of the lockers and the kind of job the four men are assigned are a racial taxonomy, the cipher of the hierarchy of the racial mosaic even within the proletarian class in the United States, as well as the indicator that the mutual understanding between the African American sharecroppers emigrated from the South of the country and the unassimilated Italian American, a status that his broken English reveals, precedes the solidarity that workers may (or may not) build inside the factory. The darker the skin, the closer to hell, metaphorically and concretely. Attaway does not describe a case of solidarity of workers as workers. There is no class determinism here. Solidarity is not the cipher of equally hideous working conditions. Instead, he paints a condition of shared identity based on each worker's singular universality. The Italian American and the African American men are able to see themselves in each other because they are able to see their difference. This is what fuels their solidarity as workers. At the end of the novel the conflicts between racial and ethnic identities and class condition, as well as the lack of a shared class identity among the workers, are presented as the cause of the defeat of the strike that the union has called, which, of course, is every worker's defeat, beginning with the strikebreakers.

What triggers the reciprocal recognition of their differentiated identity is the Italian open-hearth worker's ability to laugh about his body as a signifier of his male identity, including his masculinity, historically a potent part of the male working-class condition and an aspect that the Moss brothers share with him. The story of Mike's pants "dropping off my behind" may seem an innocent, laughable accident that the Italian recounts to make the brothers feel welcomed and comfortable in the mill, but this is precisely the reason why it works as a signifier of the workers' consciousness and identity, especially in an American working environment in the early twentieth century such as a steel mill, where an ethnically and racially diverse proletarian force was often unable to overcome cultural and language barriers, a factor that the managerial class used to divide the workers. Attaway offers a good example of this cultural separation in a verbal exchange between an Irishman and an Italian stove tender named John, who crosses himself and mutters something "in his own tongue" (186) as he hears Chinatown say that he feels something bad is going to happen in the mill on that morning:

> "You ain't superstitious, eh, John?"
> "Not me," said John. "I ain't believe nothing.'"
> "Then what was you sayin' to yourself?" (186–87)

The Moss brothers don't laugh because the story that Mike recounted is amusing, which it is. They laugh because an Italian American man is making fun of himself referencing that specific anatomical part. Moreover, there are all sorts of sexual allusions in the passage, with the hand mimicking the furnace slanting, some of the slag missing the hole, and Mike's joking about not getting his behind burned. For black men who feel like they "ain't nothing, and a man got to have somethin' he kin grin a little about hisself," hearing an Italian man making fun of himself by figuratively giving away the bodily signifier of his masculinity, to the point that his language may even include some sort of homosexual allusions, is a powerful moment of identification. Such a form of identification carries even more weight because historically in the United States white men attempted to emasculate their black counterparts.

There is a second, even more powerful racial allusion when Mike concludes his story telling the brothers, "Maybe I lucky not get burned, huh?" which the conspiratorial final "huh?" reinforces (79). No black writer, especially one born in Mississippi, as Attaway was, would have a non–African American man talk to black men about bodies getting burned without having in mind another kind of burning, the one that we have seen the ex-colored man of Johnson's novel decry by commenting, "I do not see how a people that can find in its conscience any excuse whatever for slowly burning to death a human being, or tolerate such an act, can be entrusted with the salvation of a race," where clearly the agent of the burning is whiteness, whereas what is being burned is everyone's humanity. Additionally, the fact that Attaway has an Italian, a member of an ethnic group that itself suffered a significant amount of lynching in the early part of the twentieth century, is hardly irrelevant, especially considering that the novel is set in 1919 and published during World War II.

The invisible blackness of the Italian Americans reaches its peak when another Irish worker gives Big Mat the nickname "Black Irish" because he prevented a fellow worker named O'Casey from getting injured, perhaps even killed in the furnace. "That black fella make a whole lot better Irisher than a hunky or a ginny. They been over here twenty years and still eatin' garlic like it's as good as stew meat and potatoes," a second Irishman comments (122–23). The Irishman ranks the black man above Eastern European and Mediterranean Americans in the racial ladder of America. His racial hierarchy is based on the Italians' supposed inability to give up their garlic, one of the symbols of their identity and geographical origins that includes their darker skin, and assimilate into the whiteness that the Irish food, climatically and culturally speaking a northern dish, represents. At the same time, although the Irishman absorbs Big Mat's identity in his newly found Irishness, he does not erase Big Mat's blackness from it, figuratively excluding him from full participation in Irishness, or, better yet, whiteness as he conceives of it. Big Mat may be a putative Irish, but he is still black, a "Black Irish." Big Mat cannot be praised for what he is, an African American man. In this respect, it is telling that the Irishman speaks for Big Mat. Equally telling is the fact that when O'Casey waves to Big Mat and says, "So long, Black Irish," Big Mat does not answer—and silence here does not mean approval (123).

This ethnic hierarchy is subverted later on in the novel when Melody gets hurt on the job, an event that the workers salute as a proof of his masculinity. An injury makes any worker "a kind of hero to the men who had worked beside him." Melody's injury prompts an Italian to tell him, "You stand pain like anything . . . I tell fella on night crew that you Italian. I say you gone back to Italy" (173). Previously, it was the Moss brothers who identify with Mike the Italian open-hearth worker as he told them his laughable accident. Here, when the accident is nothing to laugh about and is instead taken as a certificate of one's masculinity that grants inclusion, something that makes any worker gain the respect of his fellow workers in their male-coded communicative domain, an Italian American worker pronounces a black man

Italian *and* figuratively sends him *back* to Italy. Unlike Big Mat, Melody is not renamed a Black Italian by his African American fictional creator. He is considered an Italian. Because of it, he is sent to Italy, he is granted access to the original homeland of the Italian immigrants, the land that *they* left. One could argue that his blackness is now erased. Or maybe one could argue that Attaway acknowledges the invisible blackness of the Italians. As in the previously mentioned passage involving Big Mat and the Irish workers, the black man does not get to speak. Such an argument, however, would erase the real blackness, the black voice of the narrator, a blackness that allows him to send a black man to Italy, to send him back home (!), thereby locating the invisible blackness of the Italian Americans in Italy, transnationalizing it, just as Jerre Mangione does in *Mount Allegro*.

A previous passage further illustrates the disarticulation of the Italian Americans from the whiteness that Irish and Slav workers share in the eyes of the African Americans brothers. And here again we encounter the link between the racial dimension and the body, this time with the further connection to the mother trope that unchained Big Mat's reaction to the white riding boss in native Kentucky. One Monday a Slav worker intentionally lets a hot test block fall on the toes of the Italian worker next to him. The Italian is taken to the hospital amid the laughing of his fellow workers, "as though it were a joke that a man got a toe smashed" (118). The only person not to laugh is Big Mat. One need not be a devoted Freudian to associate the physical abuse that includes a coded message of identity-based disrespect and maltreatment that the Italian suffers with the countless physical abuses that marked the African American experience. Physical abuse is the matrix of African American history, and the body is the page where that history was written. In this case, one also need not be a devoted Freudian to connect the block that lacerates the toe of the Italian worker to the rocks that the Slavs have thrown at the Moss brothers as they arrived in Pennsylvania or to the rocks where Big Mat's mother, "a nigger woman," as the white riding boss had told Big Mat, was dragged. Ironically—and irony, like paradox, is a sign of history—at the end of the novel a young Slav kills Big Mat with a stone, linking history, exploitation, and exclusion in a generational racial circle, the violent past mirrored in an equally violent present.

Blood on the Forge offers no way out of this deadly vision that so much bothered Ralph Warner, Ralph Ellison, and Theodore Ward, who praised the story but fiercely attacked the conclusions of the novel in their reviews of the book in the *Daily Worker*, the *Negro Quarterly*, and *Mainstream* respectively. The former lamented that Attaway failed to provide a way out of the workers' division, of unity between blacks and whites. Albeit in different fashion, Ellison lamented the same thing: Attaway's failure to see a light at

the end of the black-and-white tunnel. Yet the recurring identification between the Moss brothers and the Italian workers and the way such identification is portrayed might suggest otherwise. Considered from the standpoint
of a historical category, as Herbert Gutman defines it—a category "describing people in relationship over time, and the ways in which they became
conscious of their relationship, separate, unite, enter into struggle, form institutions, and transmit values in class ways" (359)—Attaway's investment in
the Italian American invisible blackness allowed him to enact credible processes of reciprocal identification and create a fictional home for difference
with significant symbolic consequences. The protean dimension of the invisible blackness of the Italian Americans helped Attaway to enlarge the
representation of life in America at a time when such a life registered the
movement of black people from the South to the North and of others from
Eastern Europe, the Mediterranean region, and the Caribbean islands to the
United States.

   Unlike what Ellison argued, Attaway inserted more, not less American
life in *Blood on the Forge*. And so did, on an even larger scale, Willard Motley in *Knock on Any Door*, his 1947 best-selling novel centered on Nick
Romano, an altar boy in Denver whose Italian immigrant parents hope he
will become a Catholic priest. Instead, first Nick ends up in a reform school.
Then he turns into a bisexual prostitute and low-key gangster on the streets
of a multiethnic, racially mixed proletarian neighborhood of Chicago, the
city where his family moved to join Aunt Rose, his mother's sister, after los-
ing their grocery store of Italian-imported food in Denver. In the end, Nick
is executed in the electric chair for the killing of the ever-present Irish cop.
In the midst of this turbulent life, Nick marries Emma, a German American
girl who commits suicide shortly after Nick gets out of prison and quits his
newfound job in a steel mill.

   One of the achievements of *Knock on Any Door* is that Motley invests in
an Italian American as a way to reinvent blackness after the New Deal and
World War II, his contribution to the African American decentering of whiteness. One way *Knock on Any Door* achieves such a decentering is through
the number of diverse characters who surround Nick Romano. Whether one
looks at them from the ethnic, racial, gender, religious, sexual, economic, or
simply fictional standpoint, the diversity of significant characters is truly
remarkable. To name a few: white American Owen, Italian Vito, Jewish
Abe, German Emma, black Sunshine, Mexican Juan. The list could go on.
Another narrative strategy that Motley deploys is the unconventional geographical trajectory of the novel. Unlike the typical African American modern novel, from Dunbar's *The Sport of the Gods* to Ellison's *Invisible Man*,
Knock on Any Door avoids the literary convention that moves the main

characters and the action of the novel from the South to the North. Of course, this novelty is dictated by Motley's decision to build the story around an Italian American character. And yet, Motley also avoids a second formal convention, the westward movement that characterizes both classic white and ethnic American novels such as John Steinbeck's *The Grapes of Wrath* or John Fante's *Ask the Dust*, to mention two classic examples from the same period. In *Knock on Any Door*, the Romanos withdraw from the West. The immigrant family abandons the frontier, a symbolic shattering of the American dream owing to the economic failure of their grocery store and the lack of new opportunities.

Although he renounced the narrative possibilities that the northward migration and the frontier habitually offered American writers, Motley did not ignore these two thematic traditions. He reformulated them with the invisible blackness of Nick Romano that Motley locates at the center of the multiracial and multiethnic urban poverty of Chicago's proletarian streets such as the (in)famous Maxwell Avenue, where one can hear "men and women shouting their wares in hoarse, rasping voices, Jewish words, Polish and Russian words, Spanish, mixed-up English. And once in a while you heard a chicken cackling or a baby crying"—the same kind of street that reeks of "hot dog, garlic, fish, steam table, cheese, pickle, garbage can, mould and urine smells" (84).

Nick's invisible blackness becomes the way Motley reformulates the Great Migration and the frontier theme. This kid's connections to Italy are racial and sexual rather than geographical, cultural, and linguistic.

The obvious primary reason of his fictional atypical Italian American identity is that Motley was an African American, which incidentally raises the question of what is an Italian American novel and, conversely, what is an African American novel. But this variation on the theme is precisely what makes Nick Romano an interesting fictional character and *Knock on Any Door* a relevant book, perhaps today more so than in the past. Motley may not be a first-rank writer in terms of aesthetics and language execution. Ideologically, he moved more to the left of the political spectrum after the end of the New Deal and the onset of the Cold War. Stylistically, he found himself caught in between the end of modernism and the first pangs of post-modernism. In other words, Motley is a transition writer, but one who is extremely astute. Here is how he describes Nick Romano's hair: "He put water on his hair and stood in front of the mirror, combing it. It won't stay down. It's too curly" (119).[2] This is the first hint of Nick's invisible blackness, which in the reform school fuels his gradual process of racial self-realization. In the strict environment of the school, Nick, who grew up in an homoge-neous Italian American Catholic environment, cannot bring himself to say the word "nigger" when he is asked to help another kid wash the school director's "big cream-colored Cadillac, shiny with chrome and extra lights," an obvious homage to as well as a twist on *The Great Gatsby*, as Romano's first name might suggest (47). "What happened to the nig—" Nick asks the other kid, meaning the African American boy with a "scared-to-death" look on his face whom Nick tries to approach before Bricktop, the canonical racist and fascist-like thug of the school, warns him, "We don't talk to no niggers in here" (43). Nick's initial reaction mixes the typical obedience of the novice in a new environment such as a reform school and his Catholic shame for obeying Bricktop's warning, a shame that his Italian American identity unchains.

Nick does not feel that Bricktop's personal pronoun "we" includes him. Neither does he feel that he belongs to the group of people that the personal pronoun "we" identifies. Just as Nick increasingly becomes aware of his invisible blackness, so does his yearning for belonging, which time and again Motley denies him. Right after Bricktop warns him to stay away from African American kids, Nick witnesses the school's superintendent whipping Nick's friend Tommy because he attempted to escape from the school along with a group of kids that included Sam, the African American whom Nick intended to talk to before Bricktop's threat. Increasingly, Nick identifies with Tommy because the latter refuses to submit to the logic of the reform school, including its racial divide. Tommy is the exact opposite of Bricktop, to whom he responded defiantly as Bricktop ordered him not to talk to Sam, "I'll talk to anyone I want!" (57). When the kids who attempted the escape are brought back to the assembly hall, Sam sits next to Tommy, knowing that Tommy will be the one to be punished. Tommy is forced to pull down his pants, his buttocks naked for everybody to see, while the superintendent does his job with his strap, "the smack of the whip again, cutting the flesh, bringing the blood" (60). As in *Blood on the Forge*, here too the corporeal image works on a double level. In *Blood on the Forge* the story that the Italian worker tells the Moss bothers about his buttocks being burned fuels their mutual recognition. In *Knock on Any Door* the whipping of the same anatomical part triggers Nick's reaction. In both novels, a bodily injury that symbolically represents the violation of a male subject's masculinity is what fuels mutual recognition. Tommy is a white kid, but Motley was a black homosexual man, and it is right after the whipping of the one kid who crosses all sorts of racial and ethnic lines that Nick rebels against everything that the reform school stands for, beginning with racial division.

Nick starts hanging out with Sam, and the two develop a comradeship that eventually will force the young Italian American to fight and beat Bricktop. Motley presents this racial crossover as Nick's parallel, organic refusal of the school's mission, which the Anglo-Saxon director Mr. McGuire sums up as follows: "good habits—personal cleanliness, honesty, obedience, co-operation, respect for property, *and* the use of clean language" (29). The school's mission merges puritan discipline, the essential principles of a capitalist system, eugenics, and bourgeois respectability. This totality is what Nick rebels against. Nick Romano, the Italian American kid with "too curly" hair, rejects the school mission because he realizes that he does not belong to this system. The image of a white Anglo superintendent who whips colorblind Tommy is a figurative indictment of an American present that is neither too remote nor too removed from the past. From strictly a theoretical standpoint, the whipping is the cipher of capitalism's internal demand to repress any form of subversion, or even escape, that those at the margins, the multiracial and multiethnic impoverished, might attempt.

The reformatory is a microcosm of the modern capitalist world of white respectability that Nick refuses. In proper modern fashion, Nick becomes a displaced object of modernity who continuously attempts to invert his position and become a subject of the new, modern world he inhabits, which the passage to the plural microcosm of Chicago reflects. Nick's quest becomes his attempt to belong and find a home in his world. This is what Nick strives for as he gets out of the reformatory, obviously to no avail. The modern world that Nick faces reveals itself as a double estrangement. Unlike the children of the immigrants of *Mount Allegro* and other Italian American characters of the time, Nick does not inhabit two different worlds, the Italian at home and the American outside it. He inhabits neither. What he inhabits is the fictional world that Motley imagines for him(self?): the multiracial, multilingual, poor, sexually promiscuous neighborhood rotting with the filth and crime of Chicago's Maxwell Street. The world of a carnival street with a black orchestra and a racially mixed crowd, where a "lean young Negro, black as the hat he wore, came out of the crowd and asked a pretty Italian girl in her teens for a dance," which she agrees to (88). At the end of the dance, the young black American escorts the pretty Italian girl off the improvised dance floor. This world stands in place of what the reform school represents.

Nick Romano is the ideal fictional character to inhabit and show the possibilities that such a world presents and the obstacles that it faces, because his invisible blackness keeps different forms of outsiderness simultaneously in play as he descends into the underworld of West Madison Street, where there are "foreign appearing men, but lighter than the Italians" (84). Motley's original inspiration for Nick Romano was a Mexican teenager whom he had met when he visited a reform school in Denver. The switch to the Italian American Romano, then, is Motley's way to address the complexity of whiteness without falling prey to the typical color-based racial binarism. On Maxwell Street Nick forms a gang with his friends Vito, Stash, and Sleepy—the latter "a nigger kid they palled with because Vito had said that all they needed was a nigger in their gang" (103). When a cop stops them and questions their diverse ethnic background, their "different nationalities," Nick replies, "That ain't nothing, is it? . . . in this country?" (103–4). His response operates at two interconnected levels, strategically introduced by the addition of Sleepy to the gang because his blackness guarantees everyone's otherness. To begin with, like Fortunata Mancuso in the interview with the Ellis Island officer, Nick reverses the subject position of the power relations between the institutional authority that speaks the language of whiteness and the subalterns who have only their identity and each other. However momentarily, Nick's response subverts the ideological agency of white power that triggers divisive social relationships at the racial level, creating a positive and shared space for the mutual recognition of everyone's singular universality. Nick's reply displaces the condition of the rhetoric of equality and freedom that the addition of "in this country?" to his sentence implies. Second, by including "in this country?" at the end of his response, Nick erases the idea of racial hierarchies. Nick knows that inclusion, a code word for racial relations "in this country," is the precondition for everyone to be seen and belong, the public recognition that guarantees every person the possibility to make himself at home in the modern world.

Underneath Nick's skid-row verbal codes lies a theoretical presupposition that raises the political question of white normativity. Just as the addition of "a nigger kid" validates the otherness of the rest of the members of the gang, Nick's inclusive inversion validates everyone's outsiderness as the factual norm of the proletarian streets he inhabits. Nick does not speak for everyone else. Nick's rhetorical inclusive inversion is what everyone else represents, including blackness. Motley's investment in an Italian American teenager with "too curly hair" responds to this politics. In this perspective the plight of Nick Romano is also that of a black male, of which he is a surrogate because of his invisible blackness that nobody recognizes, including literary critics. After all, Motley's first novel is an African American novel by an African American writer.

Motley's inclusive inversion operates also at the formal level, as his twist on Nick's sexual conduct and the gangster trope indicates. Nick's initial homoerotic contacts with his teenager friend Tony who "crouched near him" (17) and with Mexican American Jesse in the reform school give way to his homosexual prostitution after he turns into a low-class gangster. Money and alcohol, the stuff of gangsters, so to speak, initiate Nick's descent into the underworld of homosexuality. Barney, the first man he ends up sleeping with, finally wins Nick's resistance by getting Nick drunk, after which Nick routinely prostitutes himself with other men. On West Madison, the street that is now his home, some people know where "he got his extra money" (156). However, Nick also develops a close relationship with a white middle-class man, Owen, who increasingly and genuinely cares for Nick. Nick reciprocates because "in his way, [Owen] lived outside the law, too" (189). Nick sees himself in the homosexual middle-class white man not because of class equality but because Owen lives outside the norm. Nick's queerness functions as what John C. Charles calls "an oppositional consciousness and mode of relationality" that translates the urban human topography of Nick's world across class, gender, ethnicity, and sex, a universe that mirrors Nick's reply to the cop that questioned his gang's mixed ethnic and racial composition (91).

Nick's queerness, however, extends beyond its oppositional and interconnecting modality. It becomes one way to attempt to envision a new social order. According to Alan Wald, "Motley places homosexuals squarely in the new community of human solidarity that he is constructing outside the system, alongside of criminals created by poverty and middle-class revolutionaries who take their side" (264). The way Nick relates his queerness to money is indicative of Motley's attempt to picture a different social order without avoiding the reality of the ideology of Nick's actual world. Nick is "money crazy," as he confesses to Owen (185), who in turn never misses a chance to give him some cash, thus showing the same indifference to money that Nick evidences in the way he uses money. Nick never accumulates any capital. Neither does he spend money to elevate his social status. Unlike the typical gangster who invests in high-quality clothes and luxurious places that situate him in what Ruth defines as "the sensuous urban realm of modern pleasure-seeking" (114), Nick does not change his attire. Nor does his proletarian urban environment change, the only world he inhabits and wants to inhabit. Nick either spends his money without any specific goal to modify his status or gives it out to his multiethnic and multiracial gang. On one occasion, he gives it to his mother and his wife's mother after Emma commits suicide.

Nick's queerness also modifies the typical depiction of Italian American criminal life, another major accomplishment of Motley's book. Certainly his criminality has a redemptive dimension, what Charles calls "a redemptive discourse—an honorific badge of queer nonconformity that is the source of his sense of manhood" (110). Yet Nick's homosexuality differs from the closeted one of popular Italian American fictional gangsters of the time that rises from the ethnic ghetto of big urban environments popularized by figures such as Rico in the previously mentioned *Little Caesar*, whose cinematic rendition could not have escaped Motley's mind. Obviously, the difference is that, unlike Little Caesar, Nick Romano is the product of an African American pen. Nick may as well be the only Italian American popular criminal who is not involved with organized crime in 1930s Chicago, a difference that Motley intentionally addresses early in the novel. As soon as his mother informs him that they will move to the Windy City, Nick thinks of Al Capone. Yet Nick never finds himself around any form of Italian American organized crime. His fictional world is truly a world apart.

The absence in Nick Romano of any of the typical signs of desire to access white respectability is the byproduct of his invisible blackness. Unlike typical Italian American gangsters, Nick trusts people outside his own ethnic group and culture. The most important difference, however, is his obsession with his looks, which is especially relevant in light of the lack of attempt to elevate his social status. Nick's obsession with his looks is immortalized in his signature sentence, "Live a good life, die young, and have a good-looking corpse!" (117). The sentence may be catchy, but the message is clear: beauty transcends even death. Such a beauty is not the reflection of the high-quality clothes and luxurious places of manufactured social status of gangsters seeking money, power, and white respectability—that is to say, gangsters as businessmen. The obsession with his looks is Nick Romano's way to exert control over his own self—and controlling himself is Nick's way to reject white respectability. It is also a gesture typical of black as well as of Italian American culture, what Italian Americans consider an element of the notion of respect for oneself that is also a way to acknowledge respect for the other. What is controlled in the first place is the aesthetics of one's body. For Nick, this is an affirmative gesture. By transcending death, beauty prevails over fear and subverts the continuous attempt of the world of whiteness to control and frame him. It empowers him. That is why at the beginning of Nick's trial the newspapers, which, like any mass media, are developments of the forces of production that shape social relations, nickname him Pretty Boy Romano, linking his beauty to crime with the reference to the original Pretty Boy, Charles Arthur Floyd (367). According to the newspapers his hair, the cipher of Nick's invisible blackness, typifies his beauty. And the newspapers do not fail to point out the color of his hair, Nick's "curly black hair" (367).

The trial becomes the allegory of a lynching, with the media framing Nick as the new Pretty Boy Floyd and the prosecutor linking the Italian American young man to Al Capone. "The days of gangsterism, the days of Capone, and the days of Romano—*have ended!*" the prosecutor thunders, after which Nick "knew all over again what it was like to be stared at. *White* pulpy *faces.* Eyes pressing in on him, closer; closer; hard, like a wall moving forward to crush," a spectacular image of the white gaze operating as the Foucaultian panopticon (461–62, my italics). On trial here is a black man in Italian Amer-

ican guise, and, in turn, the Italian American invisible blackness, Nick's refusal to embrace whiteness. Right before the electricity takes his life, with
his eyes shut under "the death mask," the Italian American boy who after his
arrest in a dark alley of a slum stands under the rain "staring in its whiteness" has a flashback of the scene that triggered his reaction in the reform
school, the whipping of his friend Tommy (343). Then, his eyes open, he
sobs, "seeing the lash fall, bringing blood" (504). Nick's final memory recalls the corporality of a racial past that Nick Romano, the Italian American
with "dark eyes" and a "black heart," as his accuser in the courtroom describes him, translates for his African American author. This is the same boy
who likes his African American friend Sunshine the most because he knows
that Sunshine would "give his right arm for me" (152), as if to indicate that
one's refusal to play by the rules of whiteness led to the whip in the past and
to the electric chair in the present.

The only option to stay alive in this world, Motley suggests, is another
seeming form of death: give up one's identity, one's consciousness, one's history, and pretend to embrace whiteness, as does Anthony Fontana, the Italian juror who votes to kill Nick, "proving to the world that he appreciated
his American citizenship and believed in law and order," the latter of which
two things Nick Romano hates the most (468). The night of Nick's execution, Fontana closes his print shop feeling "a warm beat of pride in himself,
in his place in business, his comfortable security, his success as a foreigner
who had come to America and made good" (489). The warmth stands in
stark contrast to the cold weather outside the shop, where the headline of the
paper announces, "PRETTY BOY AWAITS DEATH." He saw it and his eyes,
buried by too much good and rich Italian food in a swarthy and greasy face,
snapped. All the time they think we Italians are all like—*that dago!*" (489).
The dago is about to become a bad-looking electrocuted corpse. Anthony
Fontana, instead, is alive and well. And so is his "swarthy and greasy face."

IV

Like Nick Romano, Giovanni, the homosexual lover of David, the narrator
of James Baldwin's *Giovanni's Room*, is executed, this time on the guillo-
tine, the infamous way capital punishment used to be carried out in France,
where the novel takes place. Giovanni is guilty of the murder of Guillaume,
the owner of the Parisian bar where Giovanni worked as a bartender and met
David. The death penalty and homosexuality are not the only things that
Nick and Giovanni share. Poverty and loneliness play a role in Giovanni's
fatal end as well. Similarly, Giovanni in the end is considered a gangster.
Toward the end of the novel, David's American girlfriend Hella tells her

boyfriend, "That sordid little gangster has wrecked your life" (242). Giovanni himself says that Guillaume fired him and told him that he "was a gangster and a thief and a dirty little street boy," a description that would fit any of the young boys of Maxwell Street and West Madison Street (154).

David describes Giovanni to Hella in terms that also recall Motley's novel. He tells her that Giovanni is poor, that he comes "from poor folks." Like many poor people he has no opportunity and money to build "any kind of future. That's why so many of them wander the streets and turn into gigolos and gangsters and God knows what" (197). Giovanni's rebellious temper is another sign reminiscent of Nick. However, the similarities extend beyond the main characters. Baldwin's characterization of Giovanni's mother seems to respond to stereotypes just as Motley's characterization of Nick's mother does. Unlike in *Knock on Any Door*, however, Giovanni's mother never appears physically in *Giovanni's Room*. Nonetheless, in David's mind she resembles the Italian caretaker of the home that he has rented in Southern France after leaving Paris. She seems to "have gone into mourning directly the last child moved out of childhood" is David's comment (96). This woman, "a peasant from Italy, must resemble, in so many ways, the mother of Giovanni," David concludes (99). When she hears that David lost his mother at a very young age, when he was only five year old, this same caretaker exclaims, "*Pauvre bambino!*" mixing French and Italian, just as Lena Romano cries "my boy, my boy" after mixing Italian and English when Nick accepts her request to take confession before his execution: "*Oh, grazie, thank God!*" the only time she mingles the two languages in the 504 pages of the novel (486). No less important is Giovanni's "black hair," another feature that evokes Nick Romano (90). What these similarities evince is that Baldwin modeled Giovanni according to white Americans' stereotypes of Italian Americans in the northeastern region of the country, chiefly in Baldwin's native New York City.

The story of his life in Italy as Giovanni recounts it to David indicates as much. No more stereotypical Italian American can be found in modern American literature and culture than Giovanni, not even on cable TV. Giovanni tells David that in Italy he had a woman who loved him and took care of him when he went back home at the end of his working day in the fields, a description, however, that from a gender standpoint might also be a parody of the white middle-class suburban couple in 1950s America: "She loved *me*, she took care of me and she was always there when I came home from work, in from the vineyards" (202). His village is "very old and in the south, it is on a hill" (202). Good Italian immigrant that he is, Giovanni likes his village *after* he left. Indeed, he wanted to stay "there forever" and do what Italian immigrants and Italian Americans do, "eat much spaghetti and drink much wine and make many babies and grow fat" (202). One wonders where the mandolin is. The answer, of course, is that Giovanni is an amateur violinist. Giovanni remembers the day he left his Southern Italian village on the hill, when his old self died, "one wild, sweet day. I will never forget that day. It was the day of my death—I wish it had been the day of my death" (204).

From immigrant mythic nostalgia to tragedy is a short step in Baldwin's reenactment of the white imagination that hosts Italian Americans. Giovanni confesses that he left his village right after burying his stillborn boy. "It was all grey and twisted when I saw it and it made no sound—and we spanked it on the buttocks and we sprinkled it with holy water and we prayed but it never made a sound, it was dead. It was a little boy, it would have been a wonderful, strong man" (205). When even the prayers do not work, melodrama, dressed up in Protestant garments to express Catholic guilt, becomes the proper corollary to nostalgia and tragedy. "When I knew that it was dead," Giovanni continues, "I took our crucifix off the wall and I spat on it and I threw it on the floor and my mother and my girl screamed and I went out. We buried it right away, the next day, and then I left my village and I came to this city where surely God has punished me for all my sins and for spitting on His holy Son, and where I will surely die. I do not think that I will ever see my village again" (205).

Of course, this crescendo of lurid stereotypes is a joke, and hardly a bad one, especially because the joke is on the reader and, to an extent, on Baldwin himself, the black homosexual Harlemite writer who plays with the invisible blackness of Italian American men to unmask whiteness in what myopic critics unwilling to see Italian Americans as anything but white ethnics from Europe—and Europe to these critics means always and only Northern Europe—have called Baldwin's raceless novel. Quite the contrary, *Giovanni's Room* is a novel *about* race: the white race. For Baldwin, who reminded us that nobody was white before coming to America, race is not solely an inner-directed color-based issue. It is also, perhaps especially, a way to question the whiteness of Christian liberal humanism and its organic interdependence with a capitalist system of social relations, beginning with two of its interconnected pillars, heterosexuality and masculinity. Even though Baldwin replaces New York with Paris and an Italian American with an Italian, it is the trope of an Italian American man that allows him to pretend to write a raceless novel that is not raceless at all, as the closing sentence of the opening paragraph that David *voices* makes unquestionably clear: "My ancestors conquered a continent, pushing across death-laden plains, until they came to an ocean which faced away from Europe into a darker past" (3). As for Johnson, Nugent, and 1930s and '40s African American writers such as Brown, Attaway, and Motley, race in *Giovanni's Room* concerns an idea of civilization, including its idea of humanism. David's ancestors did not conquer a nation. They conquered a continent. This powerful beginning, which stood on its head Nick Carraway's final lines in *The Great Gatsby*,[3] refers to the history of black and Native Americans. In 1956, however, it also hinted at the French colonialism in Northern Africa and Indochina as well as the concomitant Korean War. As the phallic nuances of the verbs "conquer," "push," and "come" insinuate, the conquest is envisioned also as a rape, which in turn suggests the political dimension of sex and its connection to race, which is both hidden and reinscribed in the stereotypical image of an Italian American man.

Baldwin hides blackness and masculinity behind Giovanni's Italian American mask, whose chief function is to expose the nature of whiteness and the sense of guilt typical of white Americans. The transoceanic reversed trip that stands in direct opposition to the opening passage about the conquest of the American continent is a way to subtract whiteness from the logic of black-and-white binarism in a post–World War II world where European colonialism and legal segregation in the South of the United States began to crumble. The stereotypes about the Italian characters show the antihumanist humanism of middle-class culture, which is essential to the construction of the white self. The stereotypes include the economically unproductive but socially binding and culturally nonrationalized aspects of Italian culture: "In Italy we are friendly, we dance and sing and make love," Giovanni tells David when they first meet, opposing Italians to the "cold" French, to which David responds, teasing him, "But the French say . . . that the Italians are too fluid, too volatile, have no sense of measure," a description reminiscent of white Americans' mainstream characterization of black Americans (54). At the same time, these words detach the Italian Giovanni from the "cold" northern French type, factually expelling Italian Americans from whiteness. The stereotyping of the Italians ridicules Italian culture and people in order to subvert America's racial discourse and identity.

This geo-cultural encoding entails an aesthetic dimension that unveils white masculinity, which Baldwin represents through the western films and Gary Cooper, a reminder that this is a Cold War novel. In one of the many semantic twists that Baldwin injects in the narrative in typical modern fashion, Giovanni tells David that he met the man who is going to be his future victim, Guillaume, in a cinema where a cowboy movie starring Gary Cooper was playing. "C'était un film du far west, avec Gary Cooper" (It was a western movie, with Gary Cooper), says Giovanni, who continues, "The last gunshot had been fired and all the music came up to celebrate the triumph of the goodness" (88). When they do not dance, sing, eat spaghetti, or make love, Italians are gangsters. And yet the prototypical essence of the white man, the cowboy, is the one who fires gunshots, of course for the good of humankind, which is precisely why the Italians are gangsters.

Baldwin's investment in Italian Americans begins with David's first homosexual experience, which happened back home in America, with a young boy, Joey. David met Joey at the beach in Coney Island, in Brooklyn. Most commentators argue that Joey is a black kid. African American critic Trudier Harris-Lopez, however, argues that Joey "is probably Italian," which to this black critic means "darker in color than the Anglicized WASP and certainly on a lower scale of social acceptability in American society; David observes that he lives in a 'better neighborhood' than Joey does" (25). Of course, the African American critic is right. Joey is a common name among northeastern Italian Americans of the third and subsequent generations, as viewers of the sitcom *Friends* surely remember. It could also be viewed as a phonetic bastardization of Giovanni, perhaps even evoking the desire to pass as white and hide one's blackness. More important, Joey is a working-class boy from 1950s Brooklyn whose physical features point in the direction of Italian American invisible blackness. Like Nick Romano and Giovanni, whose lack of last name makes him a representative of all Italian Americans, he has "curly hair darkening the pillow" in the bed where the two sleep and has "long eyelashes" (11). His body is "brown" and "sweaty" (11). If the physical connotation does not suffice, the literary one does. The image of Joey's body that David describes as "the *black* opening of a cavern in which I would be tortured till madness came, in which I would lose my manhood," suggests the combination of blackness and a Dantesque homosexual descent to hell (12; my italics).

Leslie Fiedler criticized Baldwin for rendering David "a shade *too* pale-face, almost ladies-magazine-Saxon, gleaming blond" ("Homosexual," 204). In this case, Fiedler missed the point. David's hyper-paleness is necessary to keep color as a part of the racial equation without overshadowing other aspects, including class, sex, and heteronormative patriarchy. In Baldwin's hand, then, we have the final function that Italian Americans play in African American male literature during Jim Crow. Their invisible blackness liberates the subversive energies that a solely color-based notion of race precludes from viewing. In turn, this invisible blackness disassembles the notion of Italian Americans as simply Euro-Americans or white ethnics. In *Giovanni's Room*, Italian American men become what Harris-Lopez called one of the many despised "other 'niggers' that David can use and abuse after he has used them sexually" (25). Joey and Giovanni are "other 'niggers'" because of their invisible blackness. Yet they are also Italian American homosexuals— in terms of the chronology of publication, the first Italian American homosexuals in black literature before *Gentleman Jigger*, another stroke of the literary genius of James Baldwin, who reversed the construction of white masculinity by turning two Italian American men, traditionally presented in the exotic guise of heterosexual stallions, into two homosexuals and Puritanism into "the last stand . . . of heterosexuality," to quote again Leslie Fiedler ("Homosexual," 206).

David's continuous references to dirtiness in relation to Joey and Giovanni and the spaces that they inhabit are another indication of their invisible blackness. They foreshadow David's whiteness in the guise of his obsession with cleanliness, the old Puritan conception that what is good is what is clean, including love, and, *ça va sans dire*, for the old Puritans the only clean love, if there is such a thing for them, is heterosexual love. The chief function of this dialectics is not an aesthetic position. David's cleanliness is not a metaphor for self-care and control of his identity as it is for Nick Romano. It is white superiority in the guise of Western rationality, which Roderick Ferguson, speaking of Baldwin's *Giovanni's Room*, defines as "a technique of racialization that requires erotic subjugation" (28). This is what the Italian American homosexual men of *Giovanni's Room* continuously disrupt. They unmask the heteronormative classist patriarchal foundations of the West already announced in the very beginning of the book, the ancestors' conquest of the American continent described with the previously mentioned series of verbs that evoke rape—and the ancestors are obviously men. What ultimately stops David from embracing homosexuality is not his nonexistent attraction for Hella, whose mythological Nordic name reinforces Giovanni's invisible blackness. What stops David is the fear of his father, who David describes as a person who disdains intellectualism and teachers because he associates them with feminine subjects. This father is the exemplary embodiment of the ossified, almost congenital Western incapacity to see the other for what it is, a version of the white self. No wonder that David's beloved mother died when David was five year old. No wonder, also, that the mother figure reappears at the end of novel, in the form of the Virgin Mary that Giovanni, true to his Italian American self, invokes twice before his execution, uttering the same words, "*Mary, blessed mother of God*," while David, the white man, invokes the father of all fathers, God (246).

David's invocation foregrounds the ultimate reinscribing of whiteness in the (God)father as the center of modernity in the second half of the twentieth century that the African American literary investment in the invisible blackness of the Italian American male subject during Jim Crow tried to disassemble. This literary disassembling aims at reformulating a more inclusive and diverse class-based notion of race that ideally would dilute color and reinscribe it in a new hybrid self. The overall goal of this discourse is the decentering of the normative power of whiteness, which entails gender and heterosexuality to begin with. That is the reason why Johnson invests in the Italian complexion in order to draw a distinction between race and appearance on the one hand and, on the other, the Italian artists who literally gave visibility to the white bourgeois male self, making it aesthetically hegemonic. For the same reason, and in juxtaposition to this internal disarticulation, Johnson underscores the progress in the sciences and the arts—we might as well say the humanities broadly conceived—as conquest of nonwhite "races," again in the plural. Essentially, this is the same distinction upon which Nugent elaborates his notion of antisocial sociability that reformulates the concept of racial difference as a way to hybridize racial identity, which might as well be read as a way to prevent the possibility of imagining, let alone theorizing, a post-racial identity, if not a post-racial world altogether. However briefly, in the concise space of one poem, Sterling Brown spatializes and gives a working-class, urban dimension to this discourse in order to characterize the mutuality that such racial reformulation of hybridization necessarily entails. Brown takes the racial markers of a new sociability out in the street, in the open space where people actually meet.

Attaway's *Blood on the Forge* shares with Brown's poem this same class-based spatialization, but he uses this spatialization to historicize the racial crossovers that distinguish the social geography of his novel. Consequently, it is no coincidence that the difference-based shared identification of his characters insists more than any of the previous works do on the male body and the masculinity of the proletarian industrial environment where they act. The bodies of *Blood on the Forge* become a racial, class, and even homoerotic signifier of identity and the spaces that mold it. And so does the body of Nick Romano in Motley's underrated *Knock on Any Door*, the work among those here under consideration that does the most to avoid making diversity a fixed order and structure and to reformulate blackness as a way to decenter whiteness. Motley's popularization of his subject might as well be seen as a bridge to the post–World War II new literary context in formation, rather than an aesthetic and formal underachievement, as the transformations, if not the reinvention altogether, of by-then traditional thematic patterns of the novel (such as the Great Migration and the frontier) indicate. It would have been much more difficult, perhaps even impossible for Baldwin to conceive *Giovanni's Room* without the example of Nick Romano and *Knock on Any Door*, of which Baldwin is an astute beneficiary, as much as he is the beneficiary of the Cold War clime of his novel. *Giovanni's Room* can be seen both as a thematic compendium of the African American investment in Italian Americans, as well as the ultimate innovator of it, especially in light of the posthumous publication of Nugent's *Gentleman Jigger*, which in turn helps us see the importance of Nugent's novel and the need to address it critically. By combining the homosexuality and the invisible blackness of the Italian American man, Baldwin transnationalizes the rationalizing classist heteronormativity of Western civilization and its father-centrism. The geographical displacement and the differentiated world of *Giovanni's Room* can be seen as a first step toward a transnational normativity. Such a differentiated modern world, however, can only begin with a notion of womanhood disentangled from the modernity of twentieth-century patriarchy in which it is confined. No trope in our (post)modern culture epitomizes the cultural power of patriarchy as well as the Italian American gangster. No trope in modern American literature embodies womanhood as subversively as the Italian American woman and mother, the subjects of the next two chapters respectively.

[4]

IN THE NAME OF THE FATHER, THE SON, AND
THE HOLY GUN: MODERNITY AS THE GANGSTER

FEW TROPES, IF ANY, SUCCEED in unveiling the interplay of the development and the trajectory of modern capitalism and the hegemonic place of
whiteness in our culture as the Italian American gangster does. This synchronic unfolding made the gangster trope coterminous with our culture
since the early days of the past century, the time when the nascent film industry, then located in the city of New York and northern New Jersey where
waves of Italian immigrants arrived and many of them settled in, started
depicting the gangster as an Italian man in short films such as Wallace Mc-
Cutcheon's 1906 *The Black Hand*. The century-long continuing success of
gangster movies with an Italian American man as the main character, both
originals and remakes and, especially in more recent years, TV series, indicates how pervasive this identification is in the American psyche. *Scarface*
and *The Sopranos* are perfect examples of this phenomenon. And indeed the
international recognition of those movies and TV shows records the transnational appeal of the Italian American gangster as well. If anything, the
artistic and commercial longevity of the Italian American gangster is the sign
of its constant level of contemporaneity in our modern culture. It signals its
ability to navigate between and suture together cultures and places, to interlock cultural formations, geographic areas, and social cleavages that would
seem otherwise distant from, if not altogether foreign to, one another, suggesting the accuracy of what Giorgio Bertellini calls the Italian American
gangster's "semantic plurality [that] is absent from the binary dynamics of
whiteness" ("White Passion," 94). The gangster offers himself as the ideal
tool for a better understanding of the spectrum of the racial discourse and
twentieth-century modernity.

Culturally speaking, the Italian American gangster accommodated the
transition to the new capitalist America that emerged at the onset of the
twentieth century characterized by social and economic changes brought

about by an unprecedented set of forces. Among these forces were urbanization, which moved violence away from nature and into the city; European
and Caribbean immigration, which widened the racial, religious, linguistic,
and ethnic mosaic of America and further differentiated the American working class after the Civil War; the new imperial position of the United States
that began to move the center of world politics from the European capitals
to this side of the Atlantic in the aftermath of World War I; nativism, essentially a reaction to both the new immigration and the new geopolitics
of the United States; Prohibition, which basically created organized crime as
we came to know it; as well as the advent of mass production and the emergence of mass culture that the microphone, the radio, and the motion picture fueled.

Because of his non-solely color-based hybridity, what I have called his
invisible blackness, the Italian American man was best suited to fuse old
cultural traits and new modes of representation that started to emerge at the
end of the nineteenth century. The invisible blackness of the Italian American man allowed mainstream American culture to reassert its whiteness in
the new modern context and in different fashions. The racialization of the
Italian American man as a gangster made it possible for white people facing
the previously mentioned unprecedented social, cultural, and economic transformations to rearticulate the fear of the male other while maintaining control over those changes, a fear historically embodied by the black man in the
form of sexual threat and political nightmare (the slave rebellions) that white
people exorcized on the stage of the minstrel show. The Italian American
man allowed this reification on the new popular stage, the screen of the motion picture, and also on the written pages of popular literature. Unlike the
Italians, black people had begun to enter a Victorian bourgeois social and
mental order and had developed a sense of themselves as Americans. No less
important is the fact that they had taken full control and therefore altered
the English language necessary to represent themselves. "It is not long after
the waning of the blackface minstrel in the late nineteenth century," writes
Fred Gardaphé in his study of the Italian American gangster and masculinity, "that the Italian replaced the African as a subject of imitation in popular
culture" (*Wiseguys*, 13–14). To state it cruelly and somewhat succinctly, but
effectively, at the dawn of the new era, the gun replaced the penis, the camera the stage, and the Italian American gangster the African American man.

Of this marriage between modernity and whiteness the Godfather is the
officiator. Don Corleone remains the ultimate case study for the critical elaboration of the gangster as the quintessential modern trope, especially as Francis Ford Coppola and Mario Puzo developed him in the guise of Michael
Corleone in the second installment of the cinematic trilogy. Don Corleone

signifies the transformation of and entails the contradictions of the gangster from the racial, working-class "other" refusing to play by the capitalist rules that the gangster embodied in the first few decades of the past century to white power broker in the last part of it. The Godfather represents both the peak of this tradition and its inverted reinvention—what I see, redirecting Gardaphé's study toward the racial dimension of the Italian American gangster and Bertellini's notion of the "racial "discarding" of the Italian Americans, as his transformation from wise guy to white guy. The Godfather represents a totality, as the divinity of his name indicates, as well as the first stage of the gangster as the signifying trope of post–World War II modernity that is my focus here. For this reason, I am reading the Godfather as a modern trope rather than as a fictional and cinematic character. For the same reason, my reading triangulates among the novel and the first two movies but concentrates especially on *The Godfather Part II*, which, in agreement with Thomas J. Ferraro, I view as a rereading of both the novel and the first cinematic installment.

Part of my argument here is that as a hermeneutic act, *The Godfather Part II* opened up formal and ideological possibilities for the elaboration of the relationship between modernity and whiteness in novelistic forms for Italian American writers. Don DeLillo's *Underworld* and Frank Lentricchia's *The Music of the Inferno*, which I consider two of the chief literary responses to Puzo and Coppola, exploited some of these possibilities in postmodern neorealist fashion. Their novels reinvent the Italian American gangster to decompose the historical unfolding of modernity in America and its ideological corollary, the success story of assimilation. I view *Underworld* and *The Music of the Inferno* as the second and the third stage of the interplay between post–World War II modernity and whiteness respectively. DeLillo's modern epic stages the transformation of the gangster as the inner death of a conflicted, raw, gender-inflected, even messy and yet vital modern experience that New York City's Italian Bronx epitomizes. Lentricchia's first full novel instead unmasks the relationship between Italian Americans, the public sphere, and the American literary canon. In this way, Lentricchia provides a novelistic meditation on the role of the intellectual and the possibilities of a popular humanism.

What unites these works, in addition to the similar biographical trajectory of their Italian American authors, men raised in urban environments in the state of New York at roughly the same time, is their use of historical memory to undermine the mainstream narrative of assimilation. In Michael Corleone's case, memory elicits the process whereby the Godfather reprocesses from the perspective of his father's story the history of his family in the United States, the country for which he put his life on the line in the

Second World War, a war his native country fought also against his father's native country, as one shaped by class division, discrimination, and racial hatred. Seeking to achieve a white world, Michael Corleone finds a disturbing Italian American one. For Nick Shay, the main character of *Underworld*, memory executes the three functions that Robert Orsi in *The Madonna of 115th Street* has found to be operative within the environment of New York City's Italian Harlem, to which the Bronx of *Underworld* can reasonably be compared. Memory locates the displaced individual in a community, binds men and women together in their most intimate relations to their families, and becomes a process of self-discovery that grounds one's historically displaced self, arguably memory's most important function in *Underworld*. Finally, for the Italian Americans of *The Music of the Inferno*, memory offers the possibility of the critical recuperation of their history as a new phase in their life in America.

Although memory performs different functions in these works, its markers are the same two intertwined motifs that the gangster tries to repress but that continue to resurface. The first is a subversive mother figure, which can take the form of either a concrete presence or an artistic construct, even a visual meta-artistic representation. Regardless of form, however, memory triggers the return of the mother-directed popular humanism of the Southern Italian immigrants that distinguishes it from both father-directed Protestantism and mother-directed aristocratic Catholicism, or, which is the same, patriarchy in the Mediterranean fashion. The second is the dark skin of the gangster that reemerges to disrupt his mental universe and alert the viewer and the reader of the Italian Americans' invisible blackness. Naturally, these works share similar formal structures centered on temporality as well as a thematic and conceptual commonality that refashions the question of modernity from the perspective of those who ultimately took the bullets. In the end, for Puzo, Coppola, DeLillo, and Lentricchia, modernity is the gangster.

From this standpoint, the Italian American gangster can be viewed as a development of the gothic tale of terror and the Godfather as the postmodern heir of what Leslie Fiedler named "the Faustian man" who barters his soul with the devil, a man whose heroic ideals are "revealed as equivocal, problematic—redeemed from easy sentimental acceptance and raised to tragic power" (433). Right from the beginning we are presented with a man, Vito Corleone, who voices a sense of discomfort with his own past as an immigrant in America, in direct opposition to his fellow immigrant guest, Amerigo Bonasera. Vito Corleone feels as if he was denied that sense of belonging that America re-

fuses to its future makers as soon as they land on their new soil. Amerigo
Bonasera, the character with whom both the novel and the first film open,
is the Italian immigrant who believes in America. "You found paradise in
America," the Godfather tells him—Don Vito's way to remind himself and
the audience that unlike his guest, he did not. The Godfather did not find
paradise in America. On the contrary, he clashed against a culturally and
socially homogeneous universe as Puzo and Coppola created it. It is a world
epitomized by "the simple, direct, impersonal Anglo-Saxon gun," as the
novel defines the deadly machine, a definition that underscores one of the
subthemes of the narrative, the depiction of modernity as a technology of
racialization (221). This is the world that the Sicilian immigrant from the
"Moorish-looking village" of Corleone is forced to embrace in order to make
sense of it and survive (195). And the way to do it after experiencing the
hardship and discrimination of immigrant life for Vito Corleone is to adopt
and adapt to the structural rationality that to his eyes defines the new world.
This is the process of assimilation that Vito Corleone embraces, the only
paradise available to this Italian immigrant in America. Those who embrace
America wholeheartedly, ideally—for example Amerigo Bonasera, who believed in America and raised his daughter in the American way—end up
paying a dear price for it, one that the Godfather has already paid in his
native Sicily as a child. American boys ruined for life Bonasera's daughter,
the one possession he has. Because those American boys badly disfigured her
face, she is no longer "beautiful," as Bonasera describes her to the Godfather.
What this means is that her marriage opportunities are decreased, which in
turns indicates how Bonasera's patriarchal authority and sense of masculinity have been ruined as well. This is why Bonasera wants revenge. As much
as he has found paradise in America, Bonasera holds to the Old World's
beliefs according to which the father considers a daughter his property and
decides who and when she will marry, a belief that later on in the movie is
on display when Michael asks his future Sicilian father-in-law, Signor Vitelli,
permission to see Apollonia because he wants to marry her.

The difference between Vito Corleone and previous Italian American gangsters is the same difference that distances the Godfather from his fellow immigrants whom Bonasera represents with his broken English. The Godfather
rationalizes everything instrumentally, including, if not especially, death. The
Godfather *is* a technology of instrumental rationalization and organization.
This is the characteristic that he maximizes, the one that according to Gardaphé distinguishes him from previous gangsters. Unlike his prototypical
antecedents before World War II, for example Antonio "Scarface" Camonte,
Don Vito Corleone does not turn into a social psychopath who kills to climb
the ladder of power for the sake of it. He is the exact opposite of a psycho-

path, which of course makes him a social psychopath of a different kind. Vito Corleone calculates everything while rising to power *in order to* maintain control over an increasingly modern world that otherwise he thinks is going to destroy him and his family just like those previously mentioned American boys destroyed the life of Bonasera and his daughter. This rationalizing assimilation is what explains the lack of the classic downfall of the gangster after his rise to power, because such downfall takes a different form. In typical modern fashion, the increasingly modern world that the Godfather does everything to control ends up by increasingly controlling him. His refusal to enter the narcotics business, the forerunner of the global capitalism that his youngest son will be forced to deal with, is the don's attempt to keep total control over the modern world when such a world is actually entering *his* world, to which, eventually, it puts an end. "My father is finished. His way of doing business is finished. Even he knows it," Michael tells his American fiancée Kay Adams when he asks her to marry him after returning to the United States from Sicily, where his first wife has been killed.

Instrumental rationalization is the Godfather's modus operandi, the way he conducts himself and business, which happen to be one and the same thing. Both the novel and the first film are filled with passages and scenes that show this principle of conduct, this second nature that defines Vito Corleone. The best example of this ability of his, however, is when Tom Hagen tells him that Sonny has been assassinated on the causeway. Don Vito's instinctual reaction is to cry, the natural reaction of any father who hears of a son's death, especially when such a tragic event occurs to a Sicilian immigrant man who just lost his first child and heard the terrible news not in public, where a Sicilian man would not express his feelings, but in the private space of his home. Yet he immediately aborts his emotional reaction and tells Hagen to prepare a meeting with Barzini, the head of the rival family, to stop the mafia war that is undermining the stability of the world the don has built away from the outside world of modern America, Bonasera's paradise that to Vito Corleone is starting to look like hell.

Ever since Dante reinvented it, in the Western world hell has been visualized spatially, and Coppola is no exception to the rule. To this end, the framework of the first movie, modeled after the framework of Puzo's best-selling novel that Ferraro has indicated as the duality that defines the meaning of the novel, juxtaposes the inside and the outside.[1] In this strict spatial dichotomy, the inside—and the inside for Italian Americans like the Corleones is home—represents stability, safety, and security. On the contrary, the outside world—and the outside is always and invariably the modern world—represents the opposite: violence and death. In ancient Mediterranean fashion, the don conducts all his business inside his Long Island residence or in the closed space of his office at work, housed in his first American home, his home away from home, New York City's Little Italy. At home his sons, his *consigliere* and the *capofamiglia* Tessio and Clemenza, plan on how to react to the attempted assassination of Don Vito. One might even note how in the Long Island mansion Santino Corleone can confidently betray his wife with his sister's maid of honor Lucy Mancini on the day of his sister's wedding, while outside, at Lucy's apartment in the city, he needs his bodyguards in front of the entrance to the building to protect him.

Any time a Corleone male or even a Corleone associate puts his nose out of his home he encounters death, an attempt on his life, or the announcement of such an attempt. For these men the outside world is a deadly environment that materializes in the symbolically charged form of three pillars of twentieth-century modernity: the automobile, guns, and the newspaper. The don is almost assassinated in the street outside his olive oil business office near an automobile, upon which he falls after being repeatedly shot by Barzini's and Sollozzo's hit men under the eyes of his son Fredo, who fails to shoot back at them with his pistol. The hit is made possible by the betrayal of the don's personal driver, Paulie Gatto, which forced Fredo to go get the don's vehicle and leave him alone in the street, a perfect target for assassination. Later on Gatto too is shot to death in an automobile outside New York City. Santino Corleone, who, unlike Vito, is a father but not a god, is killed on the causeway on his way to the city by Barzini's hit men who fire a storm of bullets in his car with their machine guns. Even the new male addition to the Corleone family, Connie Corleone's husband Carlo Rizzi, ends up strangled in the automobile by Clemenza per Michael's order, in what one can read as a symbolic inversion of subject positions, of murderer and murdered, that reiterates the identification of the automobile as a deadly space. The automobile is a deadly ghost that haunts the Corleones' men even in Sicily, where Michael's first wife, Apollonia, is blown up as she starts the car in the garden of the villa where Michael is hiding, exemplifying the boundless, transnational deadly dimension of modernity. Prior to this deadly sequence, Michael finds out about the rival families' attempt on his father's life when Kay glimpses the news of the hit on the don in the front page of a newspaper as they walk by a newsstand on New York City's Broadway, after the couple has attended a show at Radio City Music Hall. And while the fabricated stories in the newspapers by journalists on the Corleones' payroll serve to expose the police captain's corruption and calm the public anger toward the mobsters, these same stories force Michael to leave his native country and hide in ancestral Sicily.

In the 1974 sequel, this spatial juxtaposition is replaced with the conflicting parallelism of past and present, which, incidentally, explains why in *The*

Godfather Part II the photography is less stunning than in the first movie. Michael's life after the death of his father in the first movie runs parallel to the story of how Vito Corleone ended up in the United States and became the Godfather. Formally speaking, and traditionally form is content, the main difference between the second and the first film and the novel is the shift from space to time. Time replaces space as the conceptual engine that drives the movie. Yet it is not simply chronological, sequential time that we are dealing with, the parts of Puzo's novel that the author and Coppola had omitted from the script of the first picture and recuperated in the sequel. It is time as historical memory that complicates the recuperated rise-and-fall plot of the gangster genre embellished with an exotic Italian American communitarian twist. The story of Vito Corleone is presented as a recollection in parallel conflict with Michael's story, as if Vito Corleone did not belong to his own story, as if he sprang out of Michael's mind, as the ghost of Michael's haunted mind. By the end of the film, even the first few minutes that show the Godfather as a child in Sicily, intentionally set in 1901 as the dawn of a new century and a new modern era, appear to be the chronological preamble necessary to develop Michael's subsequent recollection of his father's up-from-the-ghetto tale.

The switch to memory in the second movie is what turns the Godfather trope into a more cogent critique of modernity. In the first place, it allows Coppola to reinsert in the movie the racialization of the Italian Americans and the power of Italian American motherhood that the first installment, with the partial exception of the last scene, had erased in spite of the numerous markers present in the novel. Again, the Godfather's hometown of Corleone is described in the novel as "a Moorish-looking village," while the don is depicted as "short, dark, slender" (195)—hardly physical features one would associate with Marlon Brando. In this respect, we might also point out Puzo's objection to having Michael order the killing of his brother Fredo, an objection the novelist dropped when he was guaranteed that Fredo would be killed *after* the death of Mama Corleone, the "olive-skinned face" mother of the novel who takes "one of Kay's hands in her two brown ones" (235).

These elements return to undermine Michael Corleone when he is no longer engaging in an intra-ethnic war with rival mafia families. Consequently, Michael is forced to exit the home and the Italian American universe that his father had lived in. It is a move that Michael needs to make in order to execute his business plan and guarantee the expansion and the survival of his business enterprise. The Godfather is now directly engaging in what we never get to see in the first movie, the outside world of business and politics of which organized crime is as an integral part, a totality that Coppola in a 2012 documentary on the legacy of his Italian American saga in American culture has defined as "capitalism in its purest form," of which the God-father character represents its "logic" (*Godfather Legacy*). It is within this framework, that in geo-economic and cultural terms moves among the Mediterranean, the Atlantic world, the West of the United States, and the Caribbean, that Coppola, showing us a magnificent example of the inter-twining of globalization, transnationalism, and transatlantism some forty years before their academic theorizations, develops the character of Michael Corleone also as a way to reinterpret that of his father Vito and shows how the logic of "pure capitalism" needs to repress the ontology and the episte-mology of Italian American motherhood and the invisible blackness of the Italian Americans.

Mediterranean motherhood informs *The Godfather Part II* right from the beginning. Again, the film starts in Sicily in the year 1901. The date is Coppola's way to alert the average moviegoer, who knows the Godfather only as a post–World War II character, about the kind of story that is about to be shown. *The Godfather* was an American story typically structured on the father-son paradigm enriched with an ethnic twist as the basis for one's rise to power, an American version of magic realism, what Michael Denning has called a "ghetto pastoral" (230). The story of *The Godfather Part II*, instead, is a story about modern America. The future Godfather, a nine-year-old dark-haired and dark-skinned child named Vito Andolini, the written note on the screen tells the audience, is "the only male heir to stand with his mother at the funeral" of his father because his older brother Paolo has taken to the nearby mountains to organize the killing of Don Ciccio, the local mafia chief who ordered their father's assassination. The funeral pro-cession is interrupted by the sound of the shotguns that kill Paolo Andolini, upon whose bleeding body his mother kneels in tears under the silent eyes of Vito. It is the first of the two killings that Vito witnesses in a few minutes, as the next scene shows him again standing next to his mother at Don Cic-cio's villa, where she implores the mafia boss to spare Vito's life, a request that Don Ciccio promptly declines because he fears Vito's future vengeance, a prophecy that Vito will fulfill toward the end of the movie. When Don Ciccio denies her request, the dark-skinned woman pulls a knife from un-derneath her black funeral dress, puts it to Don Ciccio's throat, and tells her son to run away. One of the Don's guards disarms her, and a second guard kills her with his shotgun under the eyes of a dumbfounded Vito, who then manages to escape.

Modernity is baptized in the name of the father, the son, and the holy gun. In other words, modernity begins in and with death, the death of this dark-skinned Sicilian woman and her selfless, other-directed motherly love. Whereas the first movie begins with a man's request to another man for a

Move and I'll kill him!

Vito's mother threatens the local mafia boss Don Ciccio in *The Godfather Part II* (directed by Francis Ford Coppola).

self-interested transaction (Bonasera's demand to the Godfather to avenge his abused daughter), the second movie begins with the death of the mother of the future Godfather as she tries to save her son from the man who wants to kill him, the only thing left to her, as she tells Don Ciccio when she is inside the don's residence. We might do well, then, to take Gardaphé's definition of Vito Corleone as "a mother-based gangster, the mother of modern gangsters" literally (*Wiseguys*, 36), from the perspective of motherhood and otherness in its relationship to the development of modernity and whiteness that the movie paints, beginning by noting that in *The Godfather Part II* in prototypical modern fashion Vito Corleone does not act upon his reality. He reacts to it, instrumentally.

The birth of the Godfather is presented as an allegory that clashes with the mainstream narrative of immigration to the United States at the service of the fable of synchronic group assimilation and individual success that political and religious freedom supposedly guarantee. Vito Andolini is forced to leave Sicily because of his mother's failed attempt to win Don Ciccio's favor. Right from the beginning, the movie subverts the typical immigrant narrative, presenting the future Godfather's story as one of a propertyless, undefended fugitive escaping a death sentence. Contrary to the fable of immigration to the United States as a biblical promised land to desire and reach, Vito Andolini does not decide to leave his home. He is forced to leave Sicily. Vito Andolini is an orphan who has witnessed his mother's assassination by the mafia. He has experienced death as the result of the combination of social hierarchy, modern technology, and manhood in the worst way possible for a child, an unmatchable trauma. Because of it, he must leave his home not in search of a better life but to save his life, which is now all he has, his own capital. His forced departure also has a racial underpinning in the hands of an American filmmaker and for an American audience in the immediate aftermath of the civil rights movement, as it is reminiscent of a fugitive man trying to escape a lynching. Don Ciccio's *picciotti* spend the night and the very early morning looking for Vito in a deserted Corleone, again the "Moorish-looking village," warning the population that those who are hiding him will be punished, whereas those who help find him will be rewarded according to a typical logic of exchange value, where the values at stake are the shared love for an innocent child on the one hand and coerced, self-interested preservation on the other. In other words, love and death are commodities to be exchanged.

The point here is not to equate the experience of Italian immigrants and Vito Andolini with that of fugitive slaves. The point is to signal how the dialectics of modernity produces what will become the gangster of all gangsters as a reaction to the forced movement of people across lands and seas. In the first place the Godfather is the object of this uprooting and the modern world he has been thrust into. His whole life is an attempt, a failed one ultimately, to become a subject of modernity, to regain control over his destiny. It is no coincidence that in the first movie Vito tells Michael that he did not want his type of life for his son, that he became a criminal because he did not want to be somebody's else puppet; he did not want to be the by-product of social hierarchy and discrimination, which might as well be the saddest line ever uttered by an ethnic character in the history of American cinema, since this is exactly what Don Vito became, a puppet of the same logic that caused his mother's death, a logic of punishment and reward, of self-interested exchange aimed at keeping the established gendered hierarchy in place and, incidentally, a clue as to why in terms of political economy the mafia and capitalism fit each other to a T.

The don's early life trajectory presents Vito's self-interested, instrumental rationalizing reaction to class division that the ghost of his mother's death signifies. His transformation from proletarian clerk in a grocery store in New York City's Little Italy to a gangster and olive oil businessman, an association that reminds us that the gangster is first and foremost a businessman, and, perhaps, that the inner logic of business is the gangster, takes the form of an inverted reminiscence of his mother's assassination. Vito and his friend Genco Abbandando, a dark-skinned Sicilian with very crispy black hair, attend a play in Little Italy's immigrant theater because Genco is attracted to

Don Fanucci threatens the theater owner's daughter in *The Godfather Part II* (directed by Francis Ford Coppola).

the young actress who performs in it, who also happens to be the daughter of the owner of the theater. In the play, tellingly titled "Senza Mamma"— without mother—a male immigrant from Naples is homesick for his mother. He laments that he has not received any news from her in a long time. When the news arrives, it is in a letter that announces her death, something that we might reasonably suppose must not go unnoticed in Vito's mind, even more so when Genco drags him backstage to meet the actress but where the two witness the Black Hand's boss Fanucci extort the theater's owner by threatening his daughter's life. Fanucci grabs the young woman, holds a knife to her face, and tells her father that he will kill her if he does not pay him the agreed-upon sum. This is nothing short of Vito's past that comes back, as if his past were not past. This time, however, the local mafia boss is the one who holds the knife to the throat of a woman whose father watches, as impotent as Vito was when his mother used the same action to protect him. When later Vito asks Genco why an Italian maltreats and robs other Italians— that is to say, why there is no difference between Sicily and the United States for the immigrants—Genco replies that nobody protects them, which is precisely what propelled the reaction of Vito's mother against Don Ciccio, to protect her child. Again, the score of critics that see the Godfather movies as a glorifier of organized crime should do well to take note of how historically accurate and socially critical of both the mafia and its basic historical causes this fictional tale is. As in Sicily, the failure of the state to protect the poor and the dispossessed is a prime reason for the flourishing of organized crime. It also indicates the consequences of class division and the discrimination against the other, in this case the Italian immigrants who do not deserve the state's presence and protection. It is the same lack of protection that causes Vito to lose his job at the grocery store of his friend's father when Fanucci forces Signor Abbandando to hire his nephew in place of Vito.

Protection, or the lack thereof, at both the individual and collective level becomes the fuel of Vito's life and his rise as a gangster, what Vito Corleone reacts to. And what Vito does in reaction to this lack of protection is never for monetary reasons. It is, however, dictated by calculated, rationalized, gendered self-interest, good old-fashioned rugged individualism clothed in the semblance of ethnic communitarian garments. This mother-based gangster acts as a seeming protector of the poor and the exploited, and especially of women, without demanding an immediate financial return, in order to enhance his own self-interest as a way to have control over his life and the world he inhabits. The Godfather earns friendships and receives respect in exchange for his favors, but "never for profit," as Puzo writes at the beginning of the novel (15). A modern Robin Hood, Vito Corleone, along with his neighbor and future partner in crime and business Clemenza, steals from the rich and never abuses the poor. The killing of Fanucci is presented as a reaction to protect the people of Little Italy like the theater's owner and his daughter. Yet he protects them not in order for them to rise together with him, collectively, but in order for him to rise above them, even symbolically, as he does when he walks on the roofs of their homes, above them, to reach Fanucci at his apartment and kill him while his fellow Italians celebrate Saint Rocco.

The protection that Vito Corleone offers is always instrumental to his own self-interest and the control of the world he inhabits. But his self-interest affirms itself, or at least it is presented as an indirect consequence. It is a rung in the ladder to get to the top. And yet his ascension to godfatherhood happens by negation. The killing of Fanucci is the elimination of a competitor in the marketplace of crime. When Vito tells Clemenza and Tessio that he will take care of Fanucci, he asks that in return they will remember that he did them a favor. Upon his wife's request, Vito takes care of a widow, Signora Colombo, whose Calabrese landlord wants to evict her from her apartment. The iconography of the scene could not be any clearer in this regard. When Don Roberto, the landlord, appears in a state of terror in Vito's office at his now established olive oil business after he finds out who Vito Corleone is, the viewer can observe on the wall behind Vito a painting of the Virgin Mary with baby Jesus. Even the last name of the widow, Colombo, seems to reinforce Vito's reputation as a protector of all the immigrants of Little Italy, if not of the New World, true to the divinity of his name. However, what is left intact, along with Signora Colombo's home rental, the cost of which Don Roberto decreases, is the social hierarchy of Little Italy, which reflects the social hierarchy of America, and the position of the women and mothers of Little Italy, which replicates their position in Italy. At best, they get a painting on the wall that reinforces the symbolism of how motherly and caring their men are. If paradise did not turn into hell yet for Vito Corleone, it is also because the New World looks a lot like the Old.

Vito's trajectory comes full circle when he returns to Sicily. Now an established gangster in the United States, Vito goes back to his hometown with his wife and their children on a trip to expand his olive oil business. The trip also presents itself as the opportunity for Vito to have his vengeance on Don Ciccio, who clearly had been a good prophet of his own future, another identification between business and death that makes the two terms of this equation interchangeable. Before Vito goes to visit Don Ciccio, we see him with his Italian relatives and friends at the table having lunch. Perhaps not coincidentally, he presents some old Sicilian women with a small reproduction of the Statue of Liberty, the "mother of exiles," the symbol of the New World. It is the proper introduction to what comes after, when Don Tommasino, Vito's Sicilian business partner, takes him to Don Ciccio's villa, introduces him to the don as Vito Corleone from New York, and asks for Don Ciccio's blessing for their business, by which he means his partnership to expand the olive oil business between Sicily and the United States. Don Ciccio asks Vito who his father was. Now old and with his hearing faculties partially impaired, he cannot hear the answer and asks Vito to move closer to him and repeat the name. First, Vito repeats his father's name in the ear of the old don; then he drives a knife across Don Ciccio's upper body as he says, "*e chisto è ppe tti*"—and this is for you. Vito kills Don Ciccio with a knife, the same technology that his mother used to threaten the don to protect her son, but he does it, literally, in the name of the father. And by so doing he also secures the expansion of the oil business. In the name of the father, what Ferraro calls "the business of family" is taken care of, concretely and symbolically. Business and family are one and the same thing.

What fueled Vito's rise to power is what returns to destroy Michael, which as long as the Corleones stayed in their ethnic universe did not present itself as a conflicting issue. Rather, it served Vito well in his rise to power. But when Michael discovers his Italian American identity in reaction to his father's recollected story, the memory of it, he also realizes that the logic of capitalism in "its purest form" forces him to repress the invisible blackness and the power of motherhood that is a defining part of his identity. And the more Michael tries to repress them, the more they become disruptive forces in his life. Eventually, they will tear him apart.

The elision of his invisible blackness begins with a well-orchestrated three-part sequence that works as the second beginning of *The Godfather Part II*. The initial moment is the First Communion party for Michael and Kay's son Anthony that showcases the dissolution of the immigrant world of Vito Corleone and begins to show Michael's attempted mimicry of whiteness, an inverted minstrelsy with no dark humor, we might say. Next we hear Nevada senator Pat Geary mispronounce Anthony's second name, Vito, his paternal grandfather's first name, a wonderful example of assimilation as elision that occurs through a process of absorption that is performed linguistically. The third and final moment is the senator's racial slur against Michael.

To begin with, gone is the East Coast where most Italians first settled in the new land, their own American frontier where they built their many Little Italys; gone is the party of Costanza Corleone's wedding (a scene inspired by Luchino Visconti's *The Leopard*) in the first movie; gone is the Italian American music to celebrate the wedding, Mama Corleone singing "Zuma Zuma Baccalà" and Johnny Fontaine doing Sinatra's mythic parody; gone is the don dancing with the bride and his wife; gone are the FBI agents and the photographers outside the Long Island mansion that anger Santino Corleone; and gone are the Italian Americans in attendance, the only kind of people that the Godfather seems to know in the first movie, aside from German Irish Tom Hagen, the exception that dutifully confirms the rule. In their place are a now painstakingly boring and plastic party where the music is provided by an orchestra that manages to turn Frankie Pentangeli's attempt to have them play a tarantella into "Pop Goes the Weasel!"; a youth choir that one can take as white America's paranoid emulation of bourgeois European culture; the police outside the mansion providing security to the party; and last but not least, Nevada senator Pat Geary and his wife in attendance to celebrate Michael's financial donation to the University of Las Vegas. Instead of the family picture of the first movie, the photo taken here is that of the senator and his wife with Michael and Kay.

When the senator announces Michael's generous donation to the university, he anglicizes the pronunciation of the name Vito. In other words, he whitens it. This phonetic distortion acquires even greater meaning because prior to this moment we witnessed the immigration officer at Ellis Island changing young Vito's last name. Just as the new modern world absorbs difference by erasing the cipher of one's main form of identification, his name, so does the senator. One is tempted to emend Marx's famous observation in

The Eighteenth Brumaire of Louis Bonaparte. When history repeats itself, the second time is a tragic farce. As if the senator's phonetic elision of the don's first name were not enough, when the senator and Michael meet in the latter's office inside the house to discuss a deal for a state gambling license for a new casino that Michael needs for his expansion plans, the senator unchains all his racism against Michael. After pronouncing the last name "Corleone" with a derogatory tone, prolonging the final "e" pronounced in correct Italian, what we might define as linguistic racism, he tells him, "I don't like your kind of people. I don't like to see you come out to this clean country in your oily hair—dressed up in those silk suits—and try to pass yourselves off as decent Americans. I'll do business with you, but the fact is, I despise your masquerade—the dishonest way you pose yourself. Yourself, and your whole fucking family," to which an unperturbed Michael replies, "Senator—we're both part of the same hypocrisy. But never think it applies to my family."

The senator's words are a stunningly racist attack, one that strangely but perhaps tellingly has gone virtually unnoticed by the critical industry that the novel and the movies generated. Yet in the end what is most relevant about this exchange is not the senator's racism per se, as despicable as it might be—and it is immensely despicable. Nor is it the self-reassuring, historically fictional racial purity that the senator claims for America—America's whiteness as the true identity of the country. The point here is that the senator turns an Italian American gangster into a racial synecdoche, "your kind of people." In his eyes Michael wears a mask to pass as a "decent American," an identity that the senator reserves for white people, as if Michael were not white, which to this white man who officially represents Michael's native country clearly he is not. Equally poignant is the racial corollary of this exchange. However reluctantly, the white man can make a business deal with an Italian American man without having to sully his own supposed racial purity and without contaminating America. Money keeps America white. Money can absorb racial difference and keep America's identity racially homogeneous in the white man's fantasy. But no less important is Michael's acknowledgment that to play the game of capitalism he has to give up the invisible blackness that he recognizes as his and his family's identity, who they really are, their present as well as their past, as the temporal adverb in his answer indicates: "Never think it applies to my family," and for once the word "family" means just that.

For the rest of the movie, the family becomes a constant reminder of Michael's attempt to pass, a symptom of Americanization as a process of assimilation that dissolves one's past. Paradoxically—and paradoxes take us to the core of an issue—the fundamental and in the end only difference between Michael and his father, what marks the development of the Godfather trope, is a shift in the development of modernity. Vito Corleone could use his ethnicity to build his empire because he knew who he was. The first thing that he rationalized was that he knew where he came from, whereas Michael not only has to break up the family to expand his business, but such a breakup forces him to confront himself in relation to what his family's history means—something that, as the movie proceeds, the Corleone women, who happen now to be and act as mothers, increasingly identify. And there is nothing that the Godfather hates more than confronting an Italian American mother, because that would mean confronting his own self and history.

At dinner on the evening of Anthony's Communion, amid the family, along with Frankie Pentangeli and the ever-present Catholic priest (the sign that the Corleones have really made it), Connie explains to Fredo's utterly blond white wife that the Italian saying "*cent'anni*" is a way to invoke good health and happiness; but she adds, "It'd be true if my father were alive," a comment that ticks off Michael. The old Italian saying is actually how Connie, Fredo, Mike, Frankie Pentangeli, Tom Hagen, and Father Carmelo respond to Mama Corleone's toast "*Famiglia*." Also in Italian, Mama Corleone whispers to Tom Hagen her comment about Fredo's wife and Connie's new boyfriend, who also happens to be as white as one can be, "Ma chisti due so proprio uguali" (Why, these two are just the same), a statement that reveals the original racial distance between Italian Americans and white Americans, as well as language as a component of racial difference, something that becomes more tangible as the movie goes on. At the same time, this exchange points out how Kay Adams and Tom Hagen are not considered white in the Corleone circle. Dark-skinned Mama Corleone exposes ethnicity as neither a matter of biology nor of family, let alone one's inherited identity. It is one's choice historically determined, or, to use the vocabulary of Werner Sollors's *Beyond Ethnicity*, it is a matter of consent. Deanna is Fredo's wife after all, whereas Tom Hagen has neither biological nor ethnic connection to the Corleones. He is German Irish, probably the only such ethnic character in the history of American cinema to speak Sicilian and know the Mediterranean sociocultural codes, and as such a spectacular example of reversed assimilation as well. Perhaps Michael's reply to the senator was true. Perhaps Michael was right. Whiteness does not apply to his family, especially if by his family we intend the women of his family, the people who guarantee the family's reproduction and the preservation of the past, and who also happen to be the only Corleones except the Godfather who either die a natural death or, to say it through William Faulkner, who endure.

By the same token, the senator was right too. Michael tries to pass as somebody who he is not. At the mythic level, in the sense of the mythic power of the imagination—that is, how in terms of narrative Coppola works out the representation of each character in the movie—Michael Corleone may as well be the only Italian American who does absolutely nothing resembling the myth of an Italian American man of the 1950s, especially one who grew up in New York City's Little Italy. His clothes, contrary to Senator Geary's anti–Italian American racist statement, exude white, bourgeois respectability. They are impeccable suits that would make Michael indistinguishable from any Wall Street broker, company chief executive, or, for that matter, a United States senator. The immigrant clothes that his father wore in the first movie are not even an option in Michael's wardrobe. His body language is equally signifying of the mask he wears. When he returns from his business trip to Cuba, he asks his bodyguard Al Neri (who interestingly has the same first name as Capone and whose last name's literal translation is "blacks") for a wet towel to freshen himself with, which he does in the most meticulous way to preserve his impeccable composure. Michael, who learned from Clemenza how to make sauce, never eats any Italian food. Actually, Michael Corleone may as well be the only Italian American who never eats, except for biting an orange because of stress when he plots Hyman Roth's assassination. He even refuses food when Roth's wife offers him a sandwich, when he conducts business. Michael does drink, and quite often, in this aspect true heir to 1930s gangsters, but less compulsively in his gestures than those gangsters and always extremely careful not to spill a drop. Moreover, all he drinks is either whiskey or club soda—American drinks, or white drinks, we might say. Wine, or the Sicilian anisette that his father loved more and more as he grew older and that Frankie Pentangeli requests when he meets Michael at Anthony's Communion party, do not interest him. Pentangeli even refers to Michael drinking the occasional champagne cocktail during his son's Communion party as one of the signs that he has forgotten where he comes from. Michael's lack of interest in food is matched only by his lack of interest in sex, not exactly a typical feature of the myth of the Italian American man. Michael Corleone is a man who wants to be on top of everything and everybody, except women. The only time we see him on top of a woman is when he drags his wife not to bed but out of their bed and onto the floor to avoid a different kind of penetration, the bullets of the machine guns of Roth's hit men.

The one thing that Michael does is take antidepressants, as we see him doing when he rides the train to Florida on his way to Cuba with his bodyguard. Several decades before Harold Ramis and David Chase put an Italian American gangster on the chair of a shrink and had him take antidepressants, Michael Corleone takes antidepressant pills to keep on his mask. This is the price he pays to pass as a decent American and to be able to sit together

with his enemy Hyman Roth next to the CEOs of major American corporations in a meeting with Cuba's corrupted military dictator to get a lucrative
deal. The Anglo last names of these CEOs speak volumes about the intertwining of modernity and whiteness and Michael's attempt to pass: Shaw,
Corngold, Dant, Petty, and Allen. Equally telling are the two ways in which
the Cuban people are represented in the film. One is a revolutionary rebel
who sacrifices his life for the cause he believes will liberate his country from
a dictator; the other is a dark-skinned child in Havana who stares at Michael in a cab, just as a dark-skinned Vito Corleone of roughly the same age
stared at his mother being killed by Don Ciccio. Drugs and paranoia: this is
how Michael Corleone assimilates and Coppola's way to tell us that modernity is the gangster. Toward the end of the movie Tom Hagen asks Michael
why he feels the need to wipe everybody out now that he has won his war.
Michael gives Tom the most paranoid and yet the most logical and coherent
of the answers, because paranoia is the end product of the complete unfolding of capitalist competition, its essence. "I don't feel I have to wipe everybody out, Tom. Just my enemies." And in his mind everybody is his enemy,
or, the same, his competitor.

A ghost is haunting Michael Corleone: Michael Corleone himself, the
only enemy he has, which his use of the Italian language reveals. In this regard it is especially profitable to recall how in the novel Vito, because of his
native language, suffered racial discrimination by American and Irish men
when he worked on the railway. Equally profitable is to point out how technically English, not Italian, is Michael's native language. Whereas Sicilian
and Italian do not identify him as an Italian, English does identify Michael
as an American, which nothing else does, not even the Navy Cross he has
earned in World War II, as the members of a Senate committee make abundantly clear during his hearings. In *The Godfather*, before killing Sollozzo
and Captain McCluskey, Michael switches from his broken Italian to English to tell Sollozzo that he needs to know that there will not be any more
attempts to assassinate his father. In Sicily Michael commands one of his
two bodyguards to translate from English into Italian to make sure that
Apollonia's father understands who Michael really is and what is he doing
by revealing his identity when he asks his future father-in-law permission to
marry his daughter.

In *The Godfather Part II*, instead, the Italian language works for Michael
as a safety valve. It reassures him, however temporarily. Just as the gun is
an Anglo-Saxon technology of killing, in strict theoretical terms English is
the language of crime and money. Clemenza inquires if Vito speaks Italian
(which to Clemenza is a form of Sicilian) before asking him to hide his pis-
tols. Later on, he asks Vito if he is interested in some business, the first hint

that business equals crime. Vito, who lives in Little Italy and goes back home with *Il Progresso Italo-Americano* in the pocket of his jacket, replies, "Yeah, sure," before switching back to Sicilian, two of the thirty-one English words he speaks in 46.09 minutes while he is on the screen as an adult. At the beginning of the second movie, when Connie goes to see Michael with her new, WASP fiancé, whom Michael ignores and despises immediately, Michael turns to Italian to extract from his younger sister the truth he already knows, that Connie needs money. First, he goes around in circles in English. Suddenly, he turns to his sister and asks her, "Che vuoi!?" (What do you want?), to which Connie replies, aptly in English, "I need money!" Likewise, in Frankie Pentangeli's home in New York City, the home that used to belong to Vito Corleone, where Michael was raised, and where Pentangeli and his wife speak Italian, Michael instructs Pentangeli, in English, on how he intends to deal with Hyman Roth and the Rosato brothers, but his last words to Pentangeli are in Italian, and they are uttered with a Sicilian inflection: "Hai capito?" (Did you get it?). Finally, during the meeting to plan Roth's assassination, after Tom Hagen reassures Michael that he is not leaving him, that he turned down the job offer he has received, about which Michael has just inquired maliciously, Michael asks, "Allora tu stai?" (So you are staying?), to which Tom, in what might be, in a strictly ethnic sense, a revealing Freudian slip, responds also using the second person of the verb instead of the first, "Si, io stai" (Yes, I am staying).

The mother tongue is what brings back into the picture the mother figure literally, which sets in motion the conceptual demolition of the Godfather rather than his actual fall. Toward the end of the movie a completely displaced Michael goes to visit his mother in the penthouse where she now lives. He speaks to her in her native tongue, in Sicilian. He asks her about his father's inner feelings and thoughts. He asks her if one can ever lose his family, in a desperate, futile attempt to avoid the final confrontation with himself. When his mother tries to reassure him that a man can never lose his family, Michael switches back to Italian and says, "I tempi cambiano" (times are changing), the hippie filmmaker's reference to Bob Dylan as a way to let the 1974 audience know that the story of the Corleones is the story of America in the twentieth century.

And times do change for Don Corleone after the Senate hearings when another mother comes back in the picture, when the mother of his children tells him that she aborted the child that she was expecting. Until this moment Kay has been literally trapped in the physical site where historically Italian American women ruled, the home, which is instead the don's territory. At the beginning of the movie, the blond Anglo-Saxon upper-middle-class woman from New Hampshire continues to pretend to believe Michael's

promise to change. She is even pictured in her bedroom at the sewing machine as Michael returns from his trip to New York City, a modern-day
American Penelope, although, aptly for the wife of an Italian American
gangster, with no suitors in her home. Later in the movie she tries to leave
the estate with the kids to drive to Reno, but the guards refuse to open the
gate. Tom explains to her that it is Michael's order to protect her and the
kids. Obediently, she returns inside the house. After the Senate hearings,
however, Kay confronts her husband in the hotel room where they stay in
Washington. There, outside the home, in neutral territory, she confronts him
at face value, as it were. She tells Michael that she is leaving him and intends
to take the children with her. Initially, Michael tries to maintain the status
quo. He knows that a confrontation with Kay is precisely what he has been
avoiding since the end of the first movie. He tells her that he knows she is
upset because of the miscarriage and his failure to make the Corleone business a legitimate enterprise, but that he will change and they will have another child and move on. A hopeless and exhausted Kay replies that he has
"become blind," that she did not have a miscarriage. She had an abortion,
"just like our marriage is an abortion, something that's unholy and evil,"
Kay tells him, using a religious vocabulary that shows how she has mastered
the rhetoric of the cultural codes that supposedly Italian American women
of the 1950s lived by. She continues and tells him that the child was what
Michael wanted, a boy, completing the switch of her subject position and
forcing Michael to confront her, in what is a tribute less to the feminism of
the '60s and '70s than to the rebellious tradition of Italian American women
here represented by Vito's mother at the beginning of the movie, to whom
symbolically Kay is now connected. "I didn't want your son, Michael! I
wouldn't bring another one of your sons into this world. It was a son, a son
Michael, and I've had it killed because this must all end!" Kay goes on under
Michael's petrified eyes.

If there is an Italian American character at the end of the movie, it is this
WASP lady from New Hampshire. We can go even further and argue that if
there is a gangster left at the end this exchange, it is Kay Corleone. By "killing" what she calls Michael's son she unchains herself from the Godfather
and acquires her agency as a woman and a mother who is no longer willing
to be complicit in a world of death and betrayal, beginning with Michael's
betrayal of himself. Unlike what most critics assume, what provokes Michael
to the point that he hits his wife, something no godfather would even dream
of doing, is not the abortion that supposedly put at risk the future survival
of the business of the family. It is the fact that in the end Kay's decision is
an act of shared and disinterested love that unmasks the Godfather, the only
enemy that Michael is unable to kill. When Kay tells Michael that she had

an abortion, she is in tears and tells him that she knows he would never forgive her. More important, she thinks of the abortion as "killing," an idea that no American feminist, certainly not in the year after the Supreme Court made abortion legal, would associate with this medical procedure. Kay tells Michael that *she* would not bring another of *his* sons into *this* world, the modern world that Michael thinks he can control but that actually controls him—"capitalism in its purest form," with its patriarchal corollary. This is what "must end," in Kay's words. No wonder, then, that when she demolishes the man who tries to pass for what he is not, the super-blond WASP lady from New England has dark hair and carries a cross around her neck along with another necklace.

In one of the last scenes of the movie, Michael enters the kitchen of his home where the children and Connie have just said goodbye to Kay, who has visited with them. Standing just outside the kitchen door, she asks Anthony to kiss her. For the first time in, by then, almost three hours of the film, Michael looks the exact opposite of Senator Geary's racist description. No oily hair, no silky suits, and no masquerade. He is casually dressed, with no styling product on his dark hair. However, the skin on his face is improbably dark. He has a very notably tanned face. As he walks toward the door of the kitchen, the camera switches between Kay's and Michael's faces, highlighting the latter's dark skin that has no factual logic whatsoever in the narrative of the film. Where did the man who spends most of his life inside closed spaces get his tan? Certainly not in snowy Nevada; certainly not in the few minutes he spent on the balcony of Hyman Roth's hotel room in Havana; and certainly not on vacation, since Michael Corleone does not vacation. As dark-skinned Michael closes the door of the kitchen, the room that identifies an Italian American home, right in the face of the mother of his children, one wonders what America lost when the Godfather became the indecent American that he never wanted to be.

II

Like *The Godfather Part II*, Don DeLillo's *Underworld* tells an up-from-the-ghetto story about the interplay between modernity and whiteness, albeit one focused solely on the second half of the past century. The story spans the time from the date of the book's publication in the second half of the 1990s to the beginning of the 1950s. Nick Shay, the main character and occasional narrator of the book, is an Italian American with a managerial position in the waste industry who grew up as working-class youth in New York City's Italian Bronx, where his mother still lives. The mingling of an inverted chronology and Nick's reconstructed past is the novelist's way to narrate half a century of social, cultural, and psychic history working through the interstices of the ethnic microcosm of the Italian Bronx and the political economy of global capitalism that the waste industry represents. "The way the Indians venerate this terrain now, we'll come to see it as sacred in the next century. Plutonium National Park. The last haunt of the white gods," Nick tells his African American colleague Simeon Biggs, nicknamed Big Sims (289). Nick pretends to believe that the mafia kidnapped and killed his father in his Bronx neighborhood. The truth is that Jimmy Costanza, a "bookmaker famous for his memory" (103), walked away from home when Nick was eleven year old because "he did not want to be a father. . . . He did the unthinkable Italian crime. He walked out of his family. They don't even have a name for this," says Nick's younger brother Matt (203–4). This is the same man who left his wife for a while when she was pregnant with their first child, an action that prompted his wife to change Nick's last name legally from Costanza to Shay.

The change of last name is a strategy that DeLillo uses to divert attention from the critical banalities habitually linked to an Italian last name, especially in a book about Italian Americans with a title that in the American psyche inevitably evokes crime and gangsters, especially if authored by a novelist from New York City whose last name ends with a vowel. In this way DeLillo preserves the historical identity of the book as he repositions Italian American urban life and the meshing of crime, class, and ethnicity within the context of the development of post–World War II capitalism, which the Bronx native envisions as the gangster of his lifetime: "The word plutonium comes from Pluto, god of the dead and ruler of the underworld," the narrator comments at one point (106). Thematically speaking, then, the inner death of modernity as a vital human experience is the signifier of *Underworld*, whether such experience concerns the old-fashion communal social desire of the Italian Americans of the Bronx, aesthetic ideals associated with important female characters, or the Western sublime visualized in André Kertész's photograph of 1972 New York City on the cover of the book, where the then-standing Twin Towers loom over an old church with its cross on top of it, as if they threatened to replace it after the end of the Cold War. In the post–Cold War era, the atomic device the Soviet Union detonated the same day of Bobby Thomson's homer at the beginning of the book has become a commodity to be sold and bought by Russian men who look "half gangsterish," symptoms of "wild privatized times" (802).

The transformation of nuclear devices into commodities is an ontological shift that is paralleled by another kind of transformation, that of Nick Shay's gradual disappearance into DeLillo's version of a postmodern whiteness represented by the "quiet life" that Nick lives in an "unassuming house in a suburb of Phoenix," out west, on the frontier, like "someone in the Witness Protection Program," longing for "the days of disorder," when he was "alive on the earth," walked "real streets," and "felt angry and ready all the time, a danger to others and a distant mystery to myself" (810), a literary version of *Goodfellas*' Henry Hill,[2] an empty subject who is existing but no longer living. In the era of transnational finance and the atomization of historical time, Nick Shay's Italian American identity becomes a form of working-class memory of post–World War II urban America, one achieved through language and voices, DeLillo's realist literary tools. Even the intertwining of class, race, and gender, as well as of Catholicism in its intellectual Jesuit version, serves to build Nick's Italian American self as a form of historical memory. This memory is corporeal in the Mediterranean fashion, a repository of the popular humanism of the immigrants and their communitarian ways of being, a collective subject that defies assimilation in the heart of modernity, the city of New York. "The Italians. They sat on top of the stoop with paper fans and orangeades. They made their world. They said, Who's better than me? She could never say that. They knew how to sit there and say that and be happy" (207). These are the people to whom family "was an art . . . and the dinner table was the place it found expression" (698).

Nick's father's presence in his life asserts itself as an absence that forces Nick to dig into his memory of the Bronx, the Italians who sit out in the street and *make* their world as the street becomes the extension of their home, making the two a single unit, a whole with no physical boundaries in a world otherwise fractured in every possible way and for that very reason pulsing like the crowd at the Giants' game where Thomson hit the shot heard around the world. These people acquire their identity by making this world, by being subjects of it. On the surface, it is essentially a man's world. Old men smoke De Nobili cigars, "the perennial guinea stinker," and still speak their language of origins (759); the ever-present Frank Sinatra shows up at the historical baseball game of the opening section without "his dago service with him" (24); the Italian radio plays for the whole neighborhood, which is not a way to re-create a mythic Old World, where the radio was not available to begin with. Rather, it is the use of a technology of communication and entertainment put at the service of their capacity to think of themselves as a collective subject and take possession of their new world, be subject of it, be modern. Of these neighbors, schoolteacher Albert Bronzini, who is also Matt Shay's chess mentor, is the consciousness, "an old Roman stoic . . . too rooted" to leave the neighborhood (214). His mind is "open to absolutely anything," but his "life is not," which caused the end of his marriage to Klara Sax, a Jewish woman with whom Nick slept when he was seventeen, their "shared memory," as Nick words it (81). This same neighborhood is also home to mafia boss Mario Badalato, an acquaintance of Nick's father to whom Nick talked occasionally and whom he runs into later on in the novel, and whose voice Nick imitates in his office when he becomes a manager in the waste industry. In this neighborhood Nick accidentally killed George Manza at age seventeen.

A second marker of Nick's Italian American self, one also connected to Nick's father and that none of the numerous commentators of this most eminent Italian American literary masterpiece has pointed out is Nick's skin color, which both Nick and his non–Italian American wife do point out to the reader early in the novel. In his rental car on the way to see Klara in the Arizona desert, Nick reaches for the sunscreen that he always carries along, even though, as he explains, "I am olive-skinned, dark as my father was" (13), an observation that he repeats when he comments on the suntan lotion's sixty protection factor. "I wonder about this even though I'm olive-skinned, dark as my old man" (120), which is to say, dark as the Italian American self that his body contains, literally. Just as Nick sees his skin color as the marker of his Italian American self, so does his wife, Marian, who tells Nick's colleague Brian Glassic, with whom she has an affair, that Nick is half Italian. "You don't see it in his face?" (165). And so does DeLillo when at the end of a dialogue between Klara and her friend Acey, a black woman and fellow artist who in her paintings represents black men in the city of Chicago, concludes, "The gang members belong to their terrain, to the pale brick and iced-over windows, and in this sense they could be brothers to the olive-skinned men in the frescoed gloom of some Umbrian church"—that is to say, central Italy (394).

The racialization of Italian American identity is not limited to Nick. It also extends to his brother Matt, albeit in different fashion, one that seems to enlarge its range. Matt is described by the narrator, likely DeLillo himself here, as the perfect example of American hybridity. "Matt looked slightly Jewish, a little Hispanic maybe. . . . Back in the Bronx, people said he looked a little everything. Mexican, Italian, Japanese even" (409). There's no direct mention of blackness in this bodily depiction, but Matt attended City College, New York City's preeminent institution of higher education for black Americans and the poor.

Nick's racialization has literary connections, too. One such connection is to Motley's *Knock on Any Door*, a source for DeLillo in more than one way. In addition to carrying the first name of Nick Romano, Nick Shay too ends up in a juvenile correction center at a very young age. And like his Chicagoan predecessor, in his Bronx days Nick Shay has a friend named Vito with whom he steals a car in their neighborhood. We could even think of Nick Shay as a late twentieth-century version of Nick Romano who embraced

whiteness instead of rebelling against it, the prototypical wiseguy who becomes the prototypical white guy in prototypical American fashion. Unlike
Nick Romano, Nick Shay did not get the electric chair because he did not
kill an Irish cop. He killed a fellow Italian American. Moreover, the reformatory's experience fueled Nick Romano's rebellion. On the contrary, albeit
by way of coercion, Nick Shay surrendered to "the stern logic of correction"
that he associates with the vacuity of modern times epitomized by a minia-
ture golf concession put in in front of the upstate New York correctional
facility before the winter, hardly the time for golf, one would assume (502).
To Nick's dismay, "They unloaded the equipment in a field near the mess
hall on a sweet and clear November day. . . . I watched it all take shape with
an odd kind of disbelief. I felt tricked and betrayed. I was here on a serious
charge, a homicide by whatever name, destruction of life under whatever
bureaucratic label, and this was where I belonged, confined upstate, but the
people who put me here were trifling with my mind" (503). Those who do
not trifle with the mind of this "dark-skinned" Italian American who declares he "suffer[s] from a rare condition that afflicts Mediterranean men . . .
called self-respect," that is to say, a man who is reflecting on his identity, are
the African American inmates with whom Nick plays basketball. He is the
only non–African American in the prison to play ball with them (116). They
are members of a gang named after a Harlem movie theater who "were
doing nigger time, they said," after doing time in "a number of reformato-
ries," just like Nick Romano, one is tempted to add (502).

Nick's physical proximity to African Americans in jail is a racial taxonomy replicated when he joins the managerial world in the nuclear waste
industry, a taxonomy that unveils Nick's aesthetic sense. In part 1 of the
book we find Nick at a ball game in Los Angeles with his now fifty-five-year-
old colleague Big Sims, who operates the Los Angeles campus of the company. Originally from New York City as well, Big Sims recalls running in the
street the day Thomson hit the homer in 1951, "a black kid who didn't even
root for the Giants" (94). This scene occurs in 1992. In part 3 instead, which
takes place in spring 1978, Nick and Sims are in a Los Angeles club listening
to a blues band. They distinguish the "African blackness" of the trumpeter
and have a discussion about the number of African Americans who live in
the country (337). As they exit the club, they get into an argument and butt
each other on the forehead while waiting for their car. Shortly after, however,
Nick is at Sims's house, looking at Sims's beautiful five-year-old son Loyal
Branson Biggs, "a boy so softly handsome, so offhandedly blessed with expressive beauty that I could not stop looking at him," a way to remind his
black parents, who are experiencing a marital crisis, "to renew their sense of
amazement in the child" (339).

Beauty is black and innocent, and in the eyes of dark-skinned Italian American Nick Costanza passing as Nick Shay entails the possibilities of life and shared love. Anxiety, instead, is white, adult, male, managerial, and it seems to haunt the family life that supposedly white-collar America cherishes. The music in Nick's colleague Brian Glassic's car carries "this Ohio boy through his white anxiety and across the Jersey side" in search of the ball of Thomson's home run (168). Brian is "wary of his family" and complains of his kids who are "careless with money" (111). He perceives his children and a stepdaughter as his enemies, threatening his self-worth. To reassert his fatherhood and his masculinity Brian even buys condoms for his son David. According to Nick's wife, Brian recommends movies where "everybody ends up in a storm sewer shooting each other," which Nick interprets as Brian's way to relieve "the pressure of being Brian" (115). However, it would be an error to read this juxtaposition in the description of Brian's troubled self as the simple equation of anxiety with whiteness. Likewise, it would be mistaken to read this same juxtaposition as the fusion of male anxiety and the false appearances of family life and white-collar work toward the end of the twentieth century in America. Certainly these issues are part of the equation. But one reason to avoid focusing solely on such binarism is that initially Brian's whiteness serves to underscore Nick's otherness and the class difference that exists between Brian's and Nick's past and the worlds they inhabited as kids. When the two talk about their adolescence at the beginning of the book, Brian tells Nick that he was "scrawny and mute, barely human. You were a strapping kid who beat the crap out of kids like me." "We didn't have any kids like you," Nick replies, where Nick's use of the plural personal pronoun in response to Brian's singular "you" refers to Italian Americans in the Bronx whom the dark-skinned son of Jimmy Costanza represents (110). The absence of kids like Brian, the "Ohio boy with his white anxiety" (168) and "barely human" (110), however, bears the question not of race and class as autonomous spheres, but as parts of the larger one at the heart of *Underworld* with regard to the Italian American history that DeLillo recaptures as a sort of Dantesque *contrapasso* to Nick's present-day waste land: What did they, the Italian Americans, have in the Bronx?

One answer is the availability of an emotionally intense and pulsating way of living, a way of being modern, of experiencing modernity entangled in an equally intense inner sense of a people who belonged to a place and to each other. Life experienced and felt, including the energy of the destructive forces that produced the local mafia boss Mario Badalato and the troubled lives of individuals like Nick's father. This is the community that the displaced Italian immigrants settled in and built. The community and the actual work needed to build it provided them with a sense of place and belonging and protected them from the disorder around them, the modern life where politics is the real mafia, as DeLillo has the comedian Lenny Bruce say in the book, a way for DeLillo the Italian American author writing after *The Godfather* to interpose a non-Italian character between difficult issues such as organized crime, the failure of America to integrate immigrants, and the hegemony of whiteness in American life. "Because this is our family thing. That's it, you see. *La cosa nostra*. Only they don't have to do it with extortion and murder. They do it with names that no one else could ever think up," says Bruce in a monologue deriding Adlai Stevenson's first name (591). Once again, whiteness and names intersect. Whereas Nick's last name hides his Italian American identity, the names in the monologue expose a critique of whiteness. Like the WASP names in DeLillo's first novel, *Americana*, these too are Anglo names. They are the Anglo names of Stevenson's cabinet members, one of the many underworlds of the book. "Alexis Johnson. *Alexis*. Bromley Smith. *Bromley*. Llewellyn Thompson. *Llewellyn*," which the comedian sets in contrast to his own Jewish name, "My name is Leonard Alfred Schneider. What was I thinking when I took the name Lenny Bruce? I was moving toward the invisible middle. I'm just like you, mister. Don't bug me, man, or insult my ancestor. I'm just another Lenny" (592). The names that reflect the political power of America's whiteness make ethnicity invisible, "just another Lenny."

The critique of whiteness manifests itself in the form of the disappearance of the historical experience that ethnic names carry within themselves and evolves into a critique of the society of waste, a transfer that reveals the interplay and reciprocal identification of whiteness and the society of waste. *Underworld* is no lament for identity politics. It is a writer's subtle and yet angry refusal to surrender to the disappearance of working people's struggles in the great empty white middle, the washout of a people's historical memory, beginning with its contradictions. It is also a writer's reaffirmation of his belief in the art of writing, which he reckons even more necessary in the age of waste. This belief explains what we might call the expansive language of the novel, its stunning amount of different words as a way to open up a novel that narrates an increasingly flattening world, a shrinking modernity, as well as DeLillo's immense effort to recapture in the language of the novel the voices of the past that he lived, the immigrant past, the Italian Americans of the 1950s.

DeLillo's Bronx, in fact, is no sentimental walk down memory line. On the contrary, it is conceived primarily as a homage to his immigrant parents to whom the book is justly dedicated. *Underworld* is the magnum opus of the writer that becomes "an American—the writer equivalent of his immigrant parents and grandparents" (G. Howard, 126). *Underworld* criticizes

whiteness historically, the only true homage available to the children of immigrants in America, a narrative that "transcends the limitations of his [the
writer's] background" and embraces all of America (126). As such, it unfolds as a spectacular narrative of inversion, the object that repositions itself
as a subject by recuperating in a place and in its voices its own story as a
form of secular redemption, the past as a monument to the future in a country that historically is in "a hurry to make the future" (89).

The careful reader can hear the voiced world of the immigrants and their
children, the Bronx where Nick (and DeLillo) grew up, which is disappearing, as it should in such a scheme. "We Italians," says Bronzini (673), but to
him "English was the sound of the present and Italian took him backwards,
the merest intonation, a language marked inexhaustibly by the past" (768).
This loss is precisely the point: when the language is gone, the memory is
what remains available through a process of reconstruction that acquires
meaning once it is inserted in its larger context, which is to say, once the
story is situated in a place whose life and images the voices recall and preserve on the written page to be read aloud, as the memorable first line of the
novel invites the reader to do: "He speaks in your voice, American" (3). To
Nick, the Bronx recalled from the vantage point of the cultural history that
waste represents and the political background of the Cold War becomes the
collective social memory, the memory of a community and, as result, memory
as a community, what otherwise might end up being repressed, the "under"
of the book's title.

Of that place and that story, Nick's mother is the center. And it is all the
more noteworthy that Rosemary Shay is not Italian. Like Kay Corleone, she
has become Italian by living with the Italians for forty years, although, unlike Kay, not in economic privilege, but in an immigrant tenement, a sort of
reversed assimilation that defies the myth of one's self-advancement, and the
one is traditionally a male one. "Regards to your mother, okay?" the neighborhood butcher admonishes Nick (681). Rosemary is the center of a completely decentered narrative in which many of its micro-stories disappear
instead of end. "This woman is not afraid," Matt tells his brother who went
back to the Bronx to move her out of the neighborhood and bring her with
him and his wife to Phoenix. "She lives a free life. People know her. They
respect her. The neighborhood's still a living thing," he continues (202). In
this neighborhood mothers are generators of interpersonal relationships
fostered by their sense of the value of disinterested mutuality. They are the
connecting tissue of an enclave, as the butcher's words to Nick signify. Their
power transcends even physical disability. Bronzini's wife, Klara, attends to
Albert's mother, who suffers from a neuromuscular condition and lives with
them. Bronzini himself sits with her for hours, watching her, soaking up "her

diarrhea with bunched Kleenex, talk[ing] to her in his boyhood Italian, and he felt that the house, the flat, was suffused with a reverence, old, sad, heavy and impressive—an otherworldliness, now that she was here" (683). One Mrs. Ketchel "sat with Albert's mother that afternoon" and left her child with a girl who lives in her building "who was capable and trustworthy" (688). Respect, trust, even rigor, whenever it is necessary, emanate from these women's life. This neighborhood could be that of Jerre Mangione in *Mount Allegro* thirty years later. The motherly rigor of the Bronx is the toughness of Fortunata Mancuso when she confronts the immigration officer in *Nuovomondo*. When Rochelle, a friend of Klara, inquires if the woman in their house is Albert's mother, Klara replies, "A forceful woman actually, even in this condition. I admire her in a number of ways. Takes no crap from anybody" (689).

As the Bronx is no place for memory lane, neither is motherhood a sanctified fable to neutralize the dialectics of life, the glorification of the old days for the sake of being gone. The generational gap between characters is a question of historical memory too. Before Rochelle leaves she tells Klara, "So she takes no crap, Albert's mother. Take me to her deathbed before it's too late. Maybe she can tell me something I should know" (690). Albert's mother is a repository of a life experience that is no longer available to younger women. She contains a memory that commands respect. After Rochelle leaves, Klara goes to the kitchen. First, however, she turns the lamp near the bed "so Albert would see his mother when he came up the steps" (690). She also expresses the collective subject that the plural personal pronouns identify. There are "he"s, "she"s, and "we"s but not "I"s in these verbal exchanges that associate mothers and the idea of collective subjects.

The power of these mothers derives from the respect they earn because the men know that they keep the neighborhood centered and united. Nick fears his mother's authority because she is a respected woman. After he and Vito stole the car, Mike the Book told him that in the neighborhood word gets around, that he could picture Nick's mother at the precinct. Immediately, Nick gets rid of the stolen car. When Nick asks Loretta if he can enter her home, she replies, twice, "My mother's here" (692). The respect for these women is both the fictional one of the characters and the real one of DeLillo, the Italian American man aware of his own history. During Bronzini's visit to Matt at his home, in the building where almost all the women are Italian, the narrator, here clearly speaking for DeLillo, interjects, "How is it we did so much laughing? How is it people came over with their empty pockets and bad backs and not so good marriages and twenty minutes later we're all laughing?" (698). The respect cements the sense of community to

the point that people are able to do things that reinforce their sense of togetherness with less money, something they are equally in need of. After
Rosemary's husband loses seven hundred dollars, she wonders, "How is it
we ate a German meal on 86th Street and went dancing at the Corso down
the block, seven hundred dollars poorer?" And again DeLillo speaks directly:
"There was less of her now and more of other people. She was becoming
other people. Maybe that's why they [the Italian women in her building]
called her Rose" (701). The grocer's wife tolerates Nick and his friend Giulio
Belisario, Juju, because "she liked Nicky's mother" (707).

The ultimate test of these women's force is, aptly enough, corporeal, concrete, and concerns death. In typical Mediterranean fashion, it occurs in
front of a dead body. In part 6 of the book, called "Arrangements in Black
and Gray," Nick and Juju go to a funeral home because they want to see a
dead body. Once inside the place, Juju wants to leave almost immediately,
but Nick warns him, "Too soon. Say a prayer. Show them you're praying.
Show them respect . . . Women in black dresses. We don't show respect, they
tear us apart" (738). Even Rosemary admires the women in the neighborhood who pray all the time and her mother-in-law who speaks no English
after thirty-five years in America. "But this was a mark of her faith in a way,
an indication of what truly mattered. What mattered were the mysteries, not
the language in which you said them" (757).

In addition to depicting the neighborhood's mothers as the opposite of
the typical male characters who assimilate, *Underworld* subverts the male
literary tradition that portrays women and the other as illogical instinctual
beings. The mother is the thinking subject, in stark contrast to the emotional
men of the Bronx, including Nick Shay, whose change of thinking habits and
personality occurs under the teaching of the Jesuits in school after he leaves
the reformatory. As if this further reversal were not enough, in *Underworld*
motherhood does not deny womanhood either. DeLillo does not deny women
their female agency as American male writers traditionally did. In typical
postmodern realist style, Klara's small print of "Whistler's Mother," the
painting *Arrangement in Black and Gray*, visually identifies this thematic
rupture. Klara looks at her, "the mother, the woman, the mother herself, the
anecdotal aspect of a woman in a chair, thinking, and immensely interesting," who seems far away because she is "in the midst of a memory trance"
(748). The idea of the mother, especially of the mother of the Italian American immigrant neighborhood, as a thinking female subject, interesting to the
intellect, the working-class uneducated mother as an intellectual in the hands
of a male novelist, is a literary inversion as gigantic and revealing of the
writer's intentions as Kay Corleone's transformation toward the end of *The*

Godfather Part II is symptomatic of Coppola's goal. The excluded female subject becomes the agent who remembers. Exclusion is transformed into remembrance, bodily presence of a modern life lived and experienced collectively. That is why Nick's brother tells him that their old neighborhood is still alive, "still a living thing."

Unlike in *The Godfather Part II*, however, where Michael Corleone remembers through the recollection of his father's life, in *Underworld* the mother triggers Nick's acts of remembrance, or the narrator who remembers for him. In this way she precedes him in the taxonomy of subject position while maintaining historical faithfulness. According to Gardaphé, Nick's father is the link between Nick and the gangster that explains why Nick can mock Badalato's voice, a sign that Gardaphé reads as the indication that everybody can be a gangster in the modern world of men. This is true as long as *we remember* that everybody can be a gangster in the modern world because modernity is the gangster. Nick takes his mother out west to Arizona with the illusion that she might be able to provide him with that sense of place and being in the world that he has long lost, that the mother-centered Bronx provided for him. It is a futile move to fill a loss by attempting to re-create a past inner experience that obviously cannot return. Nick realizes this impossibility as soon as his mother dies and things change for him because her memory becomes part of him, now an indestructible link to his humanity and his story, the inner memory of the history of which his dark skin inherited from his Italian father, with whom the mother is now symbolically reunited in Nick, is the outer custodian. In one last inversion, her death regenerates his inner humanity, "she amplifies my sense of what it is to be human. She is part of me now, total and consoling. And it is no sadness to acknowledge that she had to die before I could know her fully. It is only a statement of the power of what comes after," Nick concludes (804). This triumph of love over death is the power of the story to recollect, the preservation of the past as a way to reconstruct an inner self and ground it historically. At his mother's wake Nick embraces his brother Matt, who falls against him and weeps, a gesture that is reminiscent of Michael Corleone's embracing Fredo at their mother's wake. *The Godfather Part II* finishes with Michael sitting alone in a chair, the tragedy of an American Faust. Nick Shay too ends up sitting alone at home. Unlike Michael, however, Nick is now reunited with his past. He has located his self historically and with it his people, "the Italians who make their world." Like another literary Nick, *The Great Gatsby*'s Nick Carraway, now Nick Shay can start remembering, putting the pieces together, while drinking grappa, the liquor of his people, the dark-skinned Italians like his father, listening to jazz, the modern music of the dark-skinned people of America, "longing for the days of disorder."

III

Disorder and memory, although a memory differently layered from that of *Underworld*, are the textual matrix of Frank Lentricchia's *The Music of the Inferno*, a novel that describes another type of underworld, that of the Italian Americans of Utica, New York, where the tale takes place. The upstate center is to Lentricchia what Yoknapatawpha is to Faulkner, possibly his major literary influence, a microcosm of his America, the one he (re-)creates in his novels. Lentricchia's fiction poses the following fundamental question: What happened after the immigrants' dreams of belonging vanished as they stepped into the New World? Or, to put it differently, what does it mean to become modern in America for an ancient people? For this reason, the characters of *The Music of the Inferno* are essentially voices, often dissonant voices that constitute a collective author, the cacophony of the inferno of the title. They mirror an author raised, like so many men of his and previous generations, by formally uneducated grandparents for whom orality was the main form of communication and transmission of knowledge, a trait reflected in the dialogues that sustain the rhythm of most of Lentricchia's fiction rooted in the Italian American experience.

One of the book's main characters, Gregorio Spina, acknowledges that the aforementioned question inevitably demands to deal with the fact that modernity and whiteness go hand in hand in the New World. The immigrants were literally screwed by the Anglo-Saxon Americans, Spina tells Robert Tagliaferro, the novel's main character and a necessarily ambiguous racial and ethnic character. But they learned their lesson quickly and well. "When he [Robert] asked Gregorio if they, the first fuckers, had done the job to him, Gregorio, *in culo*, Gregorio nodded, and said: 'Why do you think we came to this country, if not for that? In the old country we had no chance. Here, in America, we must spread ourselves wide open, but here we too have the opportunity to become fuckers. America is very beautiful'" (7). Of course, Lentricchia is writing after the Italian American experience moved from the immigrant phase of landing and trying to adapt in the New World into the new cultural phase, when Italian Americans can tell their story, whose foundations Lentricchia revisits in order to reconstruct and share that story. Lentricchia practices a literary humanism from the bottom up, starting with the title of the book. In *The Music of the Inferno*, a captivating title with all kinds of allusions, internal and external, from the criminal underworld of Utica and the basement where most of the story takes place in a series of dinners, to Dante's *cantica*, to the suave attractions (the music) of modernity (the inferno), Lentricchia's fictional duty is to disturb the intellectual platitude that has taken over the Italian Americans of Utica (and perhaps of American academia), which to Lentricchia are a synecdoche of all Italian Americans outside New York City, including, one suspects, Lentricchia himself. They are the "assholes [who] eat their veggie burgers in the suburbs" (160).

The literary tool that brings disorder to Utica to redeem the Italians and modern America is Robert Tagliaferro, "a curious man, all made of words" (27). The conceptual tool, instead, is play. Whereas the force that drives DeLillo's language in *Underworld* is the voice as an expression of sheer bodily energy, the fuel of Lentricchia's narrative engine is play. There is hardly a more playful contemporary novelist in America than Lentricchia. The adjective "curious" that defines Robert is to be intended both in terms of identity and epistemology. Robert is curious because he is a mulatto orphan of uncertain identity, adopted by a black couple, Melvina and Morris Reed, and beloved by Gregorio Spina and his wife, whose home on Mary Street, the center of the Italian fortress of Utica, he intends one day to buy, so Robert tells his adoptive grandparents. Robert is also curious in the sense that Lentricchia makes him a canny detective whose mission is to unearth certain strains of modern American history through the microcosm of Utica. Robert's racial ambiguity is how Lentricchia destabilizes the mainstream narrative of assimilation—in short, how the guineas became white. Robert's hybridity is first and foremost a category of historical analysis that signifies the physical proximity of blacks and the Italian immigrants in the early phase of modern America, which the novel thematizes.

The narrative moves thanks to the accumulation of examples of this taxonomy. At the beginning of the novel, Gregorio Spina, who represents the memory of Italian immigration to the United States, tells his wife that he would like to tell Robert that he is his son. "I will lie to this orphan and tell him that he is my true son, and that he should live with us. Then when we are too old, he will save us from these cretins who were born with us in Italy, and who now destroy this beautiful city," but his wife tells him that Robert is "not dark enough" to be their son, a racial paradox that functions as the first of the many subversive moves of the novel that Lentricchia succeeds in making historically plausible (4).

Morris Reed, Robert's adoptive father who had an affair with an Italian American woman, a second subversive move, albeit one not thoroughly enacted, remembers when he used to take Robert to an Italian place to eat tripe, one of Morris's favorite Italian foods that is no longer available under the new management of the restaurant. He recalls when he told the former owners that his grandmother "came over from the southern side of Sicily, where they had a considerable amount of warm interaction with the people of Africa," another historical truth that disturbs the Italian owners of the restaurant forced to face *their history as Italians* (105). Melvina instead tells

Robert that he cannot live on Mary Street. "In our colored skin? Honey, not even you could fool those people up there. So what that you're lighter than Spina's Sicilian son-in-law, whom he calls The African? Does that so-called African like to be called The African?" (5). The irony is complete when, after Melvina's death, the narrator, with the uncomfortable cynicism proper of hard truths, asks, "*What color is it now, her colored skin?*" (15). Upon his return to Utica after his forty-year-long self-imposed exile working and living in the basement of a New York City bookstore, Robert asks Morris about the identity of the people who gave him to the family that in turn handed him to his adoptive parents, to no avail. "Were the people who handed me over to the people in Pennsylvania Italian or blacks or both?" (104). All that Morris is able to tell him is that Robert was given to them by a "light-skinned black family," not by his biological parents. Later on, Morris tells him that he was not "black enough" to hide him under his last name (71). And toward the end of the novel, Alex Lucas, the man Robert meets at the bus station at the beginning of the novel, tells Robert, "You're probably black. Now that you tell me about your background, you're starting to look black to me in your features. In a subtle way, you're obviously black. On the other hand, you're obviously not" (153).

Things get even murkier as the novel moves to the politics of the present times, and the language harsher. The dialogues now resemble the blaxploitation movies of the early 1970s, re-modulated with the modernist irony typical of a modernist critic. Sebastian Spina, a mayoral candidate in Utica, rants about Utica's Italians and their supposed Italian pride in what amounts to a frontal attack on assimilation and a sanitized liberal narrative disguised in the cynical irony underlying the long passage:

We call them blacks, they have to refer to themselves as Negroes. We agree to Negro, they go back to black. These people they are breaking my balls, and yours too my friend, whether you know it or not, your balls are being broken, don't tell me they are not. And now they imagine themselves to be African-Americans because why? Because they want parity with us. Think about it, my friend. Who in this country goes by the term fill-in-the-blank hyphen American? I mean classically. Who gets the media recognition in this country as a fill-in-the-blank hyphen American? Does Dan Rather talk about the Irish-Americans? The Oriental-Americans? The Jew-Americans? Have you ever heard Dan say "Jew" the way I just said "Jew," on the network news at seven o'clock? Pardon me, this is our thing. Mr. Lucas, your background is what, Welsh? [Alex nods.] Do you refer to yourself as a Welsh-American? [Alex shakes his head.] You have education. You have respect. You don't litter the streets with fast food containers. That's my point. Those people have shit. They like to live in shit. I made my point. We, the Italian American people of this country, are the original fill-in-the-blank hyphen Americans, we invented that form ourselves alone. *Sinn fein*, as our Irish brothers say. We Italians are known for our ethnic flare, and now these people want parity? Parity, my ass. And why us is the question I put before you today, pal, and where is their flare? Tell me, where is it? [*Alex smiles.*] Why are we being singled out for a reason they have not yet told us at this time in our tragic history? They don't want equality with the yellow race or the people like yourself who do not hyphenate, and I'll tell you why. These people consider themselves above the Welsh, above the entire WASP element, and all the other coloreds. The arrogance is tremendous. They're above everybody. Except us. This is the bone in their throat. Us. [*Pause.*] Us. [*Pause.*] So they're taking the final racial step. They're saying they have equality with the Italian-Americans and then they'll be free at last, thank God almighty, to quote that cunthound they idolize. But I ask you, my friend, how can they be equal? How? [*Alex shrugs and fluffs his balls.*] They're black black black! (44–45)

The blatant, obviously overdone racism serves to bundle together racial identity and a farcical masculinity performed rhetorically. Spina's campaign slogan is "Uticans against the Further Deterioration of Our Past," where Uticans stand for Italian Americans, the bloc that should deliver Spina's election victory. And the Italians, as one of the characters that animates the four dinners of the book, Professor Louis Ayoub, discloses, show "'the obvious Middle Eastern provenance,' because what, after all, were the Sicilians culturally considered anyway? Or, for that matter, what were they considered from the genetic point of view?" (130). The man "all made of words" who returned "to realize a wish of my childhood. To be a black Italian on Mary Street" (155), the man who promised to Alex Lucas that he "will witness a destruction" (32), the man who has read all of Utica's history and "returned to tell you all," provides the answer to this rhetorical question (54). The Italians, says Robert to his hosts, Professor Ayoub, Alex Lucas, the mafia boss Paternostra, and Primo Cesso, Paternostra's gay lover, have been swallowed in American history. They disappeared as modernity developed, another phase in the never-ending conquering of the virgin land. "We never possessed the great stone mansions, they possessed us. The hospitals and the parks never bore our names, and never will. We'll be remembered as the people who added the genre of Mediterranean color to American history in its classic phase and can be identified now only on Columbus Day, as those who wear buttons saying, Kiss Me, I'm Italian" (136).

The modernist irony of this speech is essential to the knowledge that Robert accumulated over the forty years he spent working in the New York City bookstore, the weapon that he uses to deliver the destruction that he has promised to Alex Lucas. It is also essential from a conceptual standpoint, a typical example of literary tone as content, of which a gifted literary critic such as Lentricchia is mindful. This irony works in three distinct modes. First, it works as a harsh reminder of the class and racial dimensions of American history stored in the mansions, the parks, and the hospitals that map the course of such a history in Utica. Second, it is a subtle reminder of the Italians' unspoken and forgotten past in America, which vanished within the great mansions that possessed them, the parks and the hospitals that do not carry their names, the same mansions, hospitals, and parks that they helped to build. The Italians' "heritage" and their "identity as Americans," says Spina, are under "siege" (64). Third, the irony is that the Italians will be remembered for their "Mediterranean color," for adding to the racial hybridization of modern America. They will be remembered for the marker of their truncated historical memory that allowed them to become modern Americans, forget their past and become white. The modern America that they helped to build, the mansions, the hospitals, the parks, made them invisible to themselves to begin with. What they are left with is the whiteness they bought, of which, irony of all ironies, their "Mediterranean color" is the reminder.

This concrete invisibility is the obvious paradox that Robert Tagliaferro intends to destroy. And the destruction that he intends to carry on is, in typical modern fashion, an inversion. Robert wants to recompose this historical puzzle, to de-sanitize history. This is his goal. The way to achieve it is to know the past in order to subvert the present, to avoid stagnation. "This is the point of the past," Robert comments to Alex Lucas. "To unfit us for the present" (29). The weapon that Robert uses to execute his plan in the criminal underworld that controls Utica is his knowledge. Yet it is a particular form of knowledge, one that might as well have an autobiographical component to it. Robert's knowledge is his memory, which replaces his father. "I have no memory of my father," he declares at one point. "In the absence of my father, I acquired knowledge. My knowledge is my memory. . . . Instead of my father, I have knowledge" (72). Knowledge as memory replaces the father, or, better yet, displaces patriarchy, whether it is the patriarchal power and structure that governs Utica's organized crime and local politics; the patriarchy-as-a-founding-principle narrative of Utica's and America's history, which he wants to dismantle; or, perhaps, the patriarchy that informs American literary history.

One suspects that this is the ultimate play of the book, of Lentricchia the writer of fiction, in a very literal sense a "man made of words," like any fiction writer, after all. One suspects that the underworld of *The Music of the Inferno* is the world of American letters, and the father, the canon that reflects the whiteness of modernity. One suspects that modern American literature is the gangster that Lentricchia wants to disarm. Robert is a virgin at the age of sixty because, again, he is a "man made of words." His statement that he acquired his knowledge in the absence of a father reveals a process of self-acquisition, the self-construction of a subject. Moreover, by confessing that he did not have a father, Robert plays a game with and therefore gains the respect of Paternostra, the mafia boss who, faithful to the playfulness implicit in his name and his role, would never question the idea of a father figure or dismiss the lack thereof. When a people's history, the Italians', is erased from the public presence, the aforementioned hospitals and the parks from historical memory, what is left to them in the age of mass culture is how they have been represented and how they have represented themselves, which, in the end, is the outcome of modernity for an immigrant people.

The obvious fact is that first and foremost they represented themselves exactly as they have been represented by others, as gangsters, starting in 1906 with *The Black Hand* short film and up to *The Godfather* and countless other movies, novels, and TV series. And this representation is precisely what Robert's knowledge of Utica's history debunks in the second part of the novel, beginning with the unmasking of Joseph Paternostra, whom not surprisingly Lentricchia defines as "the Godfather of all Upstate New York, with the exception of Albany" (51), and his fellow Italian American, dentist Albert Cesso, as homosexual lovers, the ultimate inversion of the Italian American gangster that an Italian American novelist could engineer in light of the above-mentioned line of cultural representation. When Robert calls Paternostra "Our Mother" in public, he strips away the male power historically associated with the gangster figure, causing Alex to warn him, "Last night you spoke the words 'Our Mother' in public. This is not done in this town" (41). This comment reiterates the power of words.

Such debunking is the way Lentricchia makes his literary argument, what he calls "the American literary history of family gangsterism" that spans from William Faulkner and *The Great Gatsby* to Mario Puzo's *The Godfather* (143). What are represented here are modern American literature and its male canon as another dimension of the interplay of modernity and whiteness, the patriarchy of literary periodization, the modern(ist) canon as the gangster, one might say as the Godfather of modernity, what Fred Gardaphé has defined as "the connection between American literature and the male powers of history that have come and gone before the Italian gangster" (*Wiseguys*, 103). In the end Robert Tagliaferro, another playful name, both etymologically—iron cutter—and historically with its reference to Booker T.

(for Taliaferro) Washington, carries on Lentricchia's project to provide a the-oretical framework for an Italian American genealogy that might do away with modernity as a gangster, a project that Lentricchia had started with his first foray in the world of fiction, *Johnny Critelli*. It is also the way Lentric-chia makes a political statement as a writer, reclaiming an artistic vision as a humanist in the era of the commodification of culture. In this way, he also provides a critique of modernity and capitalism. "All wealth is guilty at the source," declares Professor Ayoub, sounding like Karl Marx talking about the original accumulation of wealth—and wealth in the modern Western world is capitalist wealth (140).

The novel dates the rise of Paternostra as a mafia chief to the 1950s, the decade of *The Godfather* saga. The name of the mafia don, Joseph Paternos-tra, conjures up these three elements that interlock crime as male powers, capitalism, and literature. The name Paternostra can be read as a subtle ref-erence to Puzo's novel, which is directly discussed in the novel in a succinct and up-tempo exchange between Professor Ayoub, Paternostra, and Alex:

AYOUB: "Behind every great family lies a crime."
PATERNOSTRA: "And a politician."
ALEX: "And eventually a writer." (139)

Because in a second exchange between Ayoub, Paternostra, and Alex, the professor quotes Balzac, Karl Marx's literary darling, it can also be read as a reference to capitalism, to the accumulation of wealth in America:

AYOUB: ". . . Behind every great fortune there is a crime. That's how they get rich. They make someone else pay."
ALEX: "Balzac, Prof, on the old world of great families."
AYOUB: "Remembered by Mario Puzo in the epigraph to *The Godfather* . . . All wealth is guilty at the source."
PATERNOSTRA: "The professor overexaggerates everything."
AYOUB: "The road of exaggeration leads to the palace of fact." (140)

Finally, the name Paternostra can also be read as a reference to the mas-culine divinity of the Godfather trope, a semantic translation, we might call it. The intertwining of crime, accumulation of wealth, and modern literature leads to history, the "palace of fact," and points to the further question of humanism that in the end is at the core of the novel. In other words, Lentric-chia asks what is the value of a culture that made Puzo a literary celebrity and a millionaire overnight by creating a fictional stereotype (and stereo-types lead to the contradictions of an entire culture), celebrates a racist mi-sogynist, William Faulkner, as a great writer (which he was), and thinks of America as a woman to conquer, as another playful moment in the novel that references Henry Nash Smith's *Virgin Land* indicates. When he describes Robert's youth in Utica and his years in high school, the narrator comments, "The history teacher said that 'Virgin Land' was what our country was before 'our forefathers came.' He wanted to ask his teacher (who was an Italian-American), 'Whose forefathers? And who were the foremothers they came into?'" (9). And toward the end of the novel, Robert quotes directly from *The Great Gatsby*: "'Borne ceaselessly into the past,' said Mr. Fitzgerald. With all due respect, beautiful but untrue" (211), as he has quoted, less directly, in the middle of the novel, during one of the dinners: "These good-looking Dutch sailors, gazing out upon the fresh, green breast of the new world, heard the heavy breathing and the dirty whisper" (93).

The literary and political de(con)struction of *The Music of the Inferno* ends, perhaps a little abruptly, in the only way possible, suggesting the possibilities of a humanism from below that does away with the hegemony of its patriarchal culture and its politics of self-interest, in favor of the democratic culture and a politics of sharing that the female relationality of the trope of the mother identifies as an artistic vision to begin with. This is the redemption that *The Music of the Inferno* celebrates and suggests at the very end. "The deepest human representation of nature is the Madonna and Child," says Robert, commenting on a vase, an art artifact, reconciling the eternal conflict between nature and art by suggesting that art can prevail over prejudice, that the politics of sharing is more rewarding than the politics of crime, that one can choose love instead of death. As he leaves Utica for Sioux City, the Indian West, a born-again mulatto Huck Finn who lights out for the territory, the man "all made of words" leaves behind a letter, words that tell Alex that now that he has witnessed the rewriting of Utica's (and America's) history and historical memory, what Robert defines as a "new-found wealth," he will feel the impulse *to share* such wealth with Darryl, a black kid who befriended Robert's adoptive father, and Darryl's mother:

> Dear Alex,
> You will feel the impulse to share a generous portion of your new-found wealth with Darryl and his mother. Give in.
>
> > Sincerely,
> > Robert Tagliaferro (216)

Alex's "impulse to share" is the proper subversive conclusion of the novel and the interplay among the Italian American gangster, whiteness, and modernity. This ending looks backward in order to move forward, both in terms of historical identity and novelistic opportunities. It addresses the evolution of the trope of the gangster that the Godfather trope epitomizes as one way for originally marginal people to access whiteness and its privileges after

World War II. Robert's final message speaks to the past, in the sense of the historical memory of a people whose spatial and racial taxonomy within the American social and cultural mosaic left them unfulfilled and displaced, both in terms of identity and as a community, as the final image of Michael Corleone pondering what has happened *to* his life in *The Godfather Part II* exemplifies.

Once the original Italian American communities are gone or approaching extinction, the Italian Americans are left with white suburbs and their reputation as gangsters, reinvented in the guise of corrupted political brokers or, in the case of *Underworld*, managers in the waste industry, where what is corrupted and wasted in the first place is their history. Robert asks Alex to avoid this Godfather-like self-isolation and concurrent loss of historical memory and identity that Nick Shay also laments in *Underworld*. He does it by inviting him to share with the other what he has found, his own self, now historically grounded. The conclusion also hints at the possibilities of a politics of sharing that begins at the personal level and represents the exact opposite of the "wild privatized times" of *Underworld*. It is a way to reground one's self and a people in their history. At the end of *The Godfather Part II* Michael is sitting on a chair outside of the home, no longer the symbolic throne of the Godfather in command of his world. He is pondering how he became the indecent gangster that he did not want to be in the first place and with nothing left in his life, not even a glimmer of hope for a possible redemption. In *Underworld* the historical loss of Nick's identity is recuperated intimately, at the inner level in the aftermath of the death of Nick's mother. In *The Music of the Inferno*, instead, the loss is recuperated through the final outward movement of the novel that the letter exemplifies, a movement that also signifies the cultural hybridization that Robert em*bodies*, literally and literarily, and which he passed on to Alex. Alex is now in the position to rediscover or recognize his identity and his historical origins, his history as an Italian American. His and the readers' "new-found wealth" is this history, of which the mother, as we are about to see, is the unsung hero and the keeper.

[5]

IN THE NAME OF THE MOTHER:
THE OTHER ITALIAN AMERICAN MODERNITY

A WOMAN NAMED MARIA towers over and distinguishes the Italian American novel. She appears in a central role since the early stage of the Italian American novelistic tradition and continues to do so in the present time. From John Fante's *Wait until Spring, Bandini* to Carol Maso's *Ghost Dance* via Mari Tomasi's *Like Lesser Gods*, Michael DeCapite's forgotten masterpiece *Maria* and Bruce Springsteen's forty-year-long attempt at writing the great American novel with his songs properly anthologized as a book called *Songs*, Maria is an ineludible character in Italian American literature, one that has not been dealt with systematically. Her recurrence among first-rank writers traverses historical periods, genders, and literary styles, turning her into a trope that is unique to Italian American literature. There is no other novelistic tradition in the literature of our country with such a central female protagonist that appears with the same frequency. Her repeated manifestations recuperate and adapt the Mediterranean, popular Catholic sense of the communal reality of men and women, their shared destiny, and their mutual responsibility and reciprocity, what Robert Orsi has called, magnificently, the Italian Americans' "abiding respect for things as they are, a humility before the givenness of reality" (*Madonna*, 230). Orsi points out that this position does not presuppose a lack of agency before the facts. On the contrary, it entails participation in the form of an active faith in the possibilities of human life and the recognition of the opportunities and limitations of such a life in the modern world. Because of this combination of openness to the possibilities of life in the modern world and the self-awareness of the concrete realities of such a world, we may say because of her humanism, the Maria trope pieces together a grill of causal relations that recalls the personal and collective history of the poor and the dispossessed in the form of places, cultural traditions, and fictional characters, as well as of an evolving self-realization of a working-class, specifically Italian American female identity that resists class and cultural oppression. By so doing, Maria crosses the color and ethnic line and embraces the other as a possible version of herself.

It is symptomatic of her protean dimension that Maria evolves thematically rather than chronologically. Increasingly, she performs multilingualism, dissects transoceanic generational crises and questions, and eventually subverts the established patriarchal symbolic order that historicizes independence as individualism, unconditioned social mobility, and political equality that supposedly all Americans would share. Maria gives voice to a different class of people, whose human condition and historical context bridge individual differences without denying them. This is how she builds the home that the (Italian) American modern man keeps searching for, the home that continues to elude him. Janet Zandy has defined such a home as "an inner geography where the ache of belonging finally quits, where there is no sense of 'otherness,' where there is, at last, community" (*Calling Home*, 1). I embrace the notion of an inner geography, but I view belonging and otherness as tools to acquire it and necessary components to maintain it, as well as reflections of the materiality of the outer, physical geography of life. As such, these tools help avoid the risk of homogeneity of communities, essentially an ahistorical realization as well as the potential stagnation of history, which would translate into the self-fulfillment of history as its own ablation, its death.

Historically speaking, the idea of a home as the fulfillment of the promises of modernity runs against the development of our post–Civil War literature, or at least its hegemonic discourse and the canon that such a discourse helped establish. One recalls Ernest Hemingway's statement in *The Green Hills of Africa* that all modern American literature comes from the book that celebrates the escape from home, *Adventures of Huckleberry Finn*. Leslie Fiedler taught us that one prominent reason why Huck (and the multitudes of his descendants) runs away from and hates home is the presence of a white woman, often a maternal figure or a surrogate for it. This woman represents the white civilization of law and order that a white male and his nonwhite male companion avoid. The American novel has been hostile territory for women and mothers on all accounts, but especially on racial and gender ones. In this perspective, Maria is the candidate least possible to succeed as a fully developed, autonomous, and mature character who performs agency in a patriarchal society. What seems to have attracted less attention, however, is the class-based, religious component of this anti-woman and anti-mother hostility, something that indeed Fiedler observes in *Love and Death in the American Novel*.

The merchant class–influenced cultural framework that fueled the encounter between America and the novel that Fiedler deconstructed in his study produced a novel that is *ideologically* white and *formally* Protestant. The sentimental tale of seduction with no final seduction characterizes this kind of American novel. In it, the heroine is the sexless, white, blue-eyed Protestant Virgin who outlives the seducer, the product of bourgeois sentimentalism that prevents the depiction of "sexual passion or a fully passionate woman" (217). Opposite to the Protestant Virgin stands the Dark Lady, whose traces Fiedler dates back to Shakespeare's sonnets, poems that present the "primeval terror of darkness, the northern fear of the swarthy southerner" (297). In place of the "sanctified virgin (Fair maiden)" we find the Dark Lady, "sinister embodiment of the sexuality denied the snow maiden," the dark double that "represents the threat of both sex and death which become one in such a symbolic world" (296). Fiedler's description is the critical equivalent of Luce Irigaray's theoretical argument that Western patriarchy and the capitalist system of exchange reduce woman to a product of man's labor and desire upon whom society imposes the roles of mother, virgin, and prostitute.

Not surprisingly, Fiedler looks at Hawthorne, for whom the dark figures are non-Anglo-Saxons and therefore gorgeous and poisonous, "Mediterraneans, Orientals, Jews—or at least given to an oriental lushness in dress and flesh, not considered quite decent in New England" (298). The point of this mapping is that the geography of the founding American novels is religious as much as it is racial, and it is grounded in class division. The Dark Lady, continues Fiedler,

> had represented the hunger of the Protestant, Anglo-Saxon male not only for the rich sexuality, the dangerous warmth he had rejected as unworthy of his wife, but also for the religions which he had excluded and despised. The black woman is typically Catholic or Jew, Latin or Oriental or Negro. Wherever the Dark Lady plays a serious role in our literature, she is likely to represent either our relationship with the enslaved Africa in our midst or with the Mediterranean Europe from which our culture began; she is surrogate for all the Otherness against which an Anglo-Saxon world attempts to define itself and a Protestant one to justify its existence. (301)

This tradition originates and fully develops in the eighteenth and nineteenth centuries with the rise of the bourgeoisie, but according to Fiedler it persists well into the twentieth century in two specific ways. The first is the anti-mother figures, of which Faulkner's *As I Lay Dying*, Penn Warren's *All the King's Men*, and Wright Morris's *Man and Boy* are emblems, literature where the mother goes from saint to devil. The second is the protest novel of the 1930s in which "disguised masochism" replaces the lack of sexual passion (262).

The benefit of these observations and of Fiedler's study in general here is what Fiedler omits. The anti-mother figures are the product of writers who react to the literature written by the children of the turn-of-the-twentieth-century immigrants, of which the Italians are an essential component, one that Southern Italian Catholicism, with includes traces of its pre-Christian, even pagan heritage, characterizes. This literature is also the product of two major historical shifts. The first is the end of slavery and the northern migration of African Americans owing to the implementation of segregation in the South on the one hand and the industrial and urban development of the North on the other. The second is the end of the immigration that brought the parents of those new American novelists to the United States. As for the protest novel, no such a label has ever been applied to Italian American novelists of the time, certainly not to the creators of the Maria character here examined, in spite of their prominence in the Italian American literary canon, which in more than one way they helped to shape. Even more surprising, this absence parallels the crucial role that Italian American workers and radicals played in the years when the protest novel was being written, a historical fact that Fred Gardaphé has examined in an essay focused on Fante, di Donato, and Mangione titled "Left Out," where he argues that old historical categories of scholarly analysis, outdated theoretical models of interpretation, and the Italian American writers' Marianist Catholicism explain such omission.

We begin to see a pattern here. We suspect that the exclusion of Italian American novelists from the established literary canon and the lack of a sustained critical assessment of their contribution to the development and the achievement of the novel in the United States result from the fact that these writers depict female characters who did not people the American novel prior to the arrival of these writers on the literary scene and caught the critical establishment off guard. These writers are pro-mother and increasingly, albeit in the complex way proper to authors who take their writing craft seriously, pro-woman. One such a case is DeCapite's *Maria*, whose lack of recognition is symptomatic of the critical void I am trying to begin to assess here, and which justifies this lengthy section of the book, including the many pages dedicated to DeCapite's masterpiece. These writers depict women who are characters in their own right. They do not position them at the service of men. These women do not fall into the position that Marianne Hirsch describes as "nature to man's culture, matter to man's spirit, emotion to man's reason, object to man's subject" (203). Increasingly, these women situate themselves at the center of their writing, mothers and women whose names bear Italian American Catholic implications, which is to say, non-Protestant implications that need to be textured. Perhaps more important for the appreciation and evaluation of these writers' artistic vision is the development of a feminine aesthetic sensibility. That no Italian American writer could depict the equivalent of the Mary of Stephen Crane's *Maggie: A Girl of the Streets* is beside the point. More to the point, instead, is the fact that no Italian American novelist managed to create a Maria even remotely close to the Mary of Thomas Bell's *Out of This Furnace*.

Three main reasons explain this absence. In the first place, an Italian American writer of the Great Depression era would rarely, if ever, anglicize the name Maria, which is in itself a sign of how the epistemology and ontology of the Maria trope inherently resists assimilation. Second, no Italian American writer, and certainly no male Italian American writer of the time, would be capable of imagining a character named Maria central to the development and the goal of the novel who dies as Mary does in *Out of This Furnace*, not even with a smile on her face, as Mihal Dobrejcak's wife does. Garibaldi Lapolla's Donna Maria, who dies "without absolution, and was buried two days later, her coffin borne behind a slow-moving band of musicians provided by Gennaro" (228) in *The Grand Gennaro*, is the exception of a (tellingly) Protestant Italian American writer who dutifully confirms the rule. When Maria Turin dies in Carol Maso's mid-1980s *Ghost Dance*, a death that unlike the other several deaths in the book Maso does not describe, she immediately becomes a living memory of her (partly) Italian American granddaughter, which is to say, she does not really die. Finally, no Italian American would bury a mother, even more so a mother named Maria, without a marker on her grave, as the lack of money forces Mary Dobrejcak's surviving children to do.

In the introduction to the anthology of Italian American women writers titled *The Dream Book*, the combination of what Helen Barolini defines as the Mediterranean Catholic emphasis on "acceptance, humility, and having an internal sense of worth and dignity without the external show of prosperity that indicates Calvinist grace" (22) and the aforementioned "humility before the givenness of reality" helps us see the three-dimensional trajectory of Maria: she exposes, resists, and subverts the conceptual foundations and material conditions of twentieth-century America. If the gangster embodies the Italian American man's quest for acceptance into whiteness as one way to enter the modern world, Maria is the Italian American woman who unravels an other modernity. She is for the Italian American novelists a shelter from the storm of the modern world that provides these novelists with the possibility to envision their art as a way to find a home in the world, which is to say, to make the world their home.

The novelistic connection between the Maria character and modernity begins with *Wait until Spring, Bandini*, John Fante's first published novel, in 1938. However, Fante had already established the link between women and modernity in *The Road to Los Angeles*, a short novel he had written between 1933 and 1936 that remained unpublished until 1985, two years after his death, when his wife found the manuscript that publishers had rejected and her husband had hidden. *The Road to Los Angeles* does not include a Maria character, but it provides us with the literary references and the philosophical premises of the connection between Maria and modernity that inform *Wait until Spring, Bandini*.

In *The Road to Los Angeles*, modernity epitomizes the declining Western civilization, a decline that is equally socioeconomic, intellectual, religious, and of mainstream cultural values. It is a totality. Arturo Bandini, the young protagonist and narrator of the novel, as well as Fante's literary alter ego, internalizes this decline as both an impediment to and the fuel for his goal to become a great writer. To him writing is the only way out of the modern crisis. In the tradition of the bildungsroman, Fante envisions literature as the tool to overcome the crisis that modern men and women experience, because in the middle of the Great Depression, when the socioeconomic machine that had propelled unprecedented levels of transformation of the conditions of human life broke down, it allows Arturo to build his identity as an Italian American writer. In this sense, *The Road to Los Angeles* responds to what Lawrence Buell has defined as "the importance of self-fashioning as a pathway to social recognition," which explains how "'growing up ethnic' became the modern American bildungsroman's single most remarkable literary success story" (123).

Arturo identifies culture with a tridimensional typology of the mother that combines a Victorian-originated sentimentality, Puritanism, and doctrinal, patriarchal Catholicism. Whereas Arturo reads the Northern European philosophers, his sister Mona reads the equally popular Kathleen Norris, a fact that does nothing but reinforce Arturo's negative view of modernity: "This was modern America! No wonder the decline of the west! No wonder the despair of the modern world" (116). For all her good will and actions, the prolific best-selling Norris was a proponent of Victorian morality and matriarchal sentimentality that she displayed in her first novella, eloquently titled *Mother*, published in 1911. In it, the protagonist, Margaret, the daughter of the mother in the title, feels the attraction of modern life and experiences its opportunities, but in the end she rejects them in order to commit to the needs of her future husband, just as her sisters do with their own husbands. Additionally, their unconditioned allegiance to their mother is presented as an antimodern position that, while acknowledging technological advancements such as electricity, new means of transportation, and even medical technologies, regrets the mythological good old days of a less complicated life, what Leo Marx would define as a simple conception of pastoralism. "Everything was so simple. All this business of sterilizing, and fumigating, and pasteurizing, and vaccinating, and boiling in boracic acid wasn't done in those days," proclaims one Mrs. Watson, who then continues, "Our grandmothers didn't have telephones, or motor-cars, or week-end affairs" (106).

The centrality of the link between the mother and the decline of Western civilization in Norris is even starker when we compare it with an earlier passage in which Arturo praises Michael Gold's *Jews without Money* because it portrays a great mother figure. "What a book that was! What a mother in that book!" The comparison is instructive. Fante selects a mother who is the polar opposite of Norris's, one whom Gold himself in the introduction to his novel calls "the heroine of 'Jews Without Money,'" to the point that he identifies his world with hers. "It was my world; it was my mother's world, too" (11, 19). *Jews without Money* describes Gold's mother as "very pious," with a great sense of dignity (68). Gold chronicles how in spite of their insurmountable poverty, his mother worked tirelessly to keep her children "fresh and neat" as a form of self-respect (71); "with female realism she tried to beat the foolish male dreams" out of her husband, who buys into the American dream of easy financial upward mobility, thinking he can easily become rich in America (81). Her dignity and commitment to her family is equaled by her class-based instinctual disregard for making money as a signifier of values, "that dark proletarian instinct that distrusts all that is connected to money-making" (214). Finally, although she "was opposed to the Italians, the Irish, Germans and every other variety of Christians with whom we were surrounded," at the same time she "was incapable of real hatred. Paradoxically she had many warm friends among the Italian and the Irish neighbors" because "these are good people" (165).

Gold's description reveals what Fante admired in a mother figure and speaks to his dislike for the antimodern view of Norris. It also helps us to see why in *The Road to Los Angeles* Fante identified the mother with the art of writing. Gold envisioned literature as a tool for his political vision, a potential cure for poverty. It was a part of what Alfred Kazin describes as his "unrelenting, unstoppable insistence that every mistake in life, every distortion of character, everything we vainly want, is due to poverty and nothing else" (Gold, 3). Gold was typical of a native New Yorker in that his world began and ended in New York City. At the time, the West did not exist for him, although, in prototypical immigrant fashion, he ended up living and dying there. The East was Nazi Europe, obviously not an option. Understandably, that was his modernity. "The dark ages had returned; modern thought was again burning in the flames of a new inquisition, the Jews again afflicted with the yellow badge of shame," he wrote in the "Author's Note" of his novel (9). Fante had hardly grown up on easy street, but he had been born in Denver. In classic American fashion, to him the West, California, represented a possibility. His people did not have to carry the burden of a millennial history of real and mythological (read biblical) oppression. In other words, as an Italian American writer he did not have the foundations, however terrible and tragic, that Gold was in a position to exploit.

The end of *The Road to Los Angeles* is exactly about writing and identity. And it is at this point that Arturo's mother reenters the scene. Arturo completes the book that he has been writing all along, a novel in which the hero, his alter ego Arthur Banning, dies committing suicide after he has love affairs "with women of every race and country in the world," because he never finds "the woman of his dreams" (139). This woman is Arturo's mother, because she reads the manuscript of his novel and likes it. "Here was a woman who understood me. Here before me, this woman, my mother. She understood me" (144). What she does not understand is the hero making love to a "Negro woman" from South Africa, a Chinese girl, and an Eskimo woman, a racial bias that triggers Arturo's utterly rational, modern reply, "Now, now. Let us eliminate Puritanism here. Let us have no prudery. Let us try to be logical and philosophical" (146).

Puritanism is individuated as the platform of racial and ethnic prejudice and displays a global dimension. At the same time, envisioning a universality of love that crosses national, racial, and ethnic lines is the "logical" and "philosophical" thing to do. When Arturo's mother insists that the hero should find "a nice clean little Catholic girl, and settle down and marry her" (146), Arturo identifies her request with institutional, patriarchal Catholicism: "Papism returns! The Catholic mind again! The Pope of Rome waves his lewd banner" (147). The mother liberates Arturo as a writer; Puritanism is viewed as the foundation of racial and ethnic discrimination; and institutional, patriarchal Catholicism is the insurmountable impediment for the logical and the philosophical subject position of Arturo as an Italian American, a people whom Fante squarely situates among the racial and ethnic people of the world, encompassing a geography whose trajectory moves from the South to the North to the East, in this way decentering whiteness. The outcome of this newfound faith in his writing ability is Arturo's decision to move to Los Angeles. He informs his mother of his decision with a letter where he states that he needs to leave home in order to become a writer, but that he has "much to thank you for, O woman who breathed the breath of life into my brain of destiny." The mother is identified as a "woman." And yet, she is not really a woman. She is the liberating force of Arturo's art, of his writing. Literature, then, is the home Arturo (and Fante) is searching for and that his mother allows him to find. Now he can leave and think about such a home, "the new novel" (164).

The new novel was *Wait until Spring, Bandini*, in which Fante gave Arturo a father, Svevo Bandini; two brothers, Augusto and Federico; a house in a poor section of Rocklin, Colorado; and a mother, named Maria. That is to say, he gave Arturo a family, as the literature of the Great Depression demanded. Of this family Maria is the epicenter, because Fante sets her in contrast to the epistemology of whiteness. The novel is built around a set of binary frames that keep together an otherwise conflicting world where harmony is absent and anxiety dominates the life of the characters. One of these frames is the opposition between Maria and the rich widow Effie Hildegarde, who seduces Maria's bricklayer husband, a contrast that develops at the interpersonal level the larger one between Maria and "the world of 'American women'" as visualized by the ladies' magazines she occasionally reads, "those sleek bright magazines that shrieked of an American paradise for women: beautiful furniture, beautiful gowns: of fair women who found romance in yeast: of smart women discussing toilet paper. These magazines, these pictures represented that vague category: 'American women.' . . . She came away drugged with the conviction of her separation from the world of 'American women'" (73).

The distance between Maria and these American women mirrors two different worlds that class and race keep separated, "the beautiful furniture and the fair women." This distance is what separates Maria from the world of whiteness. It is not a strict matter of gender. "American women" is the code name of whiteness in *Wait until Spring, Bandini*. This separation also unveils how concrete is Maria's view of the world, which is what makes her other, different. Maria is an outsider because her way of seeing the world does not belong to the universe that the pictures in those ladies' magazines portray. It concerns the ontology and the epistemology of Maria's world, her identity and the way this identity defines her relationality. In stark opposition to the sleek magazines and the vacuity that their images evoke, Maria's otherness is expressed with a bodily description that does not reflect the associations that her name commonly evokes in an Italian American context. Maria's body registers the conceptual discrepancy between her and the modern white world. It is the site onto which this discrepancy is *written*. As such, it is the physical repository of her Italian American history: "She had but to turn her hand and examine the palm, calloused from a washboard, to realize that she was not, after all, an American woman. Nothing about her, neither her complexion, nor her hands, nor her feet; neither the food she ate nor the teeth that chewed it—nothing about her, nothing gave her kinship with 'American women'" (74–75).

The differences with the mother of *The Road to Los Angeles* could not be any starker. In place of the mother of writing at the service of the aspiring writer son, which we could read as a literary version of the subjugation of the woman to the son that according to Simone de Beauvoir the Marian tradition enforced, this time the body itself is the writing. What one reads in this female body is the materiality of class difference and a non-color-based outsider position. The palms of her hands and the complexion of her face translate the discrepancy between Maria and whiteness (along with the food she chews, the cultural symbol par excellence of ethnic literature, certainly of Italian American literature), reiterated in the physical depiction of Maria that introduces her as "the beautiful white wife of Svevo Bandini" (12): and "she was so white, that Maria, and looking at her was seeing her through a film of olive oil" (13). The ethereal whiteness of her external appearance makes her outsiderness inscribed onto her body even more significant because it reveals an inner otherness, one that her "large black eyes" register (13). These eyes have the power to see through things and reverse darkness and light, almost mystically if not divinely, with a kind of power resonating of the authorial and male Catholic voice, and yet, as we shall see, in a very tangible way. "Her name was Maria, and the darkness was light before her black eyes" (16).

Her inner agency foregrounds her capacity to cross social lines and her intellectual faculty in spite of her lack of formal education, a void that in turn underlines her agency. Maria is an uneducated woman who did not complete high school because she "wanted things her own way and refused to graduate" (21). Her independence led her to escape from home as a young girl, forcing the police to search for her and bring her back. In spite of (or perhaps because of) her lack of formal education, Arturo—here Fante's direct voice in the novel—acknowledges his mother as "a pretty darned smart woman after all" (84). In addition, Maria, in this way subverting the typical asexual representation of the Italian American mother, is a sexually active and passionate female subject. As a young girl she liked to play "house with Nigger children" and received "a licking for it" (89), a detail thus racially worded in order to make visible an interracial spatial taxonomy of origins as well as her family's ability to read the social codes of American life, which dialectically reiterate such a taxonomy. As a woman she experiences sexual desire, which Fante represents with an image that combines mind and body, an image of wholeness and unity in a world where everything breaks and everybody's identity is fragmented. Maria "had only to think of the muscle in his [Svevo's] loins and her body and her mind melted like the spring snows" (13).

This depiction would seem to contradict the home-confined woman who prays the rosary waiting for the husband to return home after he has an affair with a rich, white American widow narrated in the rest of the novel; the mother who tends to the children and subjects herself to the humiliation of basically begging the owner of the grocery store next door to give her further credit to buy food; the woman who immolates herself on the altar of the family in the stereotypical fashion traditionally associated with Italian American women. In this perspective, her husband would seem to define Maria both as a woman and as a mother. Even her sexual desire is elicited by the thought of Svevo's body, after all. And there is no denying that this is the case, especially if one reads the novel from the point of view of her relationship with Svevo. The norms, the social conventions, the symbolic structures are all male, and they are described with a male-inflected rhetoric. In this perspective, Maria is nothing more than a product of Svevo's desire to make it in America, to assimilate, which is precisely what makes Maria an outsider, as her distance from the whiteness of the ladies' magazines indicates. This men's world is also what the other main female character of the novel, with whom Maria is juxtaposed, the widow Hildegarde, invests in when she gives Svevo a pair of new shoes and takes him around town in her automobile, that American symbol of masculinity par excellence, which tellingly the white woman who has lost her husband, her man, drives, a subtle inversion of subject position that on the one hand positions class ahead of gender hierarchy and on the other ethnic hierarchy below gender and class.

Svevo realizes both things when he is able to see beyond the whiteness that the widow's house and cultural references identify. The fact that these references are located in Italy is enlightening. To Effie Hildegarde Italy represents the Grand Tour, the pastoral ideology, and D'Annunzio; "the Campo Santo, the Cathedral of St. Peter's, the paintings of Michelangelo, the blue Mediterranean? The Italian Riviera?" she interrogates Svevo (176). None of these places and art objects is concrete for the widow. They are auto-referential symbols of who she is and, especially, of who Svevo is not and in her view should be. They are the flip side of the coin of the previously mentioned ladies' magazine. But the fact of the matter is that these are concrete places and art objects that to the Italian-born Svevo are instead a foreign land and a foreign language. He "was from Abruzzi," an Italian, but he "had never been . . . to Rome," let alone heard of the decadent poet (176). And we can safely assume that the only grand tour Svevo has ever taken is that in the steerage of the boat that brought him to America. Of the two, the American woman, not the Italian man, has been to Rome and has read D'Annunzio.

When Svevo finds himself in front of the widow, he realizes that between him and this rich woman stands the same difference that excludes Maria from the "American women" category. It is not only wealth and status. It is not only money or the lack thereof. It is an ontological and epistemological difference, which the class condition informs and Effie Hildegarde's representation of Arturo's native country identifies. Effie's Italy is white and bourgeois. Maria's version is her callused hands and her dark complexion.

The difference between Svevo and Maria is that Svevo has internalized this division, this sense of isolation from America. As a result, he has sold himself in the illusion to overcome this gap. "As he sat there, staring at her for what he believed to be the last time, he realized that he was not afraid of this woman. That he had never been afraid of her, that it was him she feared. The truth angered him, his mind shuddering at the prostitution to which he had subjected his flesh" (206). Read in contrast to the bodily descriptions of Maria, especially the sexual references, the reference to the "flesh" that Svevo prostituted to a white woman, another subversion of traditional gender positions, tells us something about Maria because it unveils the meaning of Svevo's sexual affair with Effie. Svevo submitted to the logic of exchange value that is integral to assimilation into white America, as he finds out at the end of the novel when the widow devalues him and Arturo by way of deploying class, culture, and identity as tools of exclusion from her America, which is to say, from white America. "You peasants! You foreigners! You're all alike, you and your dogs and all of you." "That's my boy. You can't talk to him like that. That boy's an American. He's no foreigner," responds Svevo, before Arturo calls her an animal and a whore, which tellingly he does not do in his native English, but in the language of his father's native country. "*Bruta animale! . . . Puttana!*" (265). The animal and the whore, of course, are not the widow. They represent America, the place these two Bandini men cannot make their home, as Arturo's use of the Italian language indicates, along with his father's claim about his son's Americanness. All of which is, from a strictly technical point of view, pointless. After all, Svevo too is an American. He acquired American citizenship and gave up his Italian one. More important, Svevo thinks of himself as an American. "He, for example, was a pure Italian, of peasant stock that went back deeply into the generations. Yet he, now that he had citizenship papers, never regarded himself as an Italian. No, he was an American" (74).

What matters is that after this animated verbal exchange with the widow, Svevo tells his son that it is time for them to go home, to the house that initially he hates because it is the material reminder of his poverty (265). Home is where Maria is, the place where she told Arturo his father would return, after Arturo lied to her and said that his father was in the hotel room where

his friend Rocco lived, looking sick and willing to go back home, but afraid
that she would not let him, that she would kick him out of it. "It's good for
him, . . . Maybe he'll learn what a home means after this. Let him stay away
a few more days. He'll come crawling on his knees. I know that man," Maria
replies (239). One could read this passage solely as a (stereo)typical image
of the Italian American wife retaliating against her unfaithful husband. After
all, earlier in the novel Maria scratches Svevo's eyes with her fingers when
he returns home and lies about his affair with Effie. Such a reading is obviously part of the equation but overlooks the fact that what fuels Maria's
reactions is her husband's lying to her. It is his lack of respect for her as a
woman to whom he is married. Maria's answer to Arturo is not an act of
defiance toward her husband, an attempt to put him down in front of Arturo.
She is not devaluing her husband, the father of her children, who actually
devalued himself by selling his flesh, as he realized. Neither is she pretending
to act as a matriarchal figure who dictates the rules of the family, her way to
assert the power that she does not hold outside the home. The key to this
passage, which is also the key to Maria and the novel, is the statement about
the home and the skepticism about her husband: "Maybe he'll learn what a
home means. . . . I know that man."

The vocabulary is crucial here. Maria does not say what a home is. She says
what a home represents, what the meaning of a home is for people like the
Bandinis, for Italian Americans like them in their time, for poor discriminated-
against people at the margins, which the location of their home on the impoverished outskirts of Rocklin embodies. Similarly, she does not say what
the role of a husband is, what it means to be a father. These things Maria is
fully conscious that Svevo knows. That is the reason why she refuses to align
with her own mother, Donna Toscana, who despises Svevo, when her mother
visits them. Likewise, Maria knows that the lack of work to which the title
of the novel refers causes Svevo's inner instability, his being decentered, as
well as his desperate behaviors and actions in pursuit of some form of self-
grounding. After all, Svevo is a bricklayer. He builds homes. No less significant is that by valuing the home above everything else, she stands for a
communal and inclusive point of view and the idea of a shared space, in a
novel where the sense of not belonging and ethnic isolation matches the
sense that everything seems to be under the constant threat of falling apart,
where the Italian men cannot control their lives, where a bricklayer who
fixes somebody's else house cannot repair his own home, at a time, the 1930s,
when everything is falling apart.

This view hypostatizes the exact opposite of a self-centered viewpoint, of
self-fulfillment and self-realization. At the same time, Maria recognizes that
there is no certainty that her husband will come to her same realization;

"Maybe he'll learn," she concludes. She does not impose her view. Neither does she occupy the center of the home. In this way Maria expresses her own agency within the spatial limits of a poor Italian American family. She knows that only this view of the world can maintain intact the only thing that can keep the entire family from disintegrating in the face of the economic uncertainty and the isolation that they face. Their home is their chance to preserve the one thing they have, which is themselves as individuals and each other as family. Her answer and her position are nothing more than the conscious recognition of things as they are, that their home is the only America possible for them to be who they are. When Maria pushes the "carpet sweeper back and forth" wearing "her nice blue housedress," she is not willingly submitting herself to the role of the passive housewife (239). Neither do the nice clothes she wears represent a tool to ingratiate herself to what she thinks will be her returning husband. Maria is not offering herself up as a forgiving reward for Svevo. To read these images stereotypically is to deny Fante his artistic vision. "I know that man" says Maria, where the personal pronoun identifies a woman in a sentence whose meaning is its dialectical opposite: that man does not know that woman.

The clean home and the nice clothes need to be read as an alternative to the sleek magazines of the "fair women who found romance in yeast" (73). They identify an other-directed Mediterranean epistemology of self-respect that entails a female aesthetic of self-value in spite of the adversities that as poor people they experience in America. This is one way Italian American culture infuses the class dimension in America from a female, communal position mindful of one's individual place in the world. There is nothing Marianist in the doctrinal and stereotypical sense of the word in this depiction of Maria. True, Maria dreams of her second son, August, becoming a priest and feels a kinship to the Virgin. Moreover, the kids do go to a Catholic school. But these passages too need to be read as manifestations of the force of Maria's epistemology, self-respect, and an aesthetic sense of self-value. They are active forms of participation in a world that otherwise excludes her and her family because they are poor and Italian American. It is no coincidence that at one point in the novel Maria authorizes the children to break the religious rules of Catholicism. August exclaims that on Friday they should eat fish. Arturo reprimands him in order to protect him, because he knows that they cannot afford fish, but Maria tells them, "It's no sin to eat chicken on Friday, if you can't afford fish" (240). Reality does not bend faith. Neither does reality contradict Maria's faith. Rather, faith is part of reality, its recognition, which helps to cope with the anti-Italian environment that the Bandinis inhabit and the isolation that they experience. In this perspective, even Maria's praying is an active investment in the possibilities that the future might hold, the title of the book, the spring, when a multitude of colors replaces the harsh and unavoidable presence of the real that the *white* melting snow of Colorado crystallizes.

II

The recognition of the givenness of reality and the need of belonging that informs *Wait until Spring, Bandini* also pervades Mari Tomasi's *Like Lesser Gods*, an intergenerational family story that takes place in Granitetown, Vermont, the fictional equivalent of Barre. The novel is centered on the Dalli family, Pietro, Maria, and their children, a nucleus that increases in size when the Dallis are joined by Pietro's old teacher in Northern Italy, Michele Pio Vittorini Giuseppe Tiffone, conveniently renamed Mr. Tiff by Petra, one of the children. Mr. Tiff is the voice of reason and the mediator of the developing relationships among the Dallis and the rest of the characters who revolve around their family. Rose Basile Green has elegantly defined him as "a symbol of the old frame of culture of Italy, the religious and social morality of Southern Europe, the persistent criterion of conscience" (136). At the time of the novel's publication, Tomasi, who was serving a term as a representative in the House of her native Vermont, enjoyed journalistic abilities and political connections that were of use to a female writer in the 1940s trying to publish novels, even more so for a woman of Italian descent after World War II. Those experiences helped her navigate the male-dominated publishing industry, but what shaped her second novel was her earlier participation in the WPA's Federal Writers' Project.

Tomasi had been a member of the group that put together the American Guide Series for her home state, one of the first guides in the series, published in 1937. Just like the Vermont guide and many other of the guides, *Like Lesser Gods* promotes what Mary Jo Bona has called "a vision of *cooperative* development, one that depends upon the members of the family and community to ensure successful adjustment into American society" (31). At its basic level, the novel is a New Deal vision that, however progressive and nuanced in detailing the natural landscape (another influence traceable to her experience in the FWP), nonetheless departs from the originally integral democratic vision of the people who headed the FWP, or branches of it, such as Henry G. Alsberg, the old anarchist general editor of the project; Jerre Mangione; Sterling Brown; and the man who behind the scenes made the FWP possible, Harry Hopkins. For example, whereas the book begins with a labor strike in Granitetown, the changes of working conditions that cause the death of Pietro Dalli in the second part of the novel are not portrayed as connected to a workers' movement with its demands and unrest.

They are the result of the legislative process and of technological advance-ment, neither of which the book explains.

Like Lesser Gods seems to reflect the trajectory from the labor protests of the 1910s and '20s to the legislative accomplishments and cultural inte-gration that the New Deal had achieved by the early 1940s. Book 1 of the novel takes place in 1924. The element that, albeit in the background, shapes the story and the lives of the Dalli family is American labor history—and American labor history after the Civil War is ethnic history, as the novel re-minds us. It is the history of the perpetual conflict between capital and labor that the workers' strike at the beginning of the book represents. It also al-lows for the development of the relationship between Pietro and Maria, and how Pietro's religion of work affects them. As Mr. Tiff explains to Maria, "I have seen Pietro at work. It is as if he has two hearts: one that beats for you and his family, and one that beats for his work" (149). This distinction unveils the gendered and power-inflected foundation of the notion of the family and the dynamic of the couple's relationship. As Mr. Tiff continues to explain, "Since the very beginnings of family, the husband's lot has always become the wife's. And justly so. Remember the wise Ruth who ever made her mother-in-law's lot her own, when she said—'Whither thou goest I will go.' And the Roman bride of antiquity formally promised her husband—'Where thou art Caius, there am I, Caia.' In the same measure your own promise 'for better or for worse' makes Pietro's lot your lot, and you must accept it if you would keep his love" (149).

It is a one-sided vision as explained by a man and internalized by a woman, Maria, who tells Mr. Tiff, "What kind of a woman do you think I am? Do I love Pietro the less because in this matter he has a mind of his own? Strong willed, my father and mother called me! Yet the moment Pietro touches me, I am no longer Maria—I am Pietro, thinking and feeling as Pi-etro, as rapturously as would a new bride! And me wearing a wedding ring these eleven years!" (15).

The gendered taxonomy of this subject position reflects the distinction between Maria and Pietro that Tomasi reiterates time and again in the novel. Gender is the propeller of this division, which functions also as an interethnic marker. Maria combines mind and heart, reason and instinct. Mr. Tiff describes her as "handsome and practical" (17) and "practical-minded" (128). She is considerate of her role as mother and wife, and yet she is willing to break the law and the statue that her husband is sculpting in order to force him to quit the job that she fears will kill him. She values knowledge, and she is the custodian of the family's Italian heritage, as her insistent request that Mr. Tiff teach the children the Italian language signals. "It is truly our good fortune that you came to us, *Maestro*. I would never have had the time or patience to teach the children to read Italian" (55). She is also willing to accept the change that modernity imposes on her, as she does when she accepts, not without an initial resistance that makes her final acceptance more credible, to send her sick daughter to the doctor instead of using the superstitious practice of her Italian hometown to cure her. Maria is "strong of mind and strong of heart" (148). In other words, she is a modern figure, one that Bona describes as revealing "a differentiated identity: she is both strong and weak; articulate and silent; traditional and rebellious; assertive and ineffective" (11). Women too are modern. Women too are part of modernity. Women too live modernity.

There is something else that Maria possesses and Pietro lacks, a feature that as in *Wait until Spring, Bandini* is inscribed inside her body rather than on her skin, something that might be a part of this gendered decentering of modernity. Like Maria Bandini, Maria Dalli too has "dark eyes"—"black eyes" that Tomasi juxtaposes with her beaten "white" face, eyes that are "defiantly burning against this defeat" when her plan to break the statue her husband is working on to make him leave the job fails miserably (149). Her eyes mirror her inner self, which is dialectically externalized in a specific bodily image: "Her eyes were still her soul: alert, constant, and, he [Mr. Tiff] thought uneasily, possessing a gleam of determination that was twin to the firmness of her full, red lips" (11). We recall here that the lips are exactly the part of the body of the nameless Italian woman that Sterling Brown describes in "Harlem Happiness" almost in the same exact way. Likewise, the woman's husband in the poem by Tomasi's fellow Federal Writers' Project member is also called Pietro. Maria's invisible blackness is not an isolated reference. Neither is it a product of life in the United States, a realization of the immigrants in their new environment. Nor is it a solely psychophysical attribute ascribed to Maria. It defines other Italian American characters as well as the Italians' historical identity, in the same transoceanic, transcultural, and transhistorical fashion that we saw Mangione insist on in *Mount Allegro* with his references to the Middle Eastern and African roots of his family members. For example, in one of the sheds where the Italian men work, Mr. Tiff notes "Tony Bottelli, dark of face and massive shoulder, bent over a drill in the roofed yard" (56).

The innovation of *Like Lesser Gods* in this respect is the religious source of the Italians' invisible blackness. When Mr. Tiff arrives at the Dallis' house, Petra—the one Italian American in the novel to recall how "once, just once, a smarty-pants boy called me 'wop'" (18)—first notices how each page of the calendar of the saints that the maestro brought from Italy bears "the picture of a saint in rich Moorish colors" (17). Then she points out how this is something her family and the Italians of Granitetown share. "We have a St. Michael in our church—St. Michael's church. And we have a calendar like that in Mama's room" (17). Her curiosity becomes attraction later in the novel when Mr. Tiff asks a man who lives on Lake Champlain to carve him a small wooden statue of Saint Michael. Of this statue Petra notices "the rich, Moorish colors, and the handsome, young face of the warrior saint" (67). Not only the invisible blackness is a historical component of the Italians of Granitetown, as the plural pronouns in "we have a St. Michael in our church" indicate. We also notice the connection between this form of otherness and Maria, the woman who tries to preserve the family's heritage as well as the husband's life, the woman who affirms life. To her daughter the Moorish presence is not located in her parents' room. It is in "Mama's room."

There seems to be an original discrepancy between the main female and male characters that does not pertain strictly to gender positions as an autonomous sphere disentangled from the political history of modernity. In the name of her cooperative vision, Tomasi makes no serious effort to question the structure of gender positions. If Maria Bandini rarely leaves the home, Maria Dalli rarely leaves the kitchen. When she does, she regrets it, as in the case of her attempt to destroy the statue that her husband is sculpting. This discrepancy is intertwined with Pietro's dream of modernity, his idea of work as a religion, to the point that he thinks of himself in these same terms. When he is in the shed sliding "the steel as it cut into the stone" for one Jerrod Aldrich Eckles, he thinks, "*So, Jerrod Aldrich Eckles, you are a stranger to me. Nor are you a* paesano, *not with that name! Is your skin of my whiteness, or are you black or yellow?*" (59). The use of the modernist literary device par excellence, the italicized stream of consciousness, underscores Pietro's identification with his work, his modernity, which will be the cause of his death.

The dream outlives Pietro, who dies early in the second section of the book. In it, instead of empowering the invisible blackness of the Italian American women, Tomasi opts for the cultural politics of the New Deal. This narrative move allows Tomasi to skip the Great Depression; rebuke fascism as a guarantee of the Italians' will to assimilate; avoid any interethnic conflict whatsoever in Granitetown; and, conversely, promote the professional, economic, social, and interpersonal assimilation of the Dalli children.

As book 2 opens, Father Cart, here too the perennial Irish priest in charge of the local Catholic Church that the Italians attend, asks Mr. Tiff to help the school's eighth graders as they are "putting on a Dante-Beatrice scene at graduation." When the priest follows up with an inquiry about the situation in Italy, Mr. Tiff "angrily" replies, "It is that Mussolini!" (153). The cultural representation of Italy in the guise of the world's greatest poet in opposition to Italy's fascist dictator accommodates the integrationist view of the Italians of Granitetown: "Mr. Tiff . . . loved both his native land and his adopted country. The old teacher was well aware of the fact that hundreds of others in Granitetown felt as he—Italian granite workers, and a few Germans, who led hard-working lives. No open hostility existed in Granitetown toward these workers of foreign blood, yet how could they but feel shame that their homelands had nurtured the monsters who were selfishly leading the world into another war?" (153). The way out of this shame is not political. It is economic and intergenerational. In a letter to his sister in Italy, Mr. Tiff, who by now has won the trust of the (white American) reader, a factor that gives credibility to the rest of the story, writes that Vetch Dalli is now a "quarry-man and is married to the daughter of a policeman; that Petra is a nurse; that Lucia's son, Gino, has become a doctor; that a fine sanatorium has been built on the hill above us; and that our street is now Pleasant Street instead of Pastinetti Place" (156).

The way out of their outsiderness is the way into middle-class modernity, which the up-from-the ghetto narrative with its consequential erasure of Maria's invisible blackness serves all too well. The past is literally replaced; the white line that identifies established wealth and a conflict-free community is crossed, as Petra's trajectory points out. Now a grown-up woman and the last of the Dallis' children to be single, she is courted by "dark Gino and blond Denny" after they return home from college, another sign that the Italians are assimilating and entering the white middle class (201). Inevitably, she has to get married, although she seems reluctant to do so. Inevitably, she has to choose between the two, which she also is reluctant to do. And inevitably, she picks the blond man, whose Protestant family owns a stone-working shed and whose mother is uncomfortable with Catholicism. Nonetheless, "blond Danny" embraces Petra's faith with his mother's eventual approval and thus wins Petra over (201). The deal is sealed. Whiteness can be negotiated by freezing the development of gender position in exchange for economic access and the preservation of a religious faith (devoid of the Moorish colors of a warrior) connected to the mother and appropriated as a philosophical system to hold on to during the inevitable turbulences of the modern world, as a safe anchor rather than as a potential agent of subversion: "Maybe it's the philosophic system that seems to remain changeless through the ages and has made it an institution of antiquity, something to hold on to in a world where everything changes," Denny comments about Petra's religion (285). It is the ideal conclusion to the integrationist vision of America's future predicated on an exchange: the woman who picks a male partner who allows her, and by extension her Italian American family, access to whiteness. It is a way to interpret modernity, but to paraphrase Marx, it is one step short of changing it.

What is left out of this future is Maria, whose only choice is to accommodate the cooperative vision that guarantees the children's access to privilege by retreating into her husband's vision of her. When Pietro dies in his bed, he dreams the dream of Mary in Bell's *Out of This Furnace*. "He was proud of her. As strong, as unflinching as granite she was, he reflected, in his last earthly flicker of humor" (256). It is a male vision that, similarly to Faulkner's, allows only one type of female agency in a male normative framework: endurance, which bodily images visualize. It is both a confession of defeat and an admission of the gender imbalance of modernity. For this reason, we see Maria internalizing and suppressing her feelings. When she understands that the husband will never quit his job, "a ponderous pain, sprung from the fierce throbbing at her temples, bore down into the flesh, into her face, her throat, into each member of her body" (189). The pain becomes imperturbability when everybody stands in front of Pietro's deathbed in his last moments, a condition that her formerly fiery black eyes transmit. "Of all the eyes about him only Maria's were dry, bright; her face, an inscrutable mask" (256). The repression of her feelings first requires wearing a mask, then turns into bitterness, although a reconciled bitterness, as the integrationist vision demands:

> Her friend Lucia, after those three days when Pietro lay in his coffin in the living room, had recalled her own Italo's death and she had marveled quietly at the dry-eyed Maria, "You're brave. Braver than I." But Maria had mentally shaken her graying head. Nor did she explain that it was not really braveness, but simply her way of life. In her earlier years she had even committed a criminal act to safeguard the health of the man she loved. When she learned, with pain, that neither threats, pleas, nor wits could change Pietro's deep-rooted regard for his work, she had become reconciled to it. Grimly and bitterly, perhaps, but reconciled. (262)

Only at this point, for the first and only time can Tomasi imagine Maria outside her kitchen, her own shed, where she makes the female equivalent of Pietro's granite statues, the ravioli, those "tasty morsels of meat and pastry," on the porch (211). While she can imagine Maria outside the house, she can do so only in the form of a traditional domestic image. On the porch, she watches her only son, strategically named Americo, who looks like his father, "his short, stocky figure, so much like that of a young Pietro," the man she loved "more than anything and anyone in the whole world," even "better than these children who were woven of her own flesh, blood, and bone" (261).

III

What Fante and Tomasi were not capable of achieving, Michael DeCapite accomplished in *Maria*, an extraordinary book shamefully but perhaps tellingly forgotten. On all accounts *Maria* fulfills literary achievement of the first order. Whether it is the characterization of the people who inhabit the pages, the execution of the English language and the multiple interjections in Italian and the combined rhythm that they produce, or the detailed landscapes and climatic conditions of Cleveland that move the story along when it is needed, *Maria* presents a very high level of sophisticated literariness.

The achievement is due in the first place to DeCapite's ability to envision modernity as a complex and evolving condition in interaction with the inverted trajectory of the female protagonist of the title, who goes from young daughter of immigrant parents deprived of her youth because of an arranged marriage at age sixteen, to mother and, finally, to a credibly liberated woman. The dynamic movement of modernity and an inverted path to womanhood advances the narrative and provides Maria with the depth that her character needs to escape the standard formulas of the proletarian and ethnic novel of the day that DeCapite criticized in a short essay titled "The Story Has Yet to Be Told," published in 1940 in Luis Adamic's unfortunately short-lived magazine *Common Ground*. In this regard *Maria* is closer and owes more to the end of the nineteenth-century naturalism of Norris's *McTeague* and *The Pit* and Dreiser's *Sister Carrie*, novels that *Maria* surpasses by way of advancing, in its 1940s ethnic context, what Jennifer Fleissner calls those novels' "truly new kind of narrative, one irreducible to the alternatives of sheer triumph or absolute decline" when it comes to "women's case" (22).

The spatial movement of the three-part structure of *Maria* opens up the main character's inner development in organic connection to the complexity of twentieth-century modernity in the United States. The novel's structure envelops the immigrant story and characters of the first part called "Little Italy," together with its safe but eventually untenable self-enclosed isolationism typical of immigrant America that the classmates of Maria's first son Paul represents ("Some kid called me a wop," he tells his mother [130]); the economic instability and the destructiveness of the American dream of the second section, "The South Side," which DeCapite skillfully couples with the generational differences of an evolving multiethnic society; and finally the politics of sharing of the last section, "The City," which concludes Maria's dynamic, ever-in-motion, circular movement from the margins to the plural center of her modern world.

Unlike the novels previously examined, as well as many others of its generation, especially (but not only) novels written by men, *Maria* begins with the thoughts and memories of a girl, the night before getting married: "All night Maria lay awake, tossing about, afraid lest the dawn come too quickly. And all night her mind was filled with memories, and each memory on this night seemed more joyful and more real than the morning and the day to come" (3). Immediately we are offered a metaphorical inversion of day and night, of light and darkness as figures of hope and fear with an image that in the United States necessarily entails a racial dimension. The inversion foresees the circular end of the novel, similar to what the European philologists called a poem's "ring composition," a formal device that informs the careful reader that this is exactly what Maria, the character as well as the novel, will accomplish: she will break barriers from within the totality of her world in her direct opposition to the traditional roles of the characters that surround her. If one had to pick the defining aspect of this woman in relationship to modernity, this would have to be Maria's crossing all sorts of lines: economic, gender, racial, ethnic, religious, and especially those defining the structural roles within the family and the sociocultural environment of mid-twentieth-century America. She does it without projecting herself outside of the mental and physical space of her history as an Italian American woman. If myth and folklore are what make credible and altogether memorable two of the great female characters of the literature of the time, Lena Grove in Faulkner's *Light in August* and Janie Crawford in Zora Neale Hurston's *Their Eyes Were Watching God*, what makes Maria an equally good, if not an even better character, is her simultaneous ability to move beyond and stay within her (hi)story, a feature that allows DeCapite to redefine the notion of belonging and home from the perspective of a first-generation Italian American woman in the first half of twentieth-century urban, midwestern America.

Gender nuances this aspect of Maria right from the beginning of the novel, when she recalls her aunt Annunziata giving her a piece of sugar candy not in exchange for her labor, but "for helping me, child," initiating the gendering of the political economy of the narrative by valuing a sense of intergenerational female reciprocity and togetherness (3). This dimension is also expressed in terms of color and heritage, narrative components that DeCapite employs sophisticatedly, especially in relation to the notion of space, which in America visualizes the nation's class, ethnic, and racial topography. In school, Maria "sat at the side of Lilian, a Negro girl who managed to cry before she answered any question; and behind her, Polish Anna, snapping gum and always getting fingers rapped by Miss Palmer," the proverbial Anglo teacher of non-Anglo kids in urban contexts in the early twentieth century, the time when the story begins (4). Outside school, instead, she takes candy from a German boy, the son of the rare German family that "moved into the red block," the neighborhood where the Italians live, and "always said hello to her" on his way home from work with his father. "He had a fair face with light blue eyes, and she liked him" (29).

Equally suggestive is how Maria perceives the racial dimension of her soon-to-be-husband, Dominic. To Maria, Dominic "didn't look like other Italians, he was so light skinned," a description repeated twice in the space of the first sixteen pages (6). The other Italians—and the other Italians in this novel *are* the Italians, that is to say, the racialized, dark-skin immigrants—look like Bernardine, the old shoemaker "with dark skin" who dies dreaming of going back to Italy and for whom Maria develops a genuine affection (6). Dominic's racial depiction, however, extends beyond skin color. It includes his external appearance, the mirror of his inner self. "His eyes were steel gray and Maria did not like to look into them. His face was not soft, but hard and strong looking, and his chin jutted a little. His walk was erect and his laugh was never full. It was only when he talked or when he made a gesture that she knew he was Italian, but he was different to Maria, very different from Pepi or Nuncio," the latter two Maria's father and a neighbor (23). His inner difference becomes relational; "He never kissed her when he came home from work, he never talked much about her or himself. He rarely called her by her name" (23).

Dominic's racialization foresees his epistemological opposition to the men of Little Italy. The old immigrants work to live. They content themselves with bread, wine, a game of cards, and the occasional Italian *festa* that provides relief from the tempo of the capitalist time that dictates their life outside their home, along with the traditional immigrant communitarian life and the old values, patriarchal as well as matriarchal. Unlike them, Dominic embraces individual success as the ideal of making it in America and the concomitant fable that hard work always pays off. "I like it here. One can make money in America," he tells his in-laws when he visits them to get to know his future spouse (10). Dominic is hardly mindful of his past, of which the old immigrants are a constant reminder. To him these are people "content with their places and jobs and their children. . . . They'll never get anywhere. . . . Look at them, lazy and dumb," he comments "scornfully" (74). His past reminds him of his class condition, the reason why he left Italy at age fourteen, as well as the trap he sees himself locked in in the red block. In place of the red of the block where he lives he sees the green of the dollar bill that he dreams, which becomes his credo. "I've seen how money is made. One just has to work hard for it" (75).

The embracing of this narrative initially earns him the respect of the elderly immigrants who admire his seeming assimilation and self-confidence, which contrast with their own sense of displacement and insecurity: "He did not seem to be bothered by his being Italian, he was not afraid of his new country. He seldom talked of the old world. In comparison with others, who were never sure, who flocked together because they seldom felt at home and never could acquire a hold in the new country, Dominic seemed to have his feet planted firmly on the ground. He believed, he knew where he was going; the others had no belief and they could not foretell what the future would be" (80).

As a result, Dominic increasingly abandons his language of origins. And as his economic circumstances improve, he moves the family out of the red block and into the multiethnic Literary Road of the South Side, a step closer to the center of the city, to the "business district" with "white columns shining in the sun," where "the real money is made" (136). Money is Dominic's center, what he wants for himself and, indirectly, for his family. And white columns that one might safely suspect white labor did not build symbolize this center.

Dominic's story is an attempt to reach such a center, a goal that transforms him from the "Italian working man" Maria thinks she has married to a person who increasingly looks like "a real American business man who knew where he was going and what he was doing" (135). His transformation is anthropological, epistemological, ontological, and, ultimately, paradigmatic of the larger transformation of the country. The physical description of this American businessman is revealing. "His skin was light, his being erect; his body had poise," a corporeal status that his appearance matches. "And Domenic put on a new brown suit and on his head he wore a straw hat. How handsome he looked, as if he belonged in those clothes," an aesthetic description where the key words are "as if" (135).

The lure of money trumps even the fable of the self-made man who works hard, plays by the rules, and achieves his monetary self-realization. Shortly after he moves the family to the new location on the South Side, Dominic enters the world of business, both practically and mentally with the goal of increasing his financial capital, while he continues to provide for his family as he is promoted to foreman on his daily job. On the one hand, he adopts Franklin's self-advancing utilitarian credo of frugality, perseverance, and self-education to "get ahead" (79). He saves as much money as he possibly can. He wakes up at six in the morning to walk to work instead of taking the streetcar because it "costs money" (79). When he returns home from work in the evening, he takes up writing and reading. He even asks for Maria's help, making her a utilitarian tool for his self-advancement that in his mind will benefit the entire family as a consequence of *his* success. "It is necessary to read and write, and you must help me," he tells his wife (79). On "Saturdays, when he went shopping to the market, he would often return with two or three books he had picked up in a second-hand store" (79). On the other hand, Dominic pairs his Franklinian self-education with the business of selling wine at home, breaking the law of Prohibition until one day the police find out and destroy the wine press he had invested in, a failure that costs him more than half his savings. As a result, Dominic's appearance changes, and so does his language. "The way Dominic walked, the abrupt way he had of speaking so that even his accent wasn't noticed, the way he held himself, so sure, so confident" (100).

Dominic's feverish chase of monetary success results in the drastic deterioration of his relationship with Maria and even more so with their first son, Paul. Dominic considers his business his property. When it fails, he unleashes his anger against his son to levels that leave Maria unable to react and which prompt her father, Pepi, to break the rules of an Italian patriarchal family. Pepi intervenes, as he had already done once before when Dominic had abused Maria physically: "Dominic slapped him [Paul] across the face, then, seized with uncontrollable fury, he began beating him. It was more than paternal anger and righteousness, it was pent up anger and frustration of weeks coming out on the body of Paul. It was this Maria saw in Dominic's anger, this she felt, this she was powerless to act against. Only when Paul was writhing on the floor, yelling and shrieking, did she come to her senses, but Pepi had already stepped in front of Dominic" (120).

The violence against Paul reflects the widening gap between Dominic and Maria that money fuels. The effort to accumulate money is what triggers Dominic's physical and communicative distance from Maria, the woman he thinks he owns, whom he thinks of as his property, thus revealing the absolute power of money in its etymological sense: money breaks all ties and *privatizes* the *male* self, Dominic's modernity. While Maria has helped him learn to read and write and supported his other efforts, he considers the financial loss of the wine press his own loss. "I'll lose about five hundred dollars altogether" (115). But the one who internalizes this privatization is Maria. Initially, when they move to Literary Street, she tries to question him about money. She tries to convey to him the idea that their capital is communal property at the service of the family. "How much have we—you—got in the bank?" she asks (82). Now she does not even attempt to communicate with him. As they lie in bed at night after the end of the wine business and the five-hundred-dollar loss, she wants "to talk, to ask questions, but the lips didn't move" (115).

Dominic's obsession becomes an infection as he transitions from the illegal wine business to the legal world of stocks and bonds, which he enters with the help of a white-collar coworker, who also persuades him to buy what eventually will reveal itself as a valueless lot of land on the outskirts of

Cleveland. Dominic's initial gains represent the typical initial moment of monetary fever that spreads across middle and lower classes and socio-spatial areas but that eventually reveals itself as the premise of the crashes of financial capitalism that devour those same lower and middle classes, just as Dominic is devoured. Eventually, penniless, he leaves the family and moves to Chicago with his sister Emilia.

The description of this moment partly evokes F. Scott Fitzgerald and partly re-creates the working-class tone typical of the detached 1930s streetwise writer, who here replaces the elegant style that DeCapite uses to describe the natural landscapes in *Maria*:

> But Dominic was not alone, a man alone in his neighborhood on the South Side. This feverishness, this blind activity was also changing, infecting everyone. True, the men plodded to work, mothers went to church, children played on the streets; but what had been flush of money and prosperity, was now a reckless, exaggerated hunt for something that eluded them. Girls painted themselves more brazenly, cars careened around corners, the poolroom at the corner was filled every night. Gangs of boys walked the streets together, insulting passers-by, sometimes stealing, sometimes picking fights. (152)

In a nutshell, with the exception of the post–World War II thirty-year-long hiatus provided by the New Deal's sensible regulations, this is the economic history of capitalism in the United States up to our own day, a failure that is paid for by the working people—and the working people in the United States are always ethnic and racial people: "People were worried—these immigrants, Poles, Russians, Greeks, Hungarians, Italians—they, who had had such good jobs and made such good money in the past, were being laid off and they did not know the reason" (177). The logic of business is a version of a national epistemology. "It is an American way. It is business," Dominic comments when, after his last debacle, he asks Zia Annunziata for money to make more money. "This is an opportunity to make much money. . . . But to make it, I need money to start" (174). For those who are "just Dominic, one of the thousands like him with faith and courage but no 'in,'" this logic unmasks the myth of the self-made-man, of individual monetary success that sustains the fable of assimilation (182). It reveals the essence of capitalist modernity, a forward-oriented direction that takes one back. "He was not going forward. He was trying with all his might not to go backward" (193).

Dominic's story would be another story from modern America, so to speak, a story that repeats itself time and again. One only has to think of Martin Scorsese's *The Wolf of Wall Street* or Bruce Springsteen's "Shackle and Drawn," not surprisingly two Italian American artists with a Catholic aesthetic sensibility, to find similar contemporary examples. What distinguishes Dominic's story is that it opens up the space for Maria's story without setting the two in binary opposition, as the circular movement of *their* collective story that in the end is also the story of the novel avoids such binarism. Dominic's story is not situated in opposition to Maria's. It is at its service. That is to say—and this is an important formal move with regard to the tradition of the Italian American as well as the American novel—Maria's story is the epicenter of the history of an entire immigrant ethnic group in America, a group of people that do not look "light skinned" as Dominic does. Moreover, this female character is the mobile signifier of this epicenter. Finally, the woman who identifies a people and their story in America up to the 1940s carries the female Catholic name par excellence, in Italian. *Because of it*, and this might be the novel's most significant accomplishment, Maria always acts and thinks in an entirely concrete way that eventually frees her inner self. Gradually, her trajectory becomes a form of female liberation as she crosses all possible lines in the most credible way and finds her way back home. Gradually, she starts viewing the world with the eyes of a woman, with her eyes. In other words, she begins to become conscious of her working-class, ethnic female identity and the potential agency that such identity entails.

Her recognition of the real as it presents itself to her eyes is what defines her. It becomes the source of her development as a woman. Maria holds dear the golden locket with "the Virgin Mary on the one side and Christ with a bleeding heart on the other" that her family's old friend Bernadine gave her as her wedding present (25). Her initial loneliness and emptiness become signs of an evolving identity. When she loses her first child, Father Ricci tells her that her loss is God's will, but the circumstances of her life force her to dismiss the priest's authority, the embodiment of the institutional authority of the church that obviously comes from the highest Father, the ultimate patriarch of Western culture: "But when Maria saw children in the street, alive and happy, she would not, could not believe him [Father Ricci]" (41).

The source that enables her to dismiss the priest's explanation of her child's death also enables her to cross any sort of line that she comes in contact with and break the abusive and patriarchal circle. The two movements overlap. When Dominic and Maria move to Literary Street with their first child, she feels emotionally displaced. In a way, their relocation is the equivalent of her parents' immigration to the United States. She realizes that however lonely and empty her native red block with its self-isolation was, nonetheless it provided her with a safety net that the discriminated-against immigrants needed as they internalized the fear of the outside that they commonly experienced in their workplaces. The red block "was home" (73).

As she leaves it, she realizes that "it was precious, like Bernadine's locket around her neck. Maria felt that all she held dear, closest to herself was being uprooted and sent away into some strange place" (73). She also understands, in another example of recognition of the real and another typical modern moment, that her realization is the sign that there is no going back to it because she has just started her search for a new home. As the moving truck with her furniture, the material signs of any person's home, drives "out of the hill into the city," she recognizes that "the red block, her three rooms, were left forever" (74).

As a girl in school Maria sat next to a black girl and in front of a Polish one, crossing the racial and ethnic lines. As a woman and a mother in the new neighborhood, she crosses the religious and cultural lines as she establishes lines of communication and a friendly relationship with a Jewish woman, Mrs. Gelfand. And again, the reality of her circumstances, we might as well say her modernity, becomes the driving force of her actions and supersedes even her religious agency. When Paul gets sick, all her prayers to the Virgin Mary do not work. What works is the "Jewish-looking" doctor that Mrs. Garland calls after Maria asks for her help, the same Mrs. Garland who in the following days also crosses the religious and cultural line as she "trotted over a couple of times a day, often with rich creamy soup she had made" for both Paul and Maria. "This is good for the boy—and yourself too," she tells her Italian neighbor, another example of female mutuality and comradeship that permeates the novel (89).

Whereas Dominic tries to hide his accent and pass as a white American, Maria chooses the road less traveled. For Dominic, Literary Street is the street of the dollar bill, of money, stocks, and bonds, an immaterial and intangible wealth privately accumulated through and decentered from human labor. For Maria, Literary Street is an inclusive, multiethnic, racial, and working-class female America. *This* is Maria's modernity. In symbiosis with Maria's identity in formation, this modernity too is evolving, triggered by a politics of sharing that recognizes the other as its constitutive part, as a version of herself. When Dominic asks Maria why she gave away some of their wine to Mrs. Gelfand and adds, "by the way, isn't she a Jew?" Maria promptly replies, "Yes. They're nice people. She helped me so much when Paul was sick" (105). That a woman named Maria who is mother to a son called Paul gives such an answer is even more significant from a symbolic standpoint, as it is her Saturday's foray to the street market.

Dominic thinks of the market as the place for exchanges. Maria sees it as the site of ethnic and racial difference and the possibilities that modernity offers. She views the urban environment as a shared public space. For this same reason she dresses as well as she possibly can. To an Italian American woman like Maria, a public space is also a space of public appearance, her Mediterranean version of the Italian *bella figura*. It is a form of self-respect, one that demands the recognition of everyone's dignity regardless of class condition. "Dressed in her best house apron, her hair combed carefully, her face still rosy in the sun—one easily forgot about one's self cooped up in the house, working all the time—and a brown wicker basket under her arm, Maria went to the market on Saturdays" (106). As the market is a shared public place, so is the streetcar that takes Maria, other women with their children, and even some men to the market, as if a public space were by definition differentiated because of its class alignment as well as a fundamentally democratic site that the languages, the bodies, the clothes of the people, even the diffidence of the youngsters toward some riders and the awkwardness of the occasional man riding the streetcar identify:

> The street car was filled with women going to the market, women jabbering in a hundred tongues, women in heavy black shawls, their faces puffed and lumpy; women, young and powdered too much, edging away from those who talked in Polish, Russian or Greek. There were children pressing noses against car windows; children bawling; children eyeing the wonders of the street car with beautiful curious eyes; and here and there a man who didn't have to work on Saturday, dressed in his best suit, awkwardly sitting among the others, pretending the scene before him was all very usual. (106–7)

The mix of uncommon difference translates the modernity of the city that enables Maria's spirit and takes the form of "a stir in the city, flushed with work and prosperity" (107). She observes it "in the faces of the people, the number of honking cars, the belching smoke from the factory chimneys in the flats. People hurried, sure of themselves and their intentions, unafraid. And it was good to be part of this sureness, this optimistic going and coming of the people. It seemed healthy and permanent and it filled her with strength" (107). Maria's sense of belonging among different people in a modern environment is reiterated in the market where "the women clambered out, holding onto their children," where "trucks and cars were snarled in a traffic jam" (107). The scene registers the pulsing side of modern life that combines diversity and an idea of prosperity not measured in the dollars, the stocks, and the bonds of Dominic, the light-skinned man who looks like an American businessman. "Perhaps no other thing gave so much evidence of abundance and prosperity as the market place which seemed to bulge at the seams with fruits, vegetables, meats, and people" (107). The products of nature and human labor, as well as one of the two essential elements of human life, food (the other being sexual reproduction), are associated with the idea of universal singularity, the face of a modern society as it ought to be that surrounds Maria, one not dissimilar to the Chicago of Motley's *Knock on Any Door*. "Chinese squeezing in and out of the crowds; flat-tongued Filipinos; gesticulating Jews and Italians; stolid, big-armed Slavs; pert, tailored Americans; red-faced Irishmen; black-haired Greeks; grinning Negroes," all of them "mingling and converging on the wooden stands where bright yellow lemons, golden oranges, peaches and pears and apples and corn sparkled in the sun; and endives, beans, lettuce dripping water, every vegetable and every fruit from scallions to avocado pears spilled like a horn of plenty through the market place" (107). It is an image that reverses the hegemony of capital over labor and its products. It is an image of a civic, somehow anarchically democratic economy because open to everyone, an economy where everyone can be an equally active participant without occupying the center of it, since everyone's participation prevents even the possibility of such a thing.

The economic movement and the "river of many tongues and odors" make Maria feel "excited and carried away with the others." She forgets a house on Literary Street that is not a home and her increasingly estranged husband. She recognizes herself in the other as she experiences a sense of belonging for the first time in her life; "and for the first time in her life she felt herself part of the city, that she was not alone, that the people about her were like herself" (108). This modernity elicits the mutual recognition that at least temporarily replaces her loneliness and her emptiness and brings out her mentally repressed self in the form of her youth, her beauty, even her sexual feelings that her forced marriage took away from her, as she discovers walking among the older women in the market, a mental awakening that she perceives corporeally: "She did not find herself identifying her thoughts with the mothers, the women who held children by the hand, the women fat and full of words. No, she stood above them, straight and full-bosomed. The marks of child-bearing, worry and work vanished with the blood racing through her body. She belonged with the girls and young women. Instinctively the older women made her feel this; men glanced at her as she passed, and she hurried to hide her blushing, and—yes—pleasure" (108).

Again, the sense of belonging and female self-realization takes the form of an inner opening that interacts with the external environment and causes another ethnic encounter, one that naturally combines racial otherness and a democratic sense of the aesthetics that a diversity of color traditionally associated with a pulsing life identifies. "At one end of the market, out in the street, dresses on hangers and aprons of yellow, red, and blue hung out in the open. Maria found herself walking to them. 'Yes, oh yes—a dress.' A dark-skinned Syrian woman, with shining oil on her hair, was selling" (108–9). Maria's ability to relate to Jewish Mrs. Gelfand as well as to a dark-skinned

Syrian woman is the cipher of her politics of sharing. No less significant is the fact that the combination of her inner blossoming and concomitant external crossing of ethnic and economic lines occurs "out in the street," in the open public site, the shared place of a differentiated community of people.

We gain a better understanding of Maria's evolving realization of her female self by contrasting this passage to the conscious, symmetric distance that Maria feels from her husband and his colleague George when they talk business. Hers is a conceptual, almost anthropological distance that does not pertain exclusively to the economic sphere, because such a distance is revealed first and foremost through the language, the prime tool people use to understand each other: "Money, shares, stocks, margins—they [Dominic and George] spoke in another world" (129). And Maria's different way of viewing the world and modern life comes full circle in the last section of the book, "The City," in the years of the Great Depression, after Dominic leaves her to move to Chicago with his sister Emilia because of his financial debacle, when Pepi dies and with him part of Maria, who sees in her father part of herself, "the part that was love and affection, that was laughter and goodness, was gone too" (212). It is when the economy almost annihilates her as both a mother and a woman—"mechanically she did her work, she was neither mother, nor woman" (203)—as well as a person, turning her into a machine: "Maria worked, desperately, feverishly, like a machine, with no capacity for feeling." She had always relied on men. "All her life depending on Dominic, all her life looking forward to Pepi's coming, and now she was lost, with nothing, no one to lean on" (214). She realizes that her economic condition transcends her feelings when she accepts her mother's suggestion to apply for relief as her sister Carmena does, "But it was not a golden promise or a thousand dollars that could change Maria, nor the tongue of her mother. None of these could have done so by themselves. It had to be something else, something intangible, but stronger too" (217).

This something takes the form of her daughter's simple question to her, "What's the matter, Mom?" which triggers her motherly self (217). A motherly self, however—and this distinguishes Maria from her predecessors—not *of* her children, but "for her children" (218). The inner rebuilding of Maria begins with the acknowledgment of her material circumstances that once again triggers the recognition of the other when she applies for relief. Accordingly, such recognition takes the form of racial otherness. In line before Maria stands a "giant Negro woman" who explains to the relief agent that she tried to find work unsuccessfully (219). As she hears her explaining her case, Maria understands that she *is* like this woman, as well as the fact that everybody could be her. "Could it be possible, Maria asked herself, that all these people were like herself? And she had been afraid to come!" (219).

The allegorical self-racialization that female mutuality enables also enacts Maria's inner agency, in her private life and in the textile factory where she finds employment and meets other female workers. Maria is able to put a definite end to her marriage, a subversion of the old-fashioned Italian ideal of keeping the family together at all costs, which DeCapite describes in harsh but historically resonating words:

> It was a law, unwritten and written, made holy by the church, woven into a culture centuries old—a man took his wife until death, no matter what their relationship; the father was head, in thought and deed, and family bowed to him. It was something taken for granted, accepted so completely that it was never spoken of. Any transgression, especially by the wife and mother, was unspeakable. How else to account for the humiliation so many Italian wives endured, the beatings they suffered; how else explain the patience and resignation of young girls born in America, with American words on their tongues, American desires in their heads, married to the old fashioned tyranny of their husbands? (192)

The painful but necessary breakup occurs when Maria travels to Chicago in a last, futile attempt to persuade Dominic to return home and finds out that the child of Dominic's sister Emilia died. When Emilia sees Maria, she embraces her and weeps on her shoulders. Maria struggles "against the sobs flooding her own throat," because while for Emilia the wake signifies the death of her child, for Maria it means the end of her marriage (233). But she also knows that she will need to make the next step, to embrace her own independence and agency.

The second strain of the previously mentioned female mutuality begins here. Whereas the first strain is about breaking bonds, this one is about making bonds, especially female, working-class bonds. Previously Maria crossed the ethnic and religious lines of her new neighborhood and the spatial line of the street market that triggered her self-realization. Now she bonds with other women because she recognizes herself in them. The textile factory where Maria finds employment is peopled with women of all backgrounds and from all walks of life, whose common denominator is need. "Widows with children, mothers whose men left them, women with invalid husbands, elderly women with no families, young girls with mothers to support, girls alone, waiting for husbands, old and broken women, determined and hard women, frightened girls, kind and patient wives, naïve women working for the first time, Negro, Greek, Italian, Polish, German, Irish, and Russian women, stitching and sewing" (234). In this genuinely American universe Maria befriends Irish Tillie, the epitome of the northern, working-class urban female character traditionally exploited in American popular literature and culture, especially the comedy, and the more peripheral Hungarian Bertha. It is a credible universe because it is located in the industrial, urban Midwest and because the superintendent who can "fire or re-hire or recommend layoff" is a white Anglo-Saxon woman named Miss Gibbons, another indication of how class and power are historically intertwined with ethnic lines and accordingly divided (238).

In the closed space of the factory, Maria learns the cruel reality of labor conditions under capitalism, where workers become numbers. "She [Miss Gibbons] gives out 403's," comments a young girl who sits next to Maria, where a 403 stands for "the layoff slip" (239). The possibility of a getting a layoff slip makes starkly clear to Maria the grounding power of work, in addition to its economic benefit. "I saw Mollie Belinsky the other day," comments Bertha. "She looks terrible. . . . After she got her 403 she was down and out" (240). Maria also learns the existence of the racial line that she ignored as a young Italian American living among dark-skinned people, one who in school used to sit next to a black girl. Tillie explains to her that the two African American women whom Maria notices being very quiet were the subject of a "wild" southern girl's racist rant. "'I'm not workin' next to niggers,' says she. 'I'm not talkin' next to niggers. Not me, not me!'" Maria's reply may be naïve, but underlines once again her capacity for crossing lines. "Why?" she asks Tillie, and then she glances "at the negro women, curious, wondering what feelings they had, how different they must act," a description whose key word is "feelings," the same word DeCapite employs anytime he needs to address Maria's inner self and her attempt at understanding the ultimate other in America, African American women (241). But, also, feelings are something that both Tillie and Bertha seem unwilling to express and that yet they have internalized, as they both ask Maria if she has "the blues."

From this point onward, the circular movement that characterizes Maria's development as a fictional character as well as the novel that carries her name (or is it Maria that carries the name of the novel?) intensifies for three reasons. The first reason is to move forward the action; the second is to bear the historical moment of the tale; and the third is to advance Maria's (and the novel's) troubled ultimate liberation. Maria is "impervious to life about her" (245). She does "what she had to do," and yet she is also "sharply awakened now and then; so rudely were her eyes and mind opened that life seemed deeper in its joy and sorrow" (246). And again her changing, growing self manifests itself bodily in what amounts to a taxonomy of her values: identity, work, home, her life. "At these moments Maria felt with every sense in her body, felt the blood singing, yes, yes, to her work, her home, her life. And it was good" (246). Her inner self develops, and so does her motherly love, an interaction that once again is felt corporeally in a shared space and takes the form of an outward motion to reach outside her own self, toward someone else, a gesture that fulfills her: "And Maria felt good to be mother *to* them. She understood them, grew with them, was happy when they were near" (246; my italics).

For the moment, this inner growth serves her in her attempt to protect her children from the outside world of a decaying and unsafe neighborhood where people no longer "converse" and "boys hung around the beer tavern" downstairs from her apartment, in "a city of a million" where friends are nearly impossible to make (249). They are typical images of modern alienation and of the capitalist economic cycles. A last visit to the old neighborhood reiterates what she already knows, that her past is long gone. In front of this alienating dimension, work and the care of her home become her nutrients. "And Maria felt a deep satisfaction in knowing she was working, keeping her home together" (250), which makes her realize that she "was no longer the child wife" (251). For this very reason her long-gone past lives in herself as a source of strength and deliverance. "Somewhere inside her, part of Pepi, part of Mama Rosalie, the red blood of hard-working peasants was now released and, combining with the forces of motherhood, came to her deliverance" (252). As she internalizes these values, as these values become a part of her identity, the outer environment becomes psychologically less inimical. Likewise, she is able to turn money into a tool for living, assigning to money her own *values*: "Through her struggle with the problems of everyday living, through her job and the sharing of worries with others like herself, the city was becoming less and less the strange, hostile world outside. And fifteen dollars—she knew what that meant to her home and to her family, the difference between self-respect and humiliation, the difference between dignity and cringing poverty, the difference between health and decay" (252).

It is no coincidence that the obstacles to Maria's fulfillment, both in her personal life and in the outer world more closely related to the economic dimension of her life, are male generated. It is also no coincidence that the answer to these obstacles is working-class female mutuality. When the female workers get laid off, hundreds of them gather on a Saturday, a day of rest, and a kind of infection different from the money fever of the 1920s possesses them. "A sense of comradeship infected the women. 'We're all in the same boat,' Bertha said" (254). Here the choice of words is critical. "Comradeship" evokes a communal, intentionally participatory political dimension that emphasizes the female recognition of one's self in the fellow coworker. At the same time it reflects the distance from immigrants such as Mama Rosalie who do not understand the absence of work: "*Perché*—why is there no work?" (255). Her question indicates the lack of understanding in a preindustrial people of the industrial economic cycle; she thinks of labor as a manual and manly activity. "A man works with his hands," Pepi comments (151). Female comradeship also exposes the other-directed love of the politics of sharing that entails a hierarchy of values and needs: children, ill husbands, basic food, a home, an understanding of the exploitation of one's labor and its surplus value, and the essential materiality of human life. "'What am I going to feed my kid?' one woman shouts at the factory's manager." "'My husband needs a doctor' said another. 'What are we going to eat?' said another. 'Who's going to pay my rent?' 'Robbers,' one woman cried. 'Live on air if ye can get it,' said Tillie drily" (255).

The female polyphony reveals a hierarchical ladder that reaches its universality when the women understand that nobody is going to help them. One of them comments, "We're human, ain't we?" (257). It is the spark that ignites the assault on the factory's offices once they realize that the men who try to calm them have exactly what these women need and demand, that is to say, food, heat, and economic security:

> Horse cries, shrill notes, guttural oaths, the words of a hundred tongues met in one discordant symphony of hate and revenge. . . . The police were knocked aside, the man on the steps ran into the building; and the women rushed through the door after him. Into offices, tearing papers, overturning files, belaboring helpless secretaries, flinging books through windows, the women, young and old, swept like an irresistible flood through the building. Lunch boxes were torn open, water cans crushed, carpets ripped. (258)

Even Maria surrenders to the emotions that the riot liberates in her fellow workers. "Shy, self-conscious, timid Maria found herself shaken with an emotion stronger than reason, stronger than herself, and she followed the women running up the steps of the building" (258). In the end, however, after the protest is over, her acknowledgment of the materiality of the real returns. "Well . . . we still ain't got our jobs" (259), she tells Bertha, a comment that might as well be the most concise history of the Great Depression, as well as what forces Maria to return to depend on two men.

The first is her son Paul, who gets work unloading newspapers from trucks at night. The second is Morgantonio, one of the customers at her house when Dominic ran the wine business. Eventually she marries the latter, in one last desperate attempt to find protection from the outer forces that she still perceives as determining her life. "For months she had struggled against fear and poverty and the city, and here was an answer, here was protection from them" (272). The combination of class condition and urban modernity is still too big a force for Maria to overcome; she cannot entirely let go of the patriarchal culture of her past, given her need to protect her children, especially the younger ones.

Yet her second marriage is an illusion already announced in the modalities of its celebration. "There was no music, no altar, no Virgin Mary" (280). It comes to an end not when Morgantonio decides to leave her, but when Maria secretly decides to abort the child she is pregnant with. Thomas Ferraro has indicated the possibility to read this gesture as a moment of proto–1960s and 1970s feminism that dominates "contemporary ethnic North American autobiographical fiction" by way of unconscious incorporation in a subsequent work, Helen Barolini's *Umbertina* ("Catholic Ethnicity," 345). It is not difficult to see the reasons for such a reading. Yet we should also remember that Maria aborts secretly; that she is already a mother of three children; and that her gesture is not ideologically motivated. She is not advocating for a woman's rights over her body. Neither is there an affirmative negation in her abortion, as in the case of Kay Corleone. After all, Maria acknowledges that she is bearing a child, something that the feminists whom Ferraro has in mind would never agree with. Maria is not revolting against the reality of the ideology she inhabits. She experiences the inner overcoming of the ideology of her reality that allows her in the first place to rejoin men on her own terms, be with them on her own terms for the first and only time in her whole life, in the middle of the city that attracted and alienated her at once, a modern person in her own right, now really entering modernity, as even the crossing of the bridge *on her way home*, which she does "effortlessly," with no external constraint, tells us: "The whistle of a passenger train shrilled in Maria's ears. She shook her head and started to walk over the bridge once more. Men in overalls emerged from the flats, plodding silently homeward, and Maria joined them. She did this effortlessly, and she walked as one of them. Almost instinctively, during the last years since Dominic's departure and the beginning of her own struggle, she had shed her fear of the city. Without realizing it she, unlike Dominic, had experienced and achieved a sense of belonging" (304–5). This crossing of the bridge signals the entrance of the Italian American woman into modern America and the modern American novel. It occurs neither by way of forgetting the past nor by negating it, as Dominic tried to do. It is a liberation predicated on the realization that her past is stored inside her as a sudden voice of memory that fuels for one last time her bodily feelings, the thermometer of her material existence, of her historicity, we might say. "Now a voice seemed to speak to her, coming from some distant past, talking to her alone, softly, soothingly. How often in the last few months it happened this way, the voice talking to her, bringing memories. *Yes, Maria*, it would say, *those years are not so far away*. And always she gave in to it, feeling a sort of peace in listening and remembering" (309). Those memories elicit positive feelings intertwined with a sense of permanence because they acknowledge the inescapability of her past as well as the certainty that such a past will not return, as it should not. "Across time and space memories fled, and the voice talked, and all faces and all things came together" (310).

The memories transcend time and space, faces and things. For the first time, faces and things are one and the same. Likewise, her daughter Lucy's presence, the living presence of the forward movement of history, signifies the possibilities to come: "Sixteen, the outline of her face sharper, her breast firm, her movements becoming more graceful . . . bubbling with laughter, for no good reason, perhaps, except the wonder at the changes in her. Not like the old people, few words of Italian on her lips, her very features were different; voice, gestures, words, cast in another mold" (311). As Lucy falls asleep next to her, "Maria stretched out her hand, touched her warm young body." Maria's own limbs, the organs that, during her abortion, had been "shaking, insides burning with shooting pains tearing and searing flesh" (297), are now "less tired" (312). It is the last corporeal, entirely female image of the novel that closes the circular motion typical of female narrative by a gifted male writer who clearly had read his Joyce carefully.

Like *Ulysses*, *Maria* too ends with the point of view of its female central character who lies in bed thinking about her life. Unlike *Ulysses*, however, in *Maria* there is no final yes. In the first place because there is no man left in her life; second, because DeCapite knew that it was not his job as a male writer at this point in the novel to speak for her. Consequently, unlike in Joyce's other masterpiece, *Finnegans Wake*, the last sentence of *Maria* is slightly different from the opening one. Whereas in the first line of the novel Maria "lay awake" all night fearing the coming of the dawn, in the closing sentence, as "the sounds of the night had ceased," she "lay awake for a long time in the dark," thinking thoughts undisclosed to the reader, as if DeCapite confessed that now that Maria is liberated he cannot enter her mind or, which is the same, that he does not know how to end the novel (312). And yet, whatever she is thinking, Maria is no longer fearful. Helen Barolini has written that, in the end, "by accepting the maternal role as more important, [Maria] is acting as the male author thinks she should" (16), an evaluation that on the one hand recalls what Nancy Armstrong has called the feminist "rhetoric of victimization," as if the novel happened "in a domain of experience outside of political history" (1,323). On the other hand, it entirely discounts the fact that in the realm of fiction, such a history concerns, in the first place, the production of a book. The publication of *Maria* was its male author's way to acknowledge that the future should and would be different from the present. For this reason the first page of the book carries DeCapite's dedication to the woman in whose name he wrote it: "For My Mother."

IV

Between the beginning of the 1950s and the early 1970s there are no significant characters named Maria in Italian American novels. Some of the factors to consider for this absence are the following: twenty years of Cold War, which attempted to freeze, if not reverse altogether, the evolving gender structure of our society; unprecedented economic growth enjoyed by a vast section of the population, including Italian Americans, an advancement that facilitated the birth of the civil rights movement and contributed to make whiteness easily accessible for the Eastern European and Mediterranean ethnics, especially thanks to intermarriage, of which Joe DiMaggio's and Frank Sinatra's unions with Marilyn Monroe and Ava Gardner respectively are chief examples; the election of the first Catholic president, albeit an Irish Bostonian, which is to say, a representative of that strain of Roman Catholicism that supported republicanism in opposition to the same British Crown against which the American colonies had fought; Pope Paul VI's epochal decision to implement a new doctrine that officially elevated the Virgin Mary to the desexualized role of mother of God; the access of previously excluded segments of the ethnic population to higher education, which propelled the development of Italian American female writing best chronicled in Helen Barolini's anthology *The Dream Book*, as well as the concomitant rise of the postmodern novel.

One of the many benefits of the development of Italian American female writing is the new way men started writing about men on the one hand and women wrote now about women on the other. Female writers also enriched our understanding of the immigrant phase of the Italian American experience, as well as of the Great Depression, which became the focus of important novels such as Marion Benasutti's *No Steady Job for Papa*; Julia Savarese's *The Weak and the Strong*, which includes an interesting, however brief racial twist represented by the micro-story of a female character named Belle and her husband; and Antonia Pola's *Who Can Buy the Stars?*, an unachieved spinoff of DeCapite's *Maria*. Such focus and the development of novels by women, however, did not correspond to the demands of the emerging postmodern novel that moved away from the realist style of the Depression era. The chief example of these late-realist works, though by a man, is Mario Puzo's *The Fortunate Pilgrim*, one of the most achieved ethnic novels about urban America in the early twentieth century that had the misfortune to be written in the 1960s, when that America was on its way to extinction. No wonder that it sold next to nothing. In terms of writing, the most accomplished Italian American novel written by a woman, Tina De Rosa's *Paper Fish*, appeared only in 1980. And so it is not surprising that a powerful Maria character appeared in the early 1970s, on the eve of the beginning of the disintegration of the social block and the political compact that Franklin Roosevelt built during the New Deal that essentially guaranteed thirty years of social and economic stability. This incarnation of Maria surfaces in the songs of Bruce Springsteen, a community college dropout graced with phenomenal storytelling talent, and the son of a first-generation Italian American woman.

In Springsteen's songbook, Maria returns in an interconnected number of linguistic variations, from the Mary of early compositions such as "Mary Queen of Arkansas" and the Mary Lou of "Does This Bus Stop at 82nd Street?" to the Mary of "Thunder Road"—the song that Springsteen considers an invitation to the journey of his music—via the Mary of "The River" and the one of "Maria's Bed," to name a few. The name's variations register the chronological distance between the experience of the immigrants and the integration of the post–World War II American-born generations in the social fabric of the country. The variations also address the changing ethnic composition of the country and the Italian American writers' ability and need to deal with these changes. The Maria trope embodies Springsteen's politics of sharing, the recognition of the other, as well as what might be his biggest accomplishment as a writer, the intertwining of female subjectivity with the historical memory of the United States in the forms of the musical references, the places, and the characters of his genuinely American music.

In "Thunder Road," Mary is neither a desexualized mother nor an evil whore. The narrator implores her to climb in his car and leave their "town full of losers" with him because he does not want to go back to the solitude of his home, of post-Vietnam and post-Watergate America, of 1975 rock and roll that lost many of its icons and no longer has Roy Orbison to comfort the lonely with his singing. In its place, there is now a "love filled with defeat," a radical indictment of the state of the country, as Springsteen writes in "Backstreets." The hopeless and angry narrator's search for home begins by leaving home. Unlike him, Mary is neither hopeless, nor does she intend to escape. When he sees her, she is dancing on the porch of her home, the liminal site that stands between her and the open space that traditionally in our culture promises hope for better days to come. In the eyes of the narrator, all Mary needs to do is cross that border and climb in his car. Like a modern, urban Huck Finn at the steering wheel of his automobile, the prime American symbol of male escapism (disguised as freedom), he wants to light out for the territory ahead and find the heaven that lies in wait for the two of them.

It is an unusual invitation, because the narrator lacks the assertive masculinity supposedly at the heart of rock and roll music. Equally unusual is Mary's correspondent lack of physical beauty. He is not a hero, and she is not a beauty. Their characterization is reinforced by lyrics that denote an inverted Catholic mental landscape. For example, the narrator's redemption lies underneath the hood of his motorcar, on the tangible earth, in the hidden work of the engine, not in the heavenly and unreachable sky. Yet in the end this anxious invitation subscribes to the ideology of competition that rewards a single winner that the logic of exchange value demands. The last verse of the song sets in binary opposition the previously mentioned "town full of losers" and what seems to be the narrator's psychological need to leave behind, indeed to get rid of that place: "And I am pulling out of here to win." The logic of the end of the song responds to the logic of self-interested individualism at the expenses of a community that the narrator considers lost and, more important, that he has no interest whatsoever in trying to rebuild, because he does not believe that it can be rebuilt in the first place.

Mary's presence and her position in the story, in the text, are evidence of the limit of a partial freedom, the insufficiency of the narrator's individual effort that undermines his search for companionship, even the dimension of self-delusion that his psychosocial desire entails. Naturally, the point of view of the song is that of the man. Mary has no voice in it. However, she finds a different way to speak. In *4th of July, Asbury Park*, Daniel Wolff has noted that when the text ends Mary is still on the porch, at home—perhaps still dancing, I would add, since the music continues. She resists the narrator's call. At the same time, halfway through the record the subject pronoun "I" that closes "Thunder Road" with the bombastic dichotomy between one winner against a community of losers becomes a "we." The singular "I" of "Thunder Road" turns into the plural "we" of the record's title track. The winner-and-losers dichotomy disappears. In its place there is a communal search for love. Escapism guarantees neither salvation nor a stable collective identity. Mary signals this discrepancy. Whereas the narrator wants to leave behind a community of losers, she forces him to leave behind his idea of home as the fulfillment of a limited, individual freedom as the outcome of self-interest. She forces him to face the harsh realities of a community under threat that is falling apart in *The River* when the two characters of "Thunder Road" reappear in the record's title track and find themselves in a trap different from the suicidal urban environment of "Born to Run." The trap is now Mary's unwanted pregnancy, her body, and an economic crisis that costs decent jobs. The description of her wedding, with the absence of the usual human and material choreography that traditionally is present for such an occasion, could be the description of the second wedding of Maria in DeCapite's first novel. In this context, Springsteen repositions Mary in a more central role to make the class condition and class relations shine with a dark light. If the economic forces reveal the characters' social conditions, so does Mary's pregnancy, as to indicate a causal interdependence between the two.

In "Thunder Road," Mary unmasks the vacuity of male escapism. In "The River," the story of an accidental pregnancy and the social and psychological repercussions of economic depression on a young working-class couple, she reveals her and the narrator's social origins and the nature of class conditions in the United States, encapsulated at the very beginning of the song in three short lines that link the personal "I," the "referential "they," and the collective "we" that, according to Janet Zandy, characterizes working-class narrative voices (*What We Hold*, xiv). In "Thunder Road," we are told where the narrator wants to go. In "The River," we are told where he is coming from, which is the valley of the opening line of the song where the class dimension of one's life identifies intergenerational destiny, the cold fact that sons end up doing the exact same thing that their father did, as the narrator states in the first stanza. The social origins determine the narrator's future at the moment of his birth. His future is his father's past. His class condition denies him the possibility of overcoming accidents and mistakes such as his high school girlfriend's unwanted pregnancy. His original working-class condition determines his possibilities and choices, or the lack thereof. It is his personal manifest destiny. The narrator evokes memories that haunt him because the economy provides little work. Even the union card he received on his nineteenth birthday is no longer a shelter in a society whose social contract is about to be crushed by the economic structure and forces that produce the lack of work—and the job that is available does not pay as well as the previous one. Mary's silence reflects this situation. It is the cipher of the complete lack of individual female agency in front of the ongoing dismantling of the social contract that at least kept working-class communities together. In addition, even individual salvation in the guise of the illusion of escapism is no longer available. The American dream is no longer disappearing, as it was five years earlier in *Born to Run*. It is gone. Something else will need to replace it, something to help maintain, if not a tangible and relatively stable community, a meaningful sense of such a thing.

No wonder that in "The River," unlike in "Thunder Road," Mary is not the only character who has no voice. The narrator has no direct voice all the way through the last part of the song. Halfway through the song, precisely when he says that because of the economy there is not much work for him, his voice becomes a memory that haunts both him and his wife. The factor that determines their lives and turns memories into a "curse," a word that again reflects a religious, Catholic mental landscape, is the nature of class relations among men and women. The things that previously seemed to matter now "vanish into the air," an utterly nonideological statement that echoes Marx and Engels's utterly ideological statement in *The Communist Manifesto*, according to which "all that is solid melts into air," one of the two novelties of modernity, according to the German philosophers, along with the profanation of the sacred.

As Springsteen's world is increasingly under threat, Mary returns, this time, however, as Maria in "Highway Patrolman," the woman whom the economically fallen Joe Roberts weds. Unlike in "Thunder Road," now Maria dances together with both her husband Joe and his brother, the same thing she does in "Reason to Believe," where Springsteen begins to conceive of unity as a possible starting point of rebirth for the previously mentioned disintegrated sense of a community in urgent need to be rebuilt. Springsteen seems to establish a correlation between the appearance of at least a semblance of unity and the name variations for his favorite female characters that point toward a differentiated plurality rooted in his musical sources and the forms of his music. They are ethnic names such as Maria in "Highway Patrolman" and Mary Lou in "Reason to Believe," another song in which the fable of the work ethic as the path to individual success is chastised in the refrain, the section of the song more directly indebted to the blues. By reiterating the central message of the song in the refrain, Springsteen also underlines the importance of the cultural and political value of a black musical form and the interplay between words and music. In addition, "Reason to Believe" initiates a more developed representation of its central female character. Mary Lou swears to work for her man every day and bring her salary home, another element the song shares with the blues and with female blues singers especially. When Johnny leaves her, her initial reaction is to wait for his return, which is the one fact that puzzles the narrator, whose voice mediates the relationship between Mary Lou and Johnny. More important, she now provides work and money, traditionally the stuff of men and husbands. Responsibility is no longer a man's job. It falls on the woman, who is no longer relegated to the home, as she is not in "Car Wash," where Mary becomes the helping hand for a mother of two children, her friend Catherine, who works at a car wash until it is time to pick up her kids from school.

Class alienation does not distinguish when it comes to gender. Gender does, thereby complicating and enriching the notion of class. The result is the unveiling of the brutality of a life that powerful men dominate. Men are absent both physically and from their responsibility as fathers. When they appear, they represent a gendered social structure. Catherine works for a dollar and a dime, she hates her boss, and she washes all the luxury cars that at once reflect the class dimension of her job and dictate the schedule of her life as a single mother. Catherine metaphorically rejects and erases this condition and the status that is attached to it when she sings that she washes every single car she gets, "From Mercedes to vw's/I do 'em all and I don't favor none." Once again the language individuates social identity, class, and status. Once again a low-class woman represents work. At the same time, this woman is a single mother who is forced to confront three interconnected factors: male power, which is represented by her boss at the car wash and the handsome man that she pictures handing her a million-dollar recording contract in the final part of the song;[1] the social status embodied by the European cars, traditionally a symbol of sophistication and elegance that reinforces the image of Catherine's lower social condition and the impossibility to step out of it; and the subversion of the symbolic order that commonly paired work and responsibility with man. There is, however, a fourth element. Not only is her world presented from her female standpoint. Now Springsteen also pairs the Mary character with female comradeship against a male-controlled world. This opposition is even stronger because the symbol of Catherine's condition is the most powerful symbol of male identity in America: the automobile. The car that in "Thunder Road" fueled the narrator's dream of the promised land and Mary's refusal to climb in it now identifies the way gender alters class relations, as well as Catherine's and Mary's rejection of female alienation.

As the world around him grows increasingly atomized and conflictual, Springsteen's Maria trope acknowledges this change accordingly. In such a world not even a home can provide a secure shelter from the outer brutalities. Rather, home becomes their reflection. At the same time, it also becomes a way to reject another kind of individualism: self-isolation. There is no illusion whatsoever that the tempests that invest the others in the outer space can be avoided inside, in the individual, privately owned, and supposedly safe space of one's house. The ties that link wives and husbands and, especially, mothers and sons are also altered and severed. In "Straight Time," Mary watches her husband, an ex-convict, standing on the porch pondering his half-free condition. The place the narrator of "Thunder Road" invited Mary to leave to accompany him in his search for belonging has become the site of psychological alienation. In "The Rising," Mary is the concrete memory of hope for the firefighter who climbs the stairs not to reach heaven, but to find the hell that will prevent him from returning home to his dear, as well as the place where life can begin again, where the music is played, "Mary's

Place"; whereas in "Jesus Was an Only Son," Mary represents a mother who cries at the biggest of the indignities, the loss of a child, as any mother would do. It is yet another symbolic subversion of institutional Catholicism. Nothing specifically religious attaches to a mother crying over the death of her son, especially when this is the mother of all mothers, so to speak; rather, motherhood and the severed link between a mother and a son are the elements that the song presents. In "Reno," instead, Mary is the wife the narrator lost that mere sexual intercourse cannot replace. Sex, however, is the twist of Springsteen's last transformation of the Maria character. It is the source that transforms her into the embodiment of the singer-songwriter's unshakable faith in his music, in his craft, in his art. Nothing shines like the light of Maria's bed, Springsteen sings in "Maria's Bed." And what happens under the blankets creates the music that allows Springsteen to liberate, revisit, and elaborate his heritage in dialogue and in contact with a plurality of voices and characters. Maria allows him to certify these voices' and characters' humanity; to testify to the struggling condition of an autobiographical family's past and his contemporary American present; to interlock different people and generations, their stories and their histories; to liberate one's individual memory in order to reach out to the others and deny their oblivion; to erect a shared differentiated memory, as Carol Maso also does in her first novel *Ghost Dance*, a tour de force committed to piecing together the many fragments of a multiethnic past in order to build a present identity.

Unlike Springsteen, Maso is self-conscious of her past in her literary debut. Unlike her fellow New Jerseyan, Maso focuses her narrative on one single character, nineteen-year-old college student Vanessa. However, perhaps surprisingly, the main difference between these two writers is not gender but class. Whereas Springsteen writes from the perspective of working-class marginalized people about working-class marginalized life in the present as a reconstructing process of personal and artistic self-discovery, Maso's story is about a middle-class, college-educated family whose working-class past is hidden, although not entirely lost, in the apparently successful immigrant story of the main character's Italian American grandparents, Angelo and Maria, especially Angelo's attempt to assimilate. He achieves his goal by way of erasing his Italian identity. Yet Angelo seems restless and drawn to otherness, here exemplified by African Americans and by the Native American chief he goes to visit at one point, an otherness that he seems to transmit to his son Michael and his granddaughter Vanessa. Vanessa uses her father to describe her grandfather. Michael watches Angelo "chopping the tomato plants into pieces" in the garden of his home, already a sign of being an Italian in America. The scene provides the context for a series of rhetorical questions about the assimilation process in America and historical memory:

"Are [they] Americans now, not Italians? Did his father announce that there will be no more Italian spoken in his house? No more wine drunk with lunch, as he burned the grapevines? Did he tell his wife there would be no more sad songs from the old country?" This scene makes Vanessa wonder if this is what her father "is forgetting," which is what the young girl needs to reconstruct (74).

Like Dominic in DeCapite's *Maria*, Angelo wants to learn English. He takes English classes, to which he also drags his wife. Also like Dominic, he wants his accent to disappear. "The accent must go" (77). He even tells his wife that she needs to change her name to Mary as he is changing his to Andy, a request that Maria promptly refuses. "I was given a name at birth and I will die with it, Angelo" (76). Maria's answer marks the difference between the two, a difference that at the basic level sums up the larger one between the Italian American men and women we have examined thus far. Angelo gets lost in his effort to assimilate, to make it in America, which demands he becomes white. He pretends to forget his past in spite of his aesthetic attraction to "the dress of the Negroes whom he considered the most authentic Americans" because they "were new and exotic like America itself" and because, "above all they were not Europeans" (77). On the contrary, Maria ends up resisting and even attempting to subvert the assimilation process.

If there is a generational link between the characters of *Ghost Dance*, it is the women's confrontation with the modern world and the men's observation of them doing so. From the very first line of the novel, modernity and women are interweaved. "She is standing under the great clock in Grand Central Station and she is waiting for me," says Vanessa, referring to her mother, Christine, who is returning from a trip to Maine (5). The train station is the modern urban environment, the train the equivalent of the machine age. The great clock signals the passing of time, an image that her mother reiterates later in the novel. "Just listen to that engine, Vanessa. It's the modern age, all right! There's no turning back now" (44). The final destination is death, the erasure of chronological and biological time. "Death was something we once invented long ago," quips Vanessa after meeting her mother in Grand Central (6). The triangulation between modernity, time, and death, or, modernity as temporality, is what Vanessa tries to overcome in her search for what her grandmother Maria stands for in the novel, what Vanessa tries to reach by reconstructing her own self: beauty. And beauty for Maso is the equivalent of home. "It was beauty that united us that day. Though vastly different, we were all lovers of beauty, lovers of a place called home" (47), Vanessa says at one point, recalling a rally in New York City, in so doing extending the meaning of her search for home beyond the strict family and

Italian American boundaries, a necessary move that, in the multiethnic world she inhabits, secures ethnicity as a meaningful part of one's identity.

Ethnicity, however, is not a self-enclosed, autonomous trait. It is up front in the characterization and even the politics of the grandparents. During the civil rights era, Grandpa Angelo sides with black Americans. "They are blocking the doors in the same way Negroes are being blocked from jobs and houses and schools," he protests at a rally (126). Grandpa Sarkis, Vanessa's maternal grandfather, is an Armenian who wants to return to his native land after a life of hard work in a mill under the Americanized name "Frank Wing"; he wishes to reclaim his real name, Sarkis Wingarian. Ethnicity also takes the form of the way spaces are envisioned and subject positions are inverted. Most of the novel takes place in the various homes of the family's characters and other closed environments. The outside, the modern, urban world is, in prototypical Italian American fashion, a dangerous place even in a time when old barriers no longer exist. The real breadwinner of Vanessa's family is her mother Christine, an accomplished poet who has a lesbian affair with a French woman, Sabine. Vanessa lives off the royalties of her mother's first book of poems after Christine's death. Her father, Michael, a graduate of Princeton, where he was "probably not a very popular person," is the one who adjusts his life to the needs of his wife's career (21). His adjustment foregrounds the reversal of gender and parental roles that Maso engineers: the father is the one who tends to the children as they grow as well as the person who cooks. "I loved to watch my father cook. He was so animated in the kitchen: measuring, testing, timing, my father the scientist flourishing among the food," Vanessa comments (45). Michael and the kids even welcome home the traveling mother with a dinner. "We made intricate dinners the days of my mother's homecomings with five and six courses and desserts," Vanessa recalls (45). His wife and her work define Michael because he is perfect for what she does and what he wanted. "My father was comfortable in the quiet. It made the silence in him seem not so strange. . . . Had loquaciousness and vivacity been demanded for my mother to write, my father could not have done it. For years, his speechlessness, his hushed tones, his silences have been legitimized by my mother's art" (109). Vanessa even states that her father "had already dedicated the rest of his life to her" when he first saw her "across the hall at a college dance" (174).

In one of the several radiating links of Maso's writing style that technically unite the grandmother and the granddaughter, Michael's mother Maria reiterates this comment when she says that Michael, not his wife, was the one who gave up professional achievement. "He could have been a nuclear physicist" (174). Maria even argues that Christine was the driving force in the relationship—structurally speaking, a complete displacement of the role of the Italian American husband. "He said he was happy . . . but I never saw it. It was as if your mother was dragging him further and further into her own private world" (174). His happiness came with the kids, she continues. "I don't think your father was ever really happy until you and Fletcher were born," Maria tells her granddaughter (174). And Vanessa, standing patriarchy on its head, concludes, "My father was the first feminist I ever met" (123), a statement that in turn the grandmother complements by standing Vito Corleone's ultimate patriarchal line on its head: "Your mother, it seemed, never had any time for you" (174).

And yet, Maria is the one who subverts the established culture of twentieth-century gender position when she sees her daughter-in-law and her female lover embracing and "touching each other like man and woman," an act she had witnessed already as a young girl in Italy (151). Although she writes, stamps, and seals a letter to her son to tell him what she witnessed, in the end she decides to miss the postman. Her gesture is the Italian American female equivalent of Huckleberry Finn tearing apart the letter to Miss Watson and, symbolically speaking, a liberating act for Italian American female novelists writing after *Ghost Dance*, perhaps even more so than after the traditionalist radicalism of Diane di Prima's *Memoirs of a Beatnik* and *Recollections of My Life as a Woman*. It is also a summary, a reconfiguration, and a (temporary) conclusion of the Maria trope that we have mapped. The force and the credibility of her gesture is not Maria's sudden activism for lesbian rights, which obviously is not the case. Neither does Maria miss the postman because of some false sense of bourgeois respectability. Simply put, she recognizes the givenness of reality, which is what makes the comparison with Huckleberry Finn plausible—although, of course, her gesture does not carry the burden and the historical significance of Huck's action. This is modern life as it is. And it reveals itself as old, transnational, and transcultural as it can be, as the fact that she saw the same act happen in Italy "over fifty years ago" illustrates (151). There is no point, as there should not be, in stopping it.

The recognition of the givenness of reality distinguishes Maria. When her husband brings home a piece of wood, the two grandchildren, Vanessa and Fletcher, marvel at it. To them it resembles a big slingshot or a wishbone, but to Maria "it looks like a piece of junk" (89). Likewise, she transcends the institutional version of Catholicism that is an important part of the family's heritage, as the names Angelo and Maria and that of their son Michael tell us. "My grandmother," writes Vanessa, "despite years of mass, believed that the end was the end" (80).

Paradoxically—and again paradoxes are one of the rhetorical figures that take us to the core of modernity—Maria's acknowledgment of the givenness of life is what fueled her painful respect for her husband's desire to assimilate as well as what leads her to retake ownership of her Italian self after Angelo's death, an event that aptly occurs at her home. There, shortly before Maria dies, Vanessa sees her grandmother dancing as if she had been bitten "by the tarantula of Italian folklore, the spider with a venom so potent that it had made her people crazy for centuries with the irresistible urge to dance" (222). It is the proper Dionysian conclusion that recuperates the pagan roots of Southern Italian history and culture, a reappropriation that the language, the food, and the music complete. "Your grandfather never let me speak Italian in the house. . . . He never let me cook my own food. I missed that so much. . . . My people always loved music. My father played the mandolin like an angel" (223). It is also an admission of the suffering and the loss that Italian American women experienced in America and an indication that one's culture and history neither disappear nor can they be erased. And it is a way of pointing out where to start from to make that culture and history shared memory, the precondition to move forward and go home, as Vanessa and her brother do at the end of the novel after their mother's death in a car accident, another image of modernity as a technological threat. "Her final word 'home,'" writes Maso (244); that elusive home that always escaped the mother but that her daughter finally reaches. "This is our home, Fletcher. It's ours now, too," Vanessa tells her brother (274).

In this home Vanessa experiences her last recollection before she and her brother say their final good-bye to their mother. A metaphor of whiteness introduces this final recollection. "I was up to my thighs in snow. It was exhausting to walk through so much white" (266). This is the moment of Vanessa's final liberation, the sign that she is now free and able to put together all the pieces of her identity. She understands that the pieces of her (hi)story are the people that makes her who she is: her Armenian grandfather, her mother's lover Sabine "far off in France," her "Grandpa and Grandma speaking their last words in Italian" (274), her brother Fletcher, and her father who "croons in the dark room with Frank Sinatra" (273), bodily translator of Maria's fondest memory—"my people always loved music"—as well as her suggestion for us as to where to look in order to complete our journey home.

[6]

THE DAGO AND THE DARKY: STAGING SUBVERSION

Long before there were Southerners in the U.S.A. there were Southerners in Italy, and it also meant a certain climate, a certain hospitality, a certain musicality in the language, and sometimes even a certain kind of violence and a tendency to vendetta. In the more learned circles, the European vision of the Southerner is much like that of anyone who understands our South: the feeling created is that of an easeful relationship to culture and a deep spontaneity that says, deep down—the point of learning how to cook all this food and talk this way and wear these fine clothes is to have a good goddam time, man!—Albert Murray to Stanley Crouch, in *Notes of a Hanging Judge*

I went to see The Temptations last night. They were all white.
—Dion DiMucci, in *Live New York City*, 1987

People talk about the white soul singers. You know, there's a lot of names that come up, but Eddy [Brigati] and Felix [Cavaliere], I am telling you right now: To sound that black, you had to be Italian!
—Steven Van Zandt, "The Rascals Induction into the Rock and Roll Hall of Fame,"
  1997

We were the rock and roll Rat Pack. I was Dean, Bruce was Frank, and Clarence was Sammy on steroids.—Steven Van Zandt, July 20, 2015, 6:03 p.m. Tweet

NOWHERE ELSE DOES the relationship among Italian Americans, African Americans, and modernity become as clear and tricky, and therefore as enlightening, as on the stage of popular music, to which we turn by looking at two partnerships that epitomize such relationship: Frank Sinatra and Sammy Davis Jr., and Bruce Springsteen and Clarence Clemons. Two moments crystallize the significance of these partnerships. The first is a 1958 live performance by Sinatra and Davis of "Me and My Shadow," a song that Billy Rose wrote and Dave Dreyer composed in 1927 for Al Jolson, popularized by Whispering Jack Smith, and ever since a favorite of an endless list of singers and entertainers. Among them was Ted Lewis, who gave the song a racial twist in the 1930s when he started performing it followed by a black usher named Eddy Chester in the role of his shadow, an act that functioned as the antecedent of Sinatra's and Davis's rendition, as we shall see. The second is the celebrated photograph of Springsteen and Clemons on the cover of the Jersey Devil's 1975 record *Born to Run*, which stands as the visual translation of their interaction on the stage. Several articles, speeches, and interviews that Sinatra and Springsteen wrote and gave over the years provide the context of these partnerships, especially with regard to Sinatra's and Springsteen's understanding of their roles as modern artists, the politics of their art, and their conscious consideration of the place of blackness in their development and identity as American artists of Italian descent.

Because these are staged performances, what we face when these biracial duos en*act* them is the co-participatory performance of a performance that plays out a pattern of shared symbolic investments, transfers, and sociocultural codes. The result is essential, willed (one is even tempted to say *raw*) ideological meaning that the bodies of these artists actualize. The bodies connect the stage, the music, the lyrics, as well as the technological equipment that amplifies the performance and makes it available for a mass audience. In this way, these bodies add a surplus of meaning to the songs being executed that their processes of engagement translate and historicize. If it is true that performances translate social aspects of a culture, we need to account for the fact that, at least in terms of temporality, cultural forms are also translations of one's past. Thus, what I am after here is a close reading of these biracial bodily engagements as interplays of reciprocating identities that create what historian Nancy Carnevale, speaking of early twentieth-century Italian American theater performer Farfariello, has termed "a positive space for difference," where difference is per*form*ed in order *to be seen* (135).

Sinatra and Davis and Springsteen and Clemons formed the two most important biracial artistic duos of American popular music because of the (hi)story that they em*body*. It is an American (hi)story in so far as we recognize that it begins, albeit at different times and in different ways, somewhere else. No less significant is the fact that these duos have been appropriated outside their national borders. Moreover, their partnerships lasted for decades and continue to last in the sense of artistic recognition, thus transcending whatever meaning their mere chronology might have. Their enduring recognition marks their modernity. It tells a modern tale, one that takes us to the core of the story told in this book.

Beyond the immense talent of these artists, it was technological advancements and the rise of mass culture, in parallel with the development of twentieth-century modernity, that helped propel their careers. For example, in *Why Sinatra Matters*, Peter Hamill explains how the microphone and the ways Sinatra used it were an integral part of his early success, especially with the female audience that formed a predominant part of his followers at the time. Gene Lees too stresses the importance of this technological device for Sinatra's artistic achievements. Lees relates Sinatra's playing of the microphone to his masterly "naturalistic phrasing," a technique he had drawn from Billie Holiday. "He had completely abandoned the previous approach to the microphone, that of standing bravely facing it, using the hands for dramatic emphasis. Sinatra was moving the mike in accordance with what he was singing. And he was the man who developed this technique" (96). If the microphone helped his singing, the radio helped his fame. It made him a household name from coast to coast, the first Italian American who happened not to be a gangster to earn such an achievement, much to the dislike of the Hearst Corporation. Bruce Springsteen too owes much of his success to the development of media forms. The advent of MTV and music videos in the early 1980s turned him and his E Street Band from recognized musicians, especially at the national level, to a planetary phenomenon.

Because of their transnational dimension, the context of race relations and whiteness in post–World War II American popular music intersects mass culture as it has rarely done before. The debt of white American performers to black music and musicians is a well-known and documented fact. It is the cause of a continuing debate over white appropriations of black cultural forms for financial profit, as well as the perpetuation and geographical expansion of white normativity. For all these reasons, in terms of the symbolic domains that are the appropriate framework of these kinds of acts, Sinatra and Davis and Springsteen and Clemons are uniquely relevant duos. These artists acknowledged each other's presence as necessary to their musical and personal identity, which is especially significant because their anomaly occurred within media context that either stereotyped or erased from the consideration of their artistic partnership the significance of Sinatra's and Springsteen's ethnicity, which is what I intend to account for here.

Such media representation cuts both ways. Two examples will suffice here. When Sinatra died, the outlets that habitually frame the so-called national discourse in our country recalled in typical assimilation fashion his Italian origins and, of course, his controversial connections to organized crime. The one exception was the black magazine *Jet*, the only "mainstream" publication to underscore Sinatra's lifelong relationship with and support of African Americans, as well as his racial politics. And yet, not once in the very long, informative, and politically salient June 1, 1998, *Jet* article adamantly titled "Blacks Mourn the Death of the Frank Sinatra That Nobody Knows"

can one read that Sinatra was an Italian American or the son of Italian immigrants, let alone that Sinatra considered his background and identity the
prime factor in his understanding and view of race relations, which might as
well be the reason why nobody knew *that* Sinatra.

Similarly, hardly any commentator, regardless of popular medium, has
attempted to dig into Springsteen's ethnic background and its relationship
to blackness, even when the singer-songwriter offered them a chance, as
he did when he included the last names of his Irish and Italian families in
"American Land," a late nineteenth-century poem by an Eastern European
steelworker turned to music by Pete Seeger that Springsteen rewrote, performed, and recorded on two different occasions. The first time was in *We
Shall Overcome: The Seeger Sessions* (American Land Edition), which includes a live recording of "American Land" that Springsteen introduces as
"an immigrant song"; the second time was an in-studio version bonus track
in his 2009 Great Recession record *Wrecking Ball*. When in 2012 Springsteen told *Rolling Stone* magazine that he was only one generation removed
from Southern Italy, where he had recently performed, the interviewer made
no attempt to elaborate on this information that the man universally known
for being born in the U.S.A. had just provided him with. Neither did the
journalist try to connect this immigrant past to Springsteen's working-class
iconic status. Likewise, hardly anybody has attempted to interrogate the
possibilities that such iconic status might entail if connected to his lifelong
partnership with an African American male musician.

And yet, even in this regard Springsteen offered plenty of chances to address the issue. *Born to Run* is the only album cover of a globally recognized
white American rock and roller that is defined by the presence of a black
man on it. The record that followed *Born to Run* in 1978 includes the word
"Darkness" in the title. Two years later, in "Sherry Darling," a song from his
platinum record *The River*, the singer first tells his girlfriend that he is tired
of hearing her mother complaining while he drives her to the unemployment
office as he does every Monday morning. Then, he tells her that if the woman
continues to complain she will take the subway to go back to the "ghetto
where she lives." Four years later, in "My Hometown," one of the many singles from his blockbuster *Born in the U.S.A.* record, Springsteen explicitly
addressed the racial fights in his high school in the middle of the 1960s and
the closing of the textile factory that provided job security and economic
stability to many in his hometown. No wonder that most if not all commentators were caught by surprise when Springsteen directly tackled the issue
of race in "(41 Shots) American Skin" in 2000, a song inspired by the killing
of a young black immigrant from central Africa. These kinds of critical over-
sights, which by way of negation are forms of appropriation, are even more

telling in light of the recognition and the artistic appropriation of Sinatra's and Springsteen's music by contemporary popular African American artists such as Jay Z, the Notorious B.I.G., Ben Harper, and Living Colour, as well as the NAACP's official recognition of both artists for their artistic work.

Unlike the mainstream media, for Sinatra and Springsteen neither the importance of their musical cooperation with black artists nor the role of their identity in shaping such cooperation and their music escaped their attention. Hamill reports that Sinatra justified his racial politics on historical ground. When asked about the reason for his support of black artists and the NAACP, in his typical fashion Sinatra evoked historical mutuality: "Because we've [the Italian Americans] been there too, man. It wasn't just black people hanging from the end of those fucking ropes" (45). Even after his (in)famous move to the right side of the political spectrum, Sinatra continued to voice his opposition to racism. In the summer of 1991, on the occasion of the Fourth of July celebration that followed the beating of African American Rodney King by several white policemen, Sinatra penned an op-ed for the *Los Angeles Times* titled "The Haters and Bigots Will Be Judged: Some Words from a 'Saloon Singer' to Those Who Still Haven't Figured Out the Whole Point of America." In it, he took issue with the "haters spewing their poisons" and the "flag wavers who wave it one day a year," while he made the case for "equality" as the ultimate meaning of American independence. "Equality is what *our* Independence Day is all about" (my italics).

This was not the first time that Ol' Blue Eyes had penned an article about race in the United States. In July 1945, he had published a longer, more articulated and poignant piece in *Magazine Digest* titled "Let's Not Forget We're ALL Foreigners." The then thirty-five-year-old number-one swooner begins the piece by recalling the time when in school he experienced verbal discrimination along with Jewish and African American kids. Sinatra makes the case for one's historical memory as a defining element of one's individual and collective identity. "I haven't forgotten the things that happened to me during my school days . . . a bunch of guys threw rocks at me and called me a little Dago. I know now why they used to call the Jewish kids in the neighborhood 'Kikes' and 'Sheenies' and the colored kids 'niggers'" ("Let's Not Forget," 8). Right from the beginning, Sinatra establishes his memory as an Italian American and aligns it to that of Jewish and African American kids. However, he refrains from positioning himself on the same hierarchical level of either Jewish Americans or African Americans. He knows that he is writing soon after his native country concluded a war with fascist enemies in Europe, one of them being the native country of his parents. Rather, his school memory is a tool to establish blackness as the paradigm of otherness and the point of reference for the hierarchy of social exclusion in America.

and re-centers difference and equality in order to fashion the idea of collective action. "This is our job—your job and my job, and the job of generations growing up—to stamp out the prejudices that are separating one group of American citizens from another" (10). Popular music goes beyond entertainment for entertainment's sake. Better yet, popular entertainment entails a social and political collective dimension. It has an impact on and a responsibility toward a nation's citizenry, because by virtue of its potential in helping to eradicate prejudice, in creating the conditions for such eradication, it transcends the sole status of a commodity to be consumed.

This is not an uncommon notion of the popular arts for a singer who came of age during and was part of what Michael Denning has called the "Cultural Front." However, unlike the vast majority of his fellow white and ethnic artists of the 1930s, for Sinatra the starting point of his political views is the question of the role of blackness in the history of the United States.

In a second article, titled "The Way I Look at Race," occasioned by the release of the movie *Kings Go Forth* and published in *Ebony* in 1958,[1] Sinatra further articulated his position on race. To begin with, Sinatra frames the argument that will serve him to conceptualize the relationship between arts and politics first exposed in the *Magazine Digest* piece thirteen years earlier. In the first few paragraphs he lays out a view of life that targets the rugged individualism of Protestant origins because it predisposes the terrain for racism. In its place Sinatra proposes an interpretation of friendship, which is to say of togetherness as the value that fulfills one's life, because he views life as a shared, interdependent experience. His idea of friendship combines reciprocal respect and fondness for and recognition of the other, and an inner commonality that he nuances aesthetically. "Without real friendship life would be a pretty empty experience. . . . My friendships were formed out of affection, mutual respect, and a feeling of having something strong in common. These are eternal values that cannot be racially classified. This is the way I look at race" ("Way I Look," 35). In addition to transcending chronology, these are also the values of the Mediterranean tradition that defined the experience of the Italian immigrants as we have witnessed it in *Nuovomondo*, *Mount Allegro*, and *Maria*, the experience of the people that intrigued Booker T. Washington and attracted Sterling Brown and the other African American writers we have examined.

According to Sinatra, the fact that these values cannot be classified racially does not mean that they transcend race, let alone that he intends for them to transcend race. Because they are shared values, because they cannot be classified as belonging to one specific race, they belong to all races, the black race to begin with. As such, they transcend time and point toward a transnational dimension that in the light of the previous observations we might as well read as Sinatra's further decentering of whiteness. "The world is suffering from a shortage of love, between nations and individuals," writes the Chairman of the Board (35). After the description of the movie that occasioned the piece, Sinatra transfers his view of the human dimension onto his art. He recognizes blackness as constitutive of his identity as a professional artist. "Professionally and musically, I can't begin to fully evaluate the tremendous importance of Negro singers and musicians to my development as a singer. The debt I owe them is too immense ever to be repaid" (41–42). Art and blackness conjure as an aesthetic measure that supersedes a monetary conceptualization; Sinatra recognizes the value of black artists historically and the fact that he is the beneficiary of such value and tradition. "I have been on the receiving end of inspiration from a succession of great Negro singers and jazz musicians stretching all the way back to early Louis Armstrong and Duke Ellington, who is happily at last being recognized as one of his country's most distinguished composers" (42).

The language leaves no doubt about Sinatra's position. The child of Italian immigrants, the person who, according to a woman who approached him in a restaurant "slightly drunk," was referred to in her household as "the wop singer," is the beneficiary of black music (42). By his own testimony, the "wop singer" positions himself as the interpreter who translates blackness for the rest of the country. Because of his experiences as an Italian American, he can recognize the value of black music and of bringing it to the rest of the country, which "at last" is "recognizing" Ellington, the black composer, as both an American and one of "his country's most distinguished composers," a word, this last one, that evokes the tradition of the great European composers. Finally, Sinatra adds the gender dimension to the black artistic patrimony of America. As much as he recognizes and values black male musicians, it is a black female singer who exerted the biggest influence on him as well as on most American popular singers, a recognition that confers agency to a black woman as the subject that connects the human and the artistic dimension. "But it is Billie Holiday, whom I first heard in 52nd Street clubs in the early 1930s, who was and still remains the greatest single musical influence on me. It has been a warm and wonderful influence and I am very proud to acknowledge it. Lady Day is unquestionably the most important influence on American popular singing in the last 20 years" (42).

Sinatra neither classicizes blackness, nor does he make whiteness primitive. Likewise, neither does he appropriate blackness, nor does he blacken whiteness. And he does not assign gender to art. He makes an aesthetic evaluation regardless of gender that connects singers and musicians as a way to share beauty by making it available to the rest of the country. In this way, Sinatra acknowledges all of his music's components and makers. He does this after he has dismantled and decentered conceptually the hegemonic role of whiteness in the life of Americans and before he politicizes and claims for entertainment the tool to bring his music to the entire country, an avant-garde dimension, before he claims its modernity while he condemns the so-called business side of it. "Entertainment on the whole has generally been ahead of the rest of the country in the matter of equal treatment and real democracy. There remain a few areas where a lot of work has to be done. For instance in music, it's still a tragic fact that a number of cities still have segregated locals of the musicians union" (43).

Sinatra points toward the recognition of hybridization in order to create the necessary space to identify differences and make them visible. He does not submit to the idea that black musicians are entirely responsible for his artistry, which would be a form of reversed exclusion, a denial of his commitment to his artistry as well as his being an Italian American. As a matter of fact, Sinatra's vocalization owed just as much, if not more to his Italian heritage and his multiethnic urban upbringing, along with countless hours in the swimming pool to increase his breath. Lees acknowledges that the way Sinatra was able to sustain certain semivowels (*m, n, l,* and *r*) might have had to do with his Italian background. Hamill, instead, writes that Sinatra "created something that was not there before he arrived: an urban American voice. It was the voice of the sons of the immigrants in northern cities—not simply the Italian Americans, but the children of all those immigrants who had arrived on the great tide at the turn of the century" (93). Sinatra's modernity was this voice that belonged to everyone, a voice grounded in class, urbanization, multiethnicity, and his Italian heritage fused with the blackness of American popular music.

This hybridization reflected his historical memory and identity as an Italian American. "Some people have wanted to know why I am so interested in such things as discrimination and prejudice. I've been opposed to bigotry all my life," he writes toward the end of the article (43). But he links his moral position to his identity. Discrimination and prejudice are "wrong" *and* "indecent," the latter a word that for Mediterranean people like Sinatra is the exact opposite of the "mutual respect" he evoked at the beginning of the article. "In my own experience I've known prejudice of another sort. A lot of people look down on Italians," he concludes, differentiating the kind of bigotry that he experienced from the unspeakable racism that African Americans endured, a differentiation that, as the verticality of the verb indicates, allows Sinatra to maintain a class dimension that is organic to any form of modern exclusion and discrimination (44).

Sinatra kept a lifelong commitment to social and political activism and philanthropy, but as a singer the best way for him to advocate against prejudice and discrimination remained his art, his music. As he did so many times in his career, during one episode of the *The Sinatra Show* aired on TV at the end of the 1950s he took the stage along with Sammy Davis Jr., "one of the world's most gifted entertainers and one of the most successful," as he defined him in the *Ebony* piece ("Way I Look," 38). The admiration dated back to Davis's time in the entertainment circuit with the Will Mastin Trio and lasted to the very end. In *Yes I Can*, one of his autobiographies, Davis recalls that in 1941 in a Detroit theater where both artists were scheduled to perform, Sinatra "walked over to us and held out his hand, 'Hi'ya. My name is Frank. I sing with Dorsey'" (41). A few months before Davis died of throat cancer, at a benefit for the United Negro College Fund to celebrate Davis's sixtieth anniversary in the entertainment industry, Sinatra saluted his dying friend with the following words: "My little friend, the best friend I've ever had. Sixty years! That's a lot of bourbon under the bridge baby, I tell you that. . . . I knew you would amount to something, but I didn't feel that you would amount to everything. . . . You know I love you, and I can't say any more than that. You're the greatest. You're my brother" ("Sammy Davis Jr. 60th"). The sentiments were reciprocal. According to Wyl Haygood, Davis's admiration for Sinatra extended to the point that once he brought his grandmother Rose to a show at the Capitol Theatre in New York and told her that the young Italian American singer represented "what he hoped to become. He clipped Sinatra articles and kept them in a scrapbook. And wherever he went—town to town—his Sinatra scrapbooks went with him" (91).

On *The Frank Sinatra Show* televised on January 31, 1958, Sinatra and Davis took the stage together to perform "Me and My Shadow." According to Thomas Hischak's *The Tin Pan Alley Song Encyclopedia*, this song was "the quintessential soft-shoe number, a masterful piece of restrained melody that practically dances by itself . . . in which a dejected wooer takes comfort in his shadow, his only friend and one who never fights with him over a girl. Yet as the two buddies are 'walking down the avenue' together, both are blue over her loss" (233). Unlike Lewis and Chester's previously mentioned live performance of the song, during which neither man sang, both Sinatra and Davis sang, taking turns and simultaneously. Unlike Chester, who joined Lewis in the middle of the act after the song had started, as an appendage to the act, Davis shared the stage with Sinatra right from the beginning. The performance of the song starts with Sinatra entering the stage and walking in circles. Davis follows him moving unnaturally awkwardly, in mimicry of Jerry Lewis, by then the impersonator-in-chief of physical and cognitive disability, a style that Lewis had partly modeled after his fellow Jewish performers Al Jolson and Eddie Cantor, notoriously exploiters of the minstrel tradition. In other words, Davis is mimicking Lewis and the derision in blackface of African Americans for the amusement of a white audience, as it becomes clear when Sinatra, here acting as the translator of the performance for the audience, says, "Now you see, you walk quietly and with a purpose, every move that I can make should mean something. Your own gestures should be natural, never exaggerated, the whole body must be nice and fluent." Sinatra's studied bodily moves intentionally produce a meaning: to act naturally, without exaggeration, the exact contrary of the minstrel show (and the Lewis act) that Davis is mimicking. Yet what we see here is not a white man telling a black man how to behave, as a sort of inverted minstrel. Sinatra's words are an invitation—"should be natural"—extended to both himself and Davis, as well as to the real target of his words, the audience; "should mean something," says Sinatra. The purpose and the meaning must be cooperatively intentional. They must be shared. Sinatra's words acquire their meaning at the exact moment when Davis stops acting awkwardly, like a minstrel actor, and starts walking naturally, with no racial surplus of meaning besides his own racial self. The moment he moves as who he is, as himself, as a person who happens to be a black man, the two men stop walking in circles and align on the stage. They stand next to each other and start walking from one side of the stage to the other. The symbolic difference of the verticality of the initial positioning of the white man and the black man, which is reinforced by the difference in height, is erased. Also, at this exact moment Davis taps the white man in front of him on the shoulder, takes the lead, and tells him *to follow him* and *go with him*, reciprocating the invitation he just received. "I think I am getting the picture now. Come with me," Davis says half satirically, half seriously. The initial racial hierarchy, if there was one to begin with, is subverted.

Just as Davis's natural moves give meaning to Sinatra's words, the lyrics of the song—we might think of them as the body of the song—give meaning to Davis and Sinatra's act. "Me and my shadow / Strolling down the avenue / Me and my shadow / Not a soul to tell my troubles to," sings the black man, the white man after him. Who is the shadow here? Shadows are dark, and so is Davis. Yet Davis is the one who is followed by the shadow, which happens to be a white man. Could it be, however, that Davis's shadow is the invisible blackness of the "wop singer"? After all, in a staged performance everything is calculated; everything has its own place and role. And here Sinatra wears a dark suit that under the stage lights provides a contrast to Davis's lighter suit. Or maybe the African American and the Italian American singers are each other's shadow, given that after the first stanza they begin to sing simultaneously. But also—and this question might provide the answer to the previous question, too—what are their troubles, exactly? Why is there not a soul to talk to? Whose stairs are they climbing when they both

Frank Sinatra and Sammy Davis Jr. performing "Me and My Shadow" on *The Sinatra Show*, January 1958 (directed by Kirk Browning).

mime the knocking on a door as they sing the verses, "And when it's twelve o'clock/We climb the stairs/We never knock/Because there's nobody there"? And whose door is that they are knocking on knowing that nobody is going to be there to open to the two of them *together*?

One possible answer is America and its racial and class stairs, the hierarchical divide that Sinatra and Davis had been climbing to overcome, only to find out that America is not there to answer. America would seem to be the figurative object of their desire, the loss that the two allude to. Such a reading would warrant a consideration of this performance along the line of Leslie Fiedler's thesis of the interracial homoerotic bond of two males attempting to build and experience a peaceful and loving world away from bourgeois, capitalist civilization, an "idyllic love between two males in the wilderness, one a White refugee from White civilization, the other a nonwhite member of a group which has been exploited and persecuted by his white lover's people. White women, who represent the world of Law and Order from which the renegade is in flight, when they appear in this myth at all, appear as the Ultimate Enemy" ("Malamud's Travesty," 212). The problem with this kind of interpretation, besides the fact that it is extremely difficult to imagine Sinatra fleeing from women, is that such a reading would erase, on the one hand, Sinatra's invisible blackness and its history, and, on the other, the premise that a girl who rejected them caused the sad mood of the wooer and his shadow. The end result is not to find comfort, however temporary, in an idyllic world that allows for the actualization of homo-erotic love. Quite the contrary, the two are "all alone and feeling blue" as the song concludes.

However, there is another way to read Fiedler's theory in regard to this performance, one that might reflect the theoretical presupposition of Fiedler's thesis first brought forth in the 1948 essay "Come Back to the Raft Ag'in, Huck Honey," where Fiedler acknowledges the materiality of life in America, "our unconfessed universal fear . . . that compelling anxiety, which every foreigner notes, that we may not be loved, that we are loved for our posses-sion and not our selves, that we really are—*alone*" ("Come Back," 52). In the light of this enunciation, it is reasonable to believe that the one to be "all alone and feeling blue" is America, which is absent when the biracial duo knocks on its door. The sad joke is on America, Sinatra and Davis seem to say. Their jovial, ebullient, and satirical mood throughout the performance reinforces this reading, just as the final moment of the performance does, when neither artist acts as the other's shadow, and Davis tells Sinatra, "Oh we forgot the big thing with the hat"—a reference to the classic move of vaudeville performers who used to throw their hat in the air, catch it with their right foot, roll it, and throw it up in the air again. Sinatra and Davis, who aren't wearing hats, thoroughly enjoy simulating the hat move before a number of real hats are parachuted on them from high above to close a performance of "that mulatto culture that is America's gift to itself and the rest of the world" (*Devil*, 312).

II

On the occasion of his eightieth birthday, the music industry honored Sina-tra with a concert whose revenues would benefit the Barbara Sinatra Chil-dren's Center in California and the AIDS Project Los Angeles. Among the musicians in attendance at the Los Angeles Shrine Auditorium was Sinatra's fellow New Jerseyan and Italian American Bruce Springsteen. As an intro-duction to his acoustic cover of "Angel Eyes" from Sinatra's 1958 record *Only the Lonely*, Springsteen mentioned their common ethnic heritage and recalled a story from his childhood when his Italian American mother Adele said to him that the voice that he was hearing coming out of a jukebox while walking by a bar was that of Frank Sinatra. Springsteen told the story to explain Sinatra's influence on him. "It was the deep blueness of Frank's voice that affected me the most . . . his blues voice." Artistically speaking, then, for

Springsteen, going back in time to his childhood meant reaching out to his fellow "Italian singer," as he called Sinatra on that evening. In turn, this Italian lineage meant for Springsteen to encounter blackness, the discovery of his own blackness in the form of Sinatra's "blues voice." The (Italian American) Voice equaled blackness for the Italian American kid walking down the street of Freehold, New Jersey. Blackness is what connected the artist who came of age in the post–New Deal era, what Eric Lott refers to as the age of the disappearing liberal intellectuals, to the artist who came of age during the Cultural Front. Blackness is the element that these two Italian American artists share. This is the same element that according to Amiri Baraka distinguishes Springsteen's voice, his "blues shouter vocal timber." Baraka argues that such timber allows Springsteen to cross over into blackness genuinely. Springsteen's "blues appropriation is solid and not given to minstrelsy," just like the "blues voice" of Sinatra that worked as a connection for Springsteen, we could add (87). And just like Sinatra, Springsteen shared most of his artistic life, including his legendary live performances, with an African American musician, Clarence Clemons, "The Big Man," as he nicknamed him, the saxophonist of his multiethnic and multiracial E Street Band.

It is profitable to recall that Springsteen asked Clemons to join his band at a time, the early 1970s, when the saxophone was no longer a central part of the sound of a rock and roll band. By 1973, the year of Springsteen's first record, the saxophone, an instrument historically rooted in black American music, had disappeared from important American rock and roll acts, with only a few exceptions. Springsteen's decision to make a black saxophonist a central part of his music did not have a solely musical and aesthetic dimension. It also had political ramifications, because at the time of his decision, the civil rights movement, racial riots, the Supreme Court's decision in *Roe v. Wade*, and the Watergate scandal had questioned the normative white foundations of the country's identity and torn the nation apart. For a white artist, sharing the stage with a black man and building his music and the live performances on and around such a man was even more unorthodox, if not altogether daring.

And yet, when in June 2011 Springsteen delivered the eulogy after Clemons's sudden death, he made clear what that presence had entailed for both men since the beginning of their musical partnership:

The first time I saw my pal striding out of the shadows of a half empty bar in Asbury Park, a path opening up before him; here comes my brother, here comes my sax man, my inspiration, my partner, my lifelong friend . . . in some funny way we became each other's protectors; I think perhaps I protected "C" from a world where it still wasn't so easy to be big and black. Racism was ever present and over the years together, we saw it. Clarence's celebrity and size did not make him immune. ("Eulogy")

Besides the recognition of Clemons's influence on his music, the denunciation of racism, and the celebration of their friendship, Springsteen acknowledged the force of their togetherness, which he insisted encapsulated the meaning of their artistic relationship on stage:

But, standing together we were badass, on any given night, on our turf, some of the baddest asses on the planet. We were united, we were strong, we were righteous, we were unmovable, we were funny, we were corny as hell and as serious as death itself. And we were coming to your town to shake you and to wake you up. Together, we told an older, richer story about the possibilities of friendship that transcended those I'd written in my songs and in my music. Clarence carried it in his heart. It was a story where the Scooter and the Big Man not only busted the city in half, but we kicked ass and *remade* the city, shaping it into the kind of place where our friendship would not be such an anomaly. . . . The chance to renew that vow and double down on that story on a nightly basis, because that is something, that is *the* thing that we did together . . . the two of us. ("Eulogy")

Racism, togetherness, and an atypical friendship to perform for their audiences: these are the elements of Springsteen's and Clemons's story, incidentally elements very similar to those that Sinatra mentions in his *Ebony* article.

The beginning of that story dates back to the cover of Springsteen's *Born to Run*, which replicates the two musicians' process of engagement on the stage, the thing that they did together, as part of a larger collective body, their audience, the city that they remade. Like Sinatra and Davis's performance of "Me and My Shadow," this album cover and their live performances signify the eulogy's inclusive politics of sharing that subverts the traditional perimeter of whiteness by switching and inverting subject positions. Springsteen himself seems to acknowledge this much in the foreword that he wrote for Clemons's book *Big Man*. "When you look at just the cover of *Born to Run* . . . when you open it up and see Clarence and me together, the album begins to work its magic. Who are these guys? Where did they come from? What is the joke they are sharing? A friendship and a narrative steeped in the complicated history of America begin to form and there is music already in the air." The key words here are "together" and "history," which Springsteen unites. First, he links his to his saxophonist's identity; second, he connects their identities to their past, which however he does not reveal; third, he weaves them together as pieces of "the complicated history" of the United States. The order of the questions does not prioritize identity. It historicizes and contextualizes it, interlocking individual identity, collective history, and music. Springsteen eliminates any possibility to conceive identity in auto-referential terms. He favors a mutuality that entails a kind of politics and aesthetics whose basis is reciprocal recognition. He asks the reader to think about these questions in artistic terms and historically, with regard to both the form, which is rock and roll, and content, which is American history. No wonder that when Springsteen accepted the Ellis Island Family Heritage Award, he started by paying homage to his Italian immigrant grandparents, echoing the foreword to Clemons's book penned only a year earlier. "For me Ellis Island is about [the fact that] you can't know who you are or where we're going unless you know who we were and where we came from," switching from the singular to the plural personal pronoun and from the present tense to the past, crossing over identities and history to tie together personal identity and communal history ("Ellis Island").

The same interplay that forged his relationship with Clemons and with his Italian immigrant heritage is on display on the album cover of *Born to Run*. The picture of Springsteen and Clemons portrays Springsteen in the rebel outfit that Brando immortalized in *The Wild One*. Springsteen wears black jeans and a black leather jacket over a white sleeveless T-shirt and holds his Fender Esquire electric guitar with an Elvis Fan Club pin on the strap. Visibly hanging over his chest is an Italian horn, a pre-Christian amulet that originates from the Naples area where Springsteen's Italian family originates as well as a prototypical symbol of Italian American male identity, especially among young working-class Italian American men like Springsteen at the time of *Born to Run*. With a smile on his face, Springsteen looks at and leans on a person who cannot be identified without opening up the long-playing record, as one would open a book. Springsteen's right hand is visible, but the rest of his arm and most of the individual whom Springsteen is leaning on are not.

By any standard, a photograph that cuts off one person's arm and almost the entire second person portrayed in it is not a good photograph, let alone an artistic achievement. Springsteen's truncated image, however, compels the viewer to turn the record around and look at the back of the fold-out cover, only to realize that what one actually sees is the other half of the cover, literally. This second half portrays a big black man who plays the saxophone and looks at the potential holder of the record. In other words, the album cover is the entire photograph, whose meaning is self-evident: the two people portrayed in it belong to each other. The biracial interplay is replicated in their clothes, which are integral to the photo just as much as the suits of Sinatra and Davis are integral to their performance of "Me and My Shadow."

It is at once symmetrical and dialectical. It signifies this biracial artistic duo. Clemons wears a black hat; Springsteen has no hat, but he has very black hair; they both wear black pants and a white shirt, but Springsteen also has an earring and wears a black leather jacket. Besides the musical instruments, two elements differentiate them. One is their pigmentation; the other is Springsteen's Italian horn, the visual equivalent of the Italian-inflected cadence and tone of his enunciation especially audible in the first two stanzas of "Backstreets," the fifth song of the record that celebrates the friendship between two people at the margins, two outsiders.

This is a staged photo for a record whose parent company and makers ideally want everybody to listen to and buy. As in the case of Sinatra and Davis's performance of "Me and My Shadow," every little detail is intentional and plays a role, even if (if not especially) it happened to be there by accident. The colors that naturally distinguish Springsteen and Clemons and historically divided America are the same colors that aesthetically unite the two musicians. The racial difference that distinguishes the two musicians and divided their country is the same factor that establishes the differentiated equality of their code-switched aesthetics. In terms of symbolic domains, the cover of Born to Run erases the racial perimeter of whiteness and unites a white and a black man without prioritizing color or erasing the black presence. Indeed, the white background of the cover further highlights the black man's presence and the code-switched representation. The black man looks toward the beholder of the album, whereas the white man leans on and looks at the black man with a smile that clearly signifies the shared joke that Springsteen refers to in his foreword to Clemons's book. The amicable pose makes the white man's smile and the underlying joke even more intriguing, especially in light of Springsteen's stillness that the photograph projects. Springsteen may be born to run, as the title of the record located under his name, next to him, announces, but his body shows no intention to do so. This figural contradiction is somewhat paradoxical because of the title of the record as well as of the iconography of rock and roll music, which Springsteen obviously acknowledges. The black leather jacket, the electric guitar, the Elvis pin, Springsteen's scruffy look, everything stands for the very essence of this musical genre, which is motion, movement, and good old-fashioned masculinity. A cursory look at some early rock and roll songs says it all: "Shake, Rattle, and Roll," "(We're Gonna) Rock around the Clock," "The Wanderer," "Whole Lotta Shakin' Goin' On." Springsteen would seem to identify the negation of the music he aspires to embody. Even the guitar, which he holds in front of his legs with its neck hanging laterally rather than forward, does not symbolize the traditional phallic power—incidentally, and tellingly, a remnant of the way the banjo appeared in many posters that advertised minstrel shows, thus reinforcing the veracity of Baraka's observation on Springsteen's appropriation of blackness "as solid and not given to black minstrelsy."

Yet, as one opens the album, things change. As soon as the cover is unfolded, a seeming interaction becomes self-evident to the eye of the beholder. Springsteen's stillness disappears, and the rock and roll iconography of his leather jacket, Elvis pin, and electric guitar acquire meaningful connotations, reminding us of the materiality underlying the production of a narrative. What changes things is Clemons's presence. One, traditional, binary way to read this visual dynamism is to interpret the black man as the symbolic engine (slavery/labor) at the service of the white man (master/capital). Read in this way, the photograph would be another example of the white man's absorption and exploitation of the power of blackness, albeit without the latter's elision, a reading that at once relies on and enforces a strict, we may even say pure, racial polarization. In the case of the cover of *Born to Run*, this polarization would absorb both the black presence *and* Springsteen's Italian heritage, depriving the symbol of his primary ethnic heritage of any role, especially in connection to blackness, the aesthetic and historical connection that Springsteen made at Sinatra's eightieth birthday party, as well as in his Ellis Island speech. Such a reading decontextualizes the photograph by answering Springsteen's identitarian question, "Who are these guys?"— they're obviously a white and a black man—but omitting the historical one, "Where do they come from?" The elision of Springsteen's ethnic heritage would equal the elision of what Springsteen considers the source of his music, as he reiterated at Ellis Island. Standing next to the three daughters of his Italian immigrant grandparents, his mother and his two aunts, he said of these women, "They put the rock and roll in me . . . they are my living connection to my heritage, to Ellis Island," what allowed him to "come here as an immigrant."

For more than thirty years, in their live shows Springsteen and Clemons reenacted and twisted the subversive inclusiveness of the image of *Born to Run* that signifies their individual identity and their collective history, especially in two classic moments of their concerts. The first moment was the introduction of the band members to the audience, which over the years Springsteen turned into an increasingly elaborate rhetorical effort. The introduction reached its peak when Springsteen first introduced Clemons as the "last but not least" member of the band and called him "King of the World, Master of the Universe," words that elicited the audience's delirious response, whether the performance occurred in his home state of New Jersey or in Atlanta. There is something at once tragically subversive and cynically ironic about the grandchild of Italian immigrants calling a physically

imposing black male "King" and "Master" and eliciting the delighted response of predominantly white audiences in a country whose mainstream
national narrative, the foundation of its very modernity, is the outcome of a
revolution against a monarchy and the establishment of a republic in the
name of a freedom sustained by its conceptual negation, the enslavement of
black people. As in the case of the cover of *Born to Run*, however, there is
nothing coincidental in Springsteen's introduction of Clemons. Again, this
is a performance of a performance, which is what makes authentic its manufactured spontaneity and conveys its ideological meaning. The most minus-
cule detail is rehearsed. Springsteen's rhetoric is preconceived. Clemons's
introduction to the audience is Springsteen's way to acknowledge and recognize blackness as an integral, central part of and a value in American life,
just as Sinatra did in his articles and with his art. By so doing, Springsteen
forces the predominantly white audience to be an imaginative part of it, to
share it, however briefly, which is both the power and the limitation of such
an act.

Such imaginative engagement turned into concrete bodily interaction in
the second pivotal moment of the show, when Springsteen and Clemons
kissed each other on the lips, what Dave Marsh has called their "soul kiss,"
at the end of the performance of "Thunder Road," a heterosexual love song,
here too eliciting the roaring response of the crowds (187). Brian K. Garman
has indicated two ways to interpret the "soul kiss." The first interpretation
sees the kiss as functional to "reinforce the political and economic interests
of white men by excluding women and people of color from the privileges
that these men enjoy" (224). The second option favors "notions of manly
love to question sexual conventions and create the possibility of forging social bonds based on love and mutual respect" (224–25). Martha Nell Smith
opts for this second reading. She reads Springsteen's performance as a social
commentary that signals his "feminine" position in the arms of Clemons
when the two kiss as the abandonment of white masculinity and the consequential preeminence of the black man's manhood in order to refuse "the
replication of exclusionary dichotomies" (850).

Perhaps one way to find out the meaning of this moment of the performance is to let the performers speak. Asked about the "soul kiss," the saxophonist put it this way: "It's the most passion that you have without sex.
Two androgynous beings *becoming one. It's love.* It's two men—two strong,
very virile men—*finding that space* in life where they can let go enough of
their masculinity *to feel* the passion of love and *respect* and trust. Friendships are based on those things, and you seal it with a kiss" (Classic Rock
Archive, my italics). Clemons explains the kiss as the natural result of the
fusion of two different "beings," the complete unfolding of their together-

The "soul kiss": Bruce Springsteen and Clarence Clemons, live in concert, 1985.
© Neal Preston/Corbis.

ness, "becoming one." It also indicates a shared space at the service of an aesthetics of inclusion in alignment with the aesthetic dimension of the cover of *Born to Run*. Such inclusion is based on "respect" and "trust" and "friendship"—these, too, words and values that pair the ones Sinatra used to motivate his position on race in the *Ebony* article. The same words and values, "respect for others," Springsteen used in his op-ed "Chords for Change" published in the *New York Times* to motivate his political activism in the presidential campaign of 2004 after the criminal war against the dark-skinned people of Iraq.

They are the values that Springsteen and Clemons, like Sinatra and Davis before them, performed to create a shared space that destabilized fixed orders and structures and allowed them to stage their differences by way of maintaining their own individual identity, what makes them equal and belong to each other. Their performances translated, etymologically, their (hi)stories. They acted out the simple truth that in the end we are a version of each other, as Springsteen sings in his immigrant song "American Land," contextualizing this truth in the past as well as the present of American history as a part of the world history that the geography of the lyrics visualizes. In it, Springsteen mentions last names that identify a variety of ethnic and racial groups, including the last names of his Irish and Italian families. They are the people who came or were brought (in chains) to the country. What they shared is an empty stomach and the burning desire to make something out of their life, to achieve some sort of fulfillment. They are the workers who actually died building America and that continue to die today for exactly the same reason, in spite of *their* country's hostility. "They died to get here a hundred years ago they're still dying now/The hands that built the country we're always trying to keep down."

As always, Springsteen combines personal identity and collective history, the names of his Irish and Italian families as well as those of other ethnic and racial groups that he uses to interlock past and present, individual historical memory and collective experience. They are reflections of what Antony De-Curtis has defined as the "inclusiveness that is at the heart of his [Springsteen's] vision," an inclusiveness that recognizes how difference and class are also, in different ways and historical moments, version of each other's sameness (15).

In 2009 Springsteen performed for the first time this song with the E Street Band in Southern Italy, in the city of Caserta. He was only a few miles from the coastal town of Vico Equense where his Italian grandparents came from, not far from the port of Naples where they had started their journey for the American land, dreaming, one would think, of getting to "that place where we really wanna go," as their grandson would sing in "Born to Run" decades later. It is the area where Booker T. Washington had observed women working in the field in conditions that made him associate them with the black slaves in the South of the United States before the Civil War. In that port Fortunata Mancuso, her family, and the two girls Rita and Rosa embark for their journey to the New World in *Nuovomondo*. The same harbor is reproduced on another stage, that of the theater in New York City's Little Italy where Vito Corleone watches the Neapolitan *sceneggiata* in which the lead male learns of his mother's death back in Naples. That evening, in Caserta, Springsteen's mother, Adele, one of the women who put the rock and roll in him, was in attendance. As the "immigrant song" ended, her son recognized all the musicians performing on the stage with him. Last "but not least," he named his lifelong black musical partner and friend Clarence Clemons, "the biggest Italian you've ever seen."

NOTES

Introduction

1. Gramsci's entire passage reads, "The starting-point of critical elaboration is the consciousness of what one really is, and is 'knowing thyself' as a product of the historical process to date which has deposited in you an infinity of traces, without leaving an inventory. Such an inventory must therefore be made at the outset." The Italian reads, "L'inizio dell'elaborazione critica è la coscienza di quello che è realmente, cioè un 'conosci te stesso' come prodotto del processo storico finora svoltosi che ha lasciato in te stesso un'infinità di tracce accolte senza beneficio d'inventario. Occorre fare inizialmente un tale inventario." See Antonio Gramsci, *Quaderni del carcere*, ed. Valentino Gerratana (Turin: Einaudi, 2007), 2:1375.

2. In the 2010 census 27,323,632 people identified themselves as African Americans, whereas 17,235,941 identified themselves as of Italian ancestry.

1. New World, Old Woman: Or, Modernity Upside Down

1. My translation. The Italian reads, "Li dovrebbero abbruciare tutti, quelli delle tasse!" See Verga, 44.

2. The city of departure is unnamed in the movie. However, the accent of the emigration officer points to Naples as the likely city. Obviously, the point of leaving the city unnamed is that it could be any city from where people left for the New World.

3. See Tamburri, 92–128.

2. Rochester, Sicily: The Political Economy of Italian American Life and the Encounter with Blackness

1. A branch of the Works Progress Administration, the Federal Writers' Project was created in 1935 to give work to otherwise unemployed writers and other white-collar workers. The FWP is best remembered for the American Guide Series, a set of automobile guidebooks focusing on the scenic, historical, cultural, natural, and economic resources of each state of the Union.

2. Mangione never joined the Communist Party USA, but when he moved to New York City after college he attended, however briefly, the meetings of the John Reed Clubs. A committed antifascist, he wrote for the major leftist publications of his times: the *New Republic*, *New Masses*, *Partisan Review*, and, more importantly, the Communist *Daily Worker* under the pen names of Mario Michele and Jay Gerlando.

3. See Hamill, 83.

4. Rochester has a robust union and left-leaning political tradition, which Sicilian immigrants contributed to establishing. Rudolph Vecoli informs us that in Rochester the

Workers Party had a Sicilian-dominated section that ACWA organizer and leader Nino Capraro led. See Vecoli, "Making and Un-making."

5. See Leo Marx, *Machine in the Garden*.

3. *Structures of Invisible Blackness: Racial Difference, (Homo)Sexuality, and Italian American Identity in African American Literature during Jim Crow*

1. The racist association between African Americans and apes is well documented from its beginning during slavery to various antebellum forms of popular culture, such as the minstrel show, throughout the Jim Crow era.

2. Hair straightening has a specific place in African American history and popular culture. Traditionally, it signifies an attempt to be more acceptable to the white establishment, or at least an acceptance of the white social order.

3. The last lines of *The Great Gatsby* read, "Gatsby believed in the green light, the orgastic future that year by year recedes before us. It eluded us then, but that's no matter—to-morrow we will run faster, stretch out our arms farther. . . . And then one fine morning—So we beat on, boats against the current, borne back ceaselessly into the past" (180).

4. *In the Name of the Father, the Son, and the Holy Gun: Modernity as the Gangster*

1. See Ferraro, "Blood in the Marketplace," 18–52.

2. At the end of Martin Scorsese's *Goodfellas*, the main protagonist, Henry Hill, a half Italian and half Irish gangster from a working-class Brooklyn neighborhood where most of the movie takes place, decides to enter the federal Witness Protection Program. In the last scene of the movie, we see him at his house in an undisclosed location, where he laments, "The hardest thing was to live the life," when he and his fellow gangsters "had it all. . . . Everybody had their hands out. Everything was for the taking. And now it's all over. That's the hardest part. Today everything is different. There's no action. I have to wait around like everyone else. Can't even get decent food. After I got here I ordered spaghetti with marinara sauce . . . and I got egg noodles with ketchup. I'm an average nobody. I get to live the rest of my life like a schnook."

5. *In the Name of the Mother: The Other Italian American Modernity*

1. This is also a subtle ironical protest against the now-millionaire songwriter nicknamed "The Boss," who relegates her to such a discomfiting role and, as such, affirms Springsteen's own personal alignment with women, his rejection of a divided and divisive world, and perhaps his statement on a recording industry also dominated by men.

6. *The Dago and the Darky: Staging Subversion*

1. The publication was hardly an option. *Ebony* was and still is one of, if not the most important and widely circulated mainstream black magazines. Obviously by publishing a piece concerned with race in such a magazine, Sinatra deliberately tried to connect with the mainstream black population. Perhaps he was also inviting a white audience to follow him and cross over into mainstream black life, so to speak, through the pages of *Ebony*.

BIBLIOGRAPHY

Acker, Joan. *Class Questions: Feminist Answers*. Lanham, MD: Rowman & Littlefield, 2006.

Armstrong, Nancy. "Some Call It Fiction: On the Politics of Domesticity." In *The Critical Tradition: Classic Texts and Contemporary Trends*, 2nd ed., edited by David H. Richter, 1317–31. Boston: Bedford St. Martin's, 1998.

Asbury, Herbert. *The French Quarter: An Informal History of the New Orleans Underworld*. New York: Thunder's Mouth Press, 2003.

Attaway, William. *Blood on the Forge*. New York: Monthly Review Press, 1987.

Baker, Houston A., Jr. *Modernism and the Harlem Renaissance*. Chicago: University of Chicago Press, 1987.

Baldwin, James. *Giovanni's Room*. New York: Dial, 1956.

Baraka, Imamu Amiri. "Not the Boss: Bruce Springsteen." In *Digging: The Afro-American Soul of American Classical Music*, 87–89. Berkeley: University of California Press, 2009.

Barolini, Helen, ed. *The Dream Book: An Anthology of Writings by Italian American Women*. Rev. ed. Syracuse, NY: Syracuse University Press, 2000.

———. *Umbertina*. New York: Seaview, 1979.

Basile Green, Rose. *The Italian-American Novel: A Documentation of the Interaction of Two Cultures*. Rutherford, NJ: Fairleigh Dickinson University Press, 1974.

Battat, Erin Royston. *Ain't Got No Home: America's Great Migrations and the Making of an Interracial Left*. Chapel Hill: University of North Carolina Press, 2014.

Bell, Thomas. *Out of This Furnace*. Pittsburgh: University of Pittsburgh Press, 1976.

Benasutti, Marion. *No Steady Job for Papa*. New York: Vanguard, 1966.

Bercovitch, Sacvan. *The Puritan Origins of the American Self*. New Haven, CT: Yale University Press, 1975.

Berman, Marshall. *All That Is Solid Melts into Air: The Experience of Modernity*. New York: Penguin, 1988.

Bertellini, Giorgio. *Italy in Early American Cinema: Race, Landscape, and the Picturesque*. Bloomington: Indiana University Press, 2009.

———. "White Passion: Italian New Yorker Cinema and the Temptations of Pain." In *Mediated Cinema: New Italian-American Cinema*, edited by Giuliana Muscio, Joseph Sciorra, and Giovanni Spagnoletti, 93–102. New York: John D. Calandra Italian American Institute, 2010.

The Black Hand. Directed by Wallace McCutcheon. American Mutoscope and Biograph, 1906. Film.

"Blacks Mourn the Death of the Frank Sinatra That Nobody Knows." *Jet*, June 1, 1998.

Bona, Mary Jo. *Claiming a Tradition: Italian American Women Writers*. Carbondale: Southern Illinois University Press, 1999.

Bone, Robert A. *The Negro Novel in America*. New Haven, CT: Yale University Press, 1958.

Boulard, Garry. "Blacks, Italians, and the Making of New Orleans Jazz." *Journal of Ethnic Studies* 16.1 (1988): 53–66.

Brown, Sterling A. "Harlem Happiness." In *The Collected Poems of Sterling A. Brown*, edited by Michael S. Harper, 165. Evanston, IL: TriQuarterly Books, Northwestern University Press, 1996.

———. "The Negro in Washington." In *Washington, D.C.: A Guide to the Nation's Capital*. American Guide Series. Washington, DC: Government Printing Office, 1936.

Buell, Lawrence. *The Dream of the Great American Novel*. Cambridge, MA: Belknap Press of Harvard University Press, 2014.

Cantarella, Eva. *Itaca: Eroi, donne, potere tra vendetta e diritto*. Milan: Feltrinelli, 2011.

Carnevale, Nancy. *A New Language, a New World: Italian Immigrants in the United States, 1890–1945*. Urbana: University of Illinois Press, 2009.

Chancer, Lynn S., and Beverly Xaviera Watkins. *Gender, Class, and Race: An Overview*. Malden, MA: Blackwell, 2006.

Charles, John C. *Abandoning the Black Hero: Sympathy and Privacy in the Postwar African America White-Life Novel*. New Brunswick, NJ: Rutgers University Press, 2013.

Chiavola Birnbaum, Lucia. *Black Madonnas: Feminism, Religion, and Politics in Italy*. San Jose: toExcel, 2000.

Clarke, Donald Henderson. *Louis Beretti*. New York: Vanguard, 1929.

Classic Rock Archive. *Clarence Clemons on Meeting Bruce Springsteen*. Video clip. YouTube, October 14, 2009. https://www.youtube.com/watch?v=HRFPWWoxpro.

Costa, Carlo, and Lorenzo Teodonio. *Razza partigiana: Storia di Giorgio Marincola (1923–1945)*. Roma: Edizioni Albano Laziale, 2009.

Crane, Stephen. *Maggie: A Girl of the Streets*. Auckland: Floating Press, 2009.

Crouch, Stanley. *Essays and Review, 1979–1989*. New York: Oxford University Press, 1990.

Cunningham, George. "The Italian: A Hindrance to White Solidarity in Louisiana, 1890–1898." *Journal of Negro History* 50.1 (January 1965): 22–36.

Davis, Sammy, Jr., and Jane and Burt Boyar. *Yes I Can: The Story of Sammy Davis Jr.* New York: Farrar, Straus & Giroux, 1965.

DeCapite, Michael. *Maria*. New York: John Day, 1943.

———. "The Story Has Yet to Be Told." *Common Ground* 1.1 (1940): 29–36.

DeCurtis, Anthony. "Springsteen Returns." *Rolling Stone*, January 10, 1991.

DeLillo, Don. *Americana*. Boston: Houghton Mifflin, 1971.

———. *Underworld*. New York: Scribner, 1997.

Denning, Michael. *The Cultural Front: The Laboring of American Culture in the Twentieth Century*. London: Verso, 1996.

De Rosa, Tina. *Paper Fish*. New York: Feminist Press, 2003.

Dion and Friends. *Live New York City*. Collectables, 2005. CD.

di Prima, Diane. "April Fool Birthday Poem for Grandpa." In *Pieces of a Song: Selected Poems*, 69. San Francisco: City Lights, 1990.

———. *Memoirs of a Beatnik*. New York: Penguin Books, 1998.

———. "Ode to Keats." In *Pieces of a Song: Selected Poems*, 57. San Francisco: City Lights, 1990.

———. *Recollections of My Life as a Woman: The New York Years*. New York: Penguin Books, 2001.

Douglass, Frederick. *Life and Times of Frederick Douglass: His Early Life as a Slave, His Escape from Bondage, and His Complete History, Written by Himself*. New York: Collier Book, 1962.

Dreiser, Theodore. *Sister Carrie*. Boston: Houghton Mifflin, 1959.

Du Bois, W. E. B. *The Souls of Black Folk*. New York: Barnes & Noble, 2003. First published in 1903.

Dunbar, Paul Lawrence. *The Sport of the Gods*. New York: Signet, 2011. First published in 1902.

Ellison, Ralph. *Invisible Man*. New York: Random House, 1952.

———. "Transition." *Negro Quarterly* 1.1 (1942): 87–92.

Engels, Frederick. *The Origin of the Family, Private Property, and the State: In the Light of the Researches of Lewis H. Morgan*. New York: International Publishers, 1942. First published in 1884.

Fante, John. *The Road to Los Angeles*. New York: Ecco, 2002.

———. *Wait until Spring, Bandini*. New York: Ecco, 2002.

Faulkner, William. *As I Lay Dying*. New York: Vintage, 1991.

———. *Light in August*. New York: Vintage, 1985.

Federal Writers' Project. *Massachusetts: A Guide to Its Places and People*. American Guide Series. Boston: Houghton Mifflin, 1937.

Federici, Silvia. *Caliban and the Witch: Women, the Body and Primitive Accumulation*. New York: Automedia, 2004.

Ferguson, Roderick A. *Aberrations in Black: Toward a Queer of Color Critique*. Minneapolis: University of Minnesota Press, 2004.

Ferraro, Thomas J. "Blood in the Marketplace: The Business of Family in *The Godfather* Narratives." In *Ethnic Passages: Literary Immigrants in Twentieth-Century America*, 18–52. Chicago: University of Chicago Press, 1993.

———. "Catholic Ethnicity and Modern American Arts." In *The Italian American Heritage: A Companion to Literature and Arts*, edited by Pellegrino D'Acierno, 331–51. New York: Garland, 1999.

———. *Feeling Italian: The Art of Ethnicity in America*. New York: NYU Press, 2005.

Fiedler, Leslie A. "As Free as Any Cretur . . ." In *The Devil Gets His Due: The Uncollected Essays of Leslie Fiedler*, edited by Samuele F. S. Pardini, 77–85. Berkeley, CA: Counterpoint, 2008.

———. "Come Back to the Raft A'gin, Huck Honey." In *The Devil Gets His Due: The Uncollected Essays of Leslie Fiedler*, edited by Samuele F. S. Pardini, 46–53. Berkeley, CA: Counterpoint, 2008.

———. *The Devil Gets His Due: The Uncollected Essays of Leslie Fiedler*. Edited by Samuele F. S. Pardini. Berkeley, CA: Counterpoint, 2008.

———. "A Homosexual Dilemma." In *The Devil Gets His Due: The Uncollected Essays of Leslie Fiedler*, edited by Samuele F. S. Pardini, 204–6. Berkeley: Counterpoint, 2008.

————. *Love and Death in the American Novel.* New York: Anchor Books, 1992.

————. "Malamud's Travesty Western." *Novel: A Forum on Fiction* 10.3 (Spring 1977): 212–19.

————. "Whatever Happened to Jerry Lewis? *That's Amore . . .*" In *The Devil Gets His Due: The Uncollected Essays of Leslie Fiedler,* edited by Samuele F. S. Pardini, 299–307. Berkeley: Counterpoint, 2008.

Fitzgerald, F. Scott. *The Great Gatsby.* New York: Scribner, 2004.

Fleissner, Jennifer L. *Women, Compulsion, Modernity: The Moment of American Naturalism.* Chicago: University of Chicago Press, 2004.

Foley, Barbara. *Specters of 1919: Class and Nation in the Making of the New Negro.* Urbana: University of Illinois Press, 2003.

Foner, Eric. *The Story of American Freedom.* New York: W. W. Norton, 1998.

Gabaccia, Donna. *Italy's Many Diasporas.* Seattle: University of Washington Press, 2000.

Gambino, Richard. *Blood of My Blood: The Dilemma of Italian-Americans.* Toronto: Guernica, 2003.

————. *Vendetta: The True Story of the Largest Lynching in U.S. History.* Toronto: Guernica, 2000.

Gardaphé, Fred L. *From Wiseguys to Wise Men: The Gangster and Italian American Masculinity.* New York: Routledge, 2006.

————. "Invisible People: Shadows and Light in Italian American Culture." In *Anti-Italianism: Essays on a Prejudice,* edited by William J. Connell and Fred Gardaphé, 1–10. New York: Palgrave Macmillan, 2010.

————. *Italian Signs, American Streets: The Evolution of Italian American Narrative.* Durham, NC: Duke University Press, 1996.

————. "Left Out: Three Italian American Writers of the 1930s." In *Leaving Little Italy: Essaying Italian American Culture,* 53–66. Albany: SUNY Press, 2004.

Garman, Bryan K. *A Race of Singers: Whitman's Working-Class Hero from Guthrie to Springsteen.* Chapel Hill: University of North Carolina Press, 2000.

Gates, Henry Louis, Jr. *Figures in Black: Words, Signs, and the Racial Self.* New York: Oxford University Press, 1989.

Gennari, John. "Passing for Italian: Crooners and Gangsters in Crossover Culture." *Transition* 72 (1996): 36–48.

Gerstner, David A. *Queer Pollen: White Seduction, Black Male Homosexuality, and the Cinematic.* Urbana: University of Illinois Press, 2011.

Gilroy, Paul. *The Black Atlantic: Modernity and Double Consciousness.* Cambridge, MA: Harvard University Press, 1993.

The Godfather. Directed by Francis Ford Coppola. Paramount Pictures, 1972. Film.

The Godfather II. Directed by Francis Ford Coppola. Paramount Pictures, 1974. Film.

The Godfather Legacy. Directed by Kevin Burns. The History Channel, 2012. Documentary.

Gold, Michael. *Jews without Money.* Introduction by Alfred Kazin. New York: Carroll & Graf, 1996.

Goodfellas. Directed by Martin Scorsese. Warner Bros., 1990. Film.

Goux, Jean-Joseph. *Symbolic Economies: After Marx and Freud.* Translated by Jennifer Curtiss Gage. Ithaca, NY: Cornell University Press, 1990.

Gramsci, Antonio. *The Gramsci Reader: Selected Writings, 1916–1935.* Edited by David Forgacs. Introduction by Eric Hobsbawm. New York: NYU Press, 2000.

The Grapes of Wrath. Directed by John Ford. Twentieth Century-Fox, 1940. Film.

Guerri, Giordano Bruno. *Il sangue del sud: Antistoria del Risorgimento e del brigantaggio.* Milan: Arnoldo Mondadori Editore, 2010.

Guglielmo, Jennifer. *Living the Revolution: Italian Women's Resistance and Radicalism in New York City, 1880–1945.* Chapel Hill: University of North Carolina Press, 2010.

Guglielmo, Thomas J. *White on Arrival: Italians, Race, Color, and Power in Chicago, 1890–1945.* New York: Oxford University Press, 2004.

Gutman, Herbert. *Power and Culture: Essays on the American Working Class.* Edited by Ira Berlin. New York: New Press, 1987.

Hale, Grace Elizabeth. *Making Whiteness: The Culture of Segregation in the South, 1890–1940.* New York: Pantheon, 1998.

Hamill, Pete. *Why Sinatra Matters.* Boston: Little, Brown, 1998.

Hamington, Maurice. *Hail Mary? The Struggle for Ultimate Womanhood in Catholicism.* New York: Routledge, 1995.

Harris-Lopez, Trudier. *South of Tradition: Essays on African American Literature.* Athens: University of Georgia Press, 2002.

Harrison-Kahan, Lori. *The White Negress: Literature, Minstrelsy, and the Black-Jewish Imaginary.* New Brunswick, NJ: Rutgers University Press, 2011.

Haygood, Wil. *On Black and White: The Life and Times of Sammy Davis Jr.* New York: Knopf, 2003.

Heller, Agnes. *A Theory of Modernity.* Oxford: Blackwell, 1999.

Hemingway, Ernest. *The Green Hills of Africa.* New York: Scribner, 1935.

Hingham, John. *Strangers in the Land: Patterns of American Nativism, 1860–1925.* New Brunswick, NJ: Rutgers University Press, 1955.

Hirsch, Marianne. "Mothers and Daughters." *Signs* 7.1 (1981): 200–222.

Hischak, Thomas S. *The Tin Pan Alley Song Encyclopedia.* Westport, CT: Greenwood, 2002.

Howard, Gerald. "The American Strangeness: An Interview with Don DeLillo." In *Conversations with Don DeLillo,* edited by Thomas DePietro, 119–30. Jackson: University Press of Mississippi, 2005.

Howard, Police Captain. "The New Orleans Mafia; or, Chief of Police Hennessy Avenged." *New Detective Library* 1.439 (April 25, 1891): 3–31.

Howells, William Dean. *Suburban Sketches.* Boston: James R. Osgood, 1872.

Hurston, Zora Neale. *Their Eyes Were Watching God.* Foreword by Edwidge Danticat. New York: HarperCollins, 2006.

Jackson, Lawrence P. *The Indignant Generation: A Narrative History of African American Writers and Critics, 1934–1960.* Princeton, NJ: Princeton University Press, 2011.

Jacobson, Matthew Frye. *Whiteness of a Different Color: European Immigrants and the Alchemy of Race.* Cambridge, MA: Harvard University Press, 1998.

Johnson, James Weldon. *The Autobiography of an Ex-Colored Man.* Compiled and edited by William L. Andrews. New York: Library of America, 2004. First published in 1912.

Joyce, James. *Finnegans Wake*. New York: Viking, 1939.
———. *Ulysses*. Edited by Hans Walter Gabler, with Wolfhard Steppe and Klaus Melchior. New York: Vintage, 1986.
Kaplan, James. *Frank: The Voice*. New York: Doubleday, 2010.
Kings Go Forth. Directed by Delmer Daves. United Artists, 1959. Film.
Klein, Marcus. *Foreigners: The Making of American Literature, 1900–1940*. Chicago: University of Chicago Press, 1981.
La Polla, Garibaldi M. *The Grand Gennaro*. Edited by Steven J. Belluscio. New Brunswick, NJ: Rutgers University Press, 2009.
Lee, Julia H. *Interracial Encounters: Reciprocal Representations in African American and Asian American Literatures, 1896–1937*. New York: NYU Press, 2011.
Lees, Gene. "The Paradox: Frank Sinatra." In *Singers and the Song II*, 77. New York: Oxford University Press, 1998.
Lentricchia, Frank. *The Edge of Night*. New York: Random House, 1994.
———. *"Johnny Critelli" and "The Knifeman": Two Novels*. New York: Scribner, 1996.
———. *The Music of the Inferno*. Albany: SUNY Press, 1999.
The Leopard. Directed by Luchino Visconti. Titanus. Société Nouvelle Pathé Cinéma, Société Générale de Cinématographie, 1963. Film.
Leverenz, Davis. "Booker T. Washington's Strategies of Manliness, for Black and White Audiences." In *Booker T. Washington and Black Progress: "Up from Slavery" 100 Year Later*, edited by W. Fitzhugh Brundage, 149–76. Gainesville: University Press of Florida, 2003.
Levine, Lawrence W. *Black Culture and Black Consciousness: Afro-American Folk Thought from Slavery to Freedom*. Oxford: Oxford University Press, 1977.
Little Caesar. Directed by Mervyn LeRoy. Warner Bros., 1931. Film.
Looney, Dennis. *Freedom Readers: The African American Reception of Dante Alighieri and the "Divine Comedy."* Notre Dame, IN: University of Notre Dame Press, 2011.
Lott, Eric. *The Disappearing Liberal Intellectual*. New York: Basic Books, 2006.
———. *Love and Theft: Blackface Minstrelsy and the American Working Class*. New York: Oxford University Press, 1993.
Mangione, Jerre. "Brief Summary of *Mount Allegro*." N.d. Jerre Mangione Archives, box 18, folder 10. Rush Rhees Library, University of Rochester, Rochester, NY.
———. *The Dream and the Deal: The Federal Writers' Project, 1935–1943*. Boston: Little, Brown, 1972.
———. "The Federal Writers' Project." Lecture presented at Harvard University, March 20, 1990.
———. *Mount Allegro: A Memoir of Italian American Life*. Syracuse, NY: Syracuse University Press, 1998.
———. "Sterling A. Brown and the Federal Writers' Project." N.d. Jerre Mangione Archives, box 74, folder 20. Rush Rhees Library, University of Rochester, Rochester, NY.
Manzoni, Alessandro. *The Betrothed* [*I promessi sposi*]. Translated by Archibald Colquhoun. New York: E. P. Dutton, 1959.
Marsh, Dave. *Glory Days: Bruce Springsteen in the 1980s*. New York: Pantheon, 1987.
Marx, Karl. *The Eighteenth Brumaire of Louis Bonaparte*. Electric Book, 2001. Online.

Marx, Karl, and Friedrich Engels. "The Communist Manifesto." In *The Marx-Engels Reader*, edited by Robert C. Tucker, 469–500. New York: W. W. Norton, 1978.

Marx, Leo. *The Machine in the Garden: Technology and the Pastoral Ideal in America*. New York: Oxford University Press, 1964.

Maso, Carol. *Ghost Dance*. San Francisco: North Point Press, 1986.

Michaels, Walter Benn. *Our America: Nativism, Modernism, Pluralism*. Durham, NC: Duke University Press, 1995.

Mormino, Gary R., and George E. Pozzetta. *The Immigrant World of Ybor City: Italians and Their Latin Neighbors in Tampa, 1885–1985*. Gainesville: University Press of Florida, 1987.

Morrison, Toni. "On the Backs of Blacks." *Time*, December 2, 1993, 57.

Moses, Wilson J. "More Than an Artichoke: The Pragmatic Religion of Booker T. Washington." In *Booker T. Washington and Black Progress: "Up from Slavery" 100 Year Later*, edited by W. Fitzhugh Brundage, 107–30. Gainesville: University Press of Florida, 2003.

Motley, Willard. *Knock on Any Door*. New York: D. Appleton-Century, 1947.

Norris, Frank. *McTeague: A Story of San Francisco*. New York: Doubleday & McClure, 1899.

———. *The Pit: A Story of Chicago*. 1903. Project Gutenberg. Online.

Norris, Kathleen Thompson. *Mother*. 1911. Project Gutenberg. Online.

Nugent. Richard Bruce. *Gentleman Jigger*. Edited by Thomas H. Wirth. Philadelphia: Da Capo, 2008.

Nuovomondo [Golden Door]. Directed by Emanuele Crialese. Rai Cinema. Respiro. Memento Films Production, 2006. Film.

Orsi, Robert. *The Madonna of 115th Street: Faith and Community in Italian Harlem*. New Haven, CT: Yale University Press, 1988.

———. "The Religious Boundaries of an Inbetween People: Street *Feste* and the Problem of the Dark-Skinned Other in Italian Harlem, 1920–1990." *American Quarterly* 44.3 (September 1992): 313–47.

Pola, Antonia. *Who Can Buy the Stars?* New York: Vantage, 1957.

Polanyi, Karl. *The Great Transformation: The Political and Economic Origins of Our Time*. Foreword by Joseph E. Stiglitz. Boston: Beacon, 2001.

Pugliese, Stanislao, ed. *Frank Sinatra: History, Identity, and Italian American Culture*. New York: Palgrave Macmillan, 2004.

Puzo, Mario. *The Fortunate Pilgrim*. New York: Random House, 1997.

———. *The Godfather*. New York: Putnam, 1969.

Rampersad, Arnold. Foreword to *Gentleman Jigger* by Richard Bruce Nugent, v–iv. Edited by Thomas H. Wirth. Philadelphia: Da Capo, 2008.

"The Rascals Induction into the Rock and Roll Hall of Fame—Part 1." Video clip. YouTube. https://www.youtube.com/watch?v=HYZlOodmbwI.

Reich, Steven A. *A Working People: A History of African American Workers since Emancipation*. Lanham, MD: Rowman & Littlefield, 2013.

Rinelli, Lorenzo. "A Boat Called Hope." JGCinema.com. March 3, 2015. Online.

Rocco and His Brothers. Directed by Luchino Visconti. Titanus. Les Films Marceau, 1960. Film.

Roediger, David R., ed. *Black on White: Black Writers on What It Means to Be White*. New York: Schocken, 1998.

———. *The Wages of Whiteness: Race and the Making of the American Working Class*. Rev. ed. London: Verso, 2003.

Rogin, Michael. *Blackface, White Noise: Jewish Immigrants in the Hollywood Melting Pot*. Berkeley: University of California Press, 1996.

Ruotolo, Onorio. "In Union Square Park." In *The Magna Carta Manifesto: Liberties and Commons for All*, by Peter Linebaugh, 231. Berkeley: University of California Press, 2009.

Russo, John Paul, and Robert Casillo. *The Italian in Modernity*. Toronto: University of Toronto Press, 2010.

Ruth, David E. *Inventing the Public Enemy: The Gangster in American Culture, 1918–1934*. Chicago: University of Chicago Press, 1996.

Said, Edward W. *Humanism and Democratic Criticism*. New York: Columbia University Press, 2004.

"Sammy Davis Jr. 60th Anniversary Special—Frank Sinatra Sings to Sammy." Video clip. YouTube, May 27, 2012. https://www.youtube.com/watch?v=t9PQHfmWk84.

Sammy Davis Jr. World. "Me and My Shadow." Video clip. YouTube, November 28, 2011. https://www.youtube.com/watch?v=i-4uKgXRnpI.

Savarese, Julia. *The Weak and the Strong*. New York: G. P. Putnam's Sons, 1952.

Scarface. Directed by Howard Hawks. United Artists, 1932. Film.

Schindler's List. Directed by Steven Spielberg. Universal Pictures, 1993. Film.

Scott, William R. "Black Nationalism and the Italo-Ethiopian Conflict." *Journal of Negro History* 63.2 (1978): 118–34.

Shankman, Arnold. *Ambivalent Friends: Afro-Americans View the Immigrant*. Westport, CT: Greenwood, 1982.

Sinatra, Frank. *Frank Sinatra Sings for Only the Lonely*. Capitol Records, 1958. LP.

———. "The Haters and Bigots Will Be Judged: Some Words from a 'Saloon Singer' to Those Who Still Haven't Figured Out the Whole Point of America." *Los Angeles Times*, July 4, 1991. http://articles.latimes.com/1991-07-04/local/me-2202_1_saloon-singer.

———. "Let's Not Forget We're *ALL* Foreigners." *Magazine Digest*, July 1945.

———. "The Way I Look at Race (as Told to Allan Morrison)." *Ebony*, July 1958.

Smith, Henry Nash. *Virgin Land: The American West as Symbol and Myth*. New York: Vintage, 1957.

Smith, Martha Nell. "Sexual Mobilities in Bruce Springsteen: Performance as Commentary." *South Atlantic Quarterly* 90.4 (1991): 833–54.

Sollors, Werner. *Beyond Ethnicity: Consent and Descent in American Culture*. New York: Oxford University Press, 1986.

———. *Ethnic Modernism*. Cambridge, MA: Harvard University Press, 2009.

———. *Neither Black nor White yet Both: Thematic Exploration of Interracial Literature*. New York: Oxford University Press, 1997.

The Sopranos. Creator David Chase. HBO. 1999–2007. TV series.

Springsteen, Bruce. "American Skin (41 Shots)." *High Hopes*. Columbia, 2014. CD.

———. "American Land." *Wrecking Ball*. Columbia, 2012. CD.

———. "Angel Eyes." Video clip. YouTube, September 29, 2011. https://www.youtube .com/watch?v=5QtjLEqK2oM&list=PLA1u11D8whiNzwZnnYnKeI8vq-KmZWEHR.

———. "Backstreets." *Born to Run*. Columbia, 1975. LP.

———. *Born to Run*. Columbia, 1975. LP.

———. "Bruce Springsteen Accepting the 2010 Ellis Island Family Heritage Award." Video clip. YouTube, July 16, 2014. https://www.youtube.com/watch?v=oAmVK4 JCHbA.

———. "Bruce Springsteen's Eulogy for Clarence Clemons." June 21, 2011. *RollingStone.com*, June 29, 2011. http://www.rollingstone.com/music/news/bruce -springsteens-eulogy-for-clarence-clemons-20110629.

———. "Car Wash." *Tracks*. Columbia, 1998. CD.

———. "Chords for Change." *New York Times*, April 5, 2004. http://www.nytimes .com/2004/08/05/opinion/chords-for-change.html?_r=0.

———. Foreword to *Big Man: Real Life and Tall Tales*, by Clarence Clemons and Don Reo. New York: Grande Central, 2009.

———. "Highway Patrolman." *Nebraska*. Columbia, 1982. LP.

———. "Jesus Was an Only Son." *Devils and Dust*. Columbia, 2005. CD.

———. Maria's Bed." *Devils and Dust*. Columbia, 2005. CD.

———. "Mary Lou." *Tracks*. Columbia, 1998. CD.

———. "Mary Queen of Arkansas." *Greetings from Asbury Park, NJ*. Columbia, 1973. LP.

———. "Mary's Place." *The Rising*. Columbia, 2002. CD.

———. "My Hometown." *Born in the U.S.A.* Columbia, 1984. LP.

———. "Reason to Believe." *Nebraska*. Columbia, 1982. LP.

———. "Reno." *Devils and Dust*. Columbia, 2005. CD.

———. "The Rising." *The Rising*. Columbia, 2002. CD.

———. *The River*. Columbia, 1980. LP.

———. "The River." *The River*. Columbia, 1980. LP.

———. *The Seeger Sessions (American Land Edition)*. Columbia, 2006. CD.

———. "Shackle and Drawn." *Wrecking Ball*. Columbia, 2012. CD.

———. "Sherry Darling." *The River*. Columbia, 1980. LP.

———. *Songs*. New York: HarperCollins, 1998.

———. "Straight Time." *The Ghost of Tom Joad*. Columbia, 1995. CD.

———. "Thunder Road." *Born to Run*. Columbia, 1975. LP.

———. *Wrecking Ball*. Columbia, 2012. CD.

Stallybrass, Peter, and Allon White. *The Politics and Poetics of Transgression*. Ithaca, NY: Cornell University Press, 1986.

Sundquist, Eric J. "Mark Twain and Homer Plessy." In *Mark Twain's "Pudd'nhead Wilson": Race, Conflict, and Culture*, edited by Susan Gillman and Forrest G. Robinson, 46–72. Durham, NC: Duke University Press, 1990.

Susman, Warren. *Culture as History: The Transformation of American Society in the Twentieth Century*. New York: Pantheon, 1984.

Tamburri, Anthony Julian. "Old World versus New; or, Opposites Attract: Emanuele Crialese's *Nuovomondo*." In *Re-Viewing Italian Americana: Generalities and Specificities on Cinema*, 92–128. New York: Bordighera Press, 2011.

Tateo, Francesco. *Modernità dell'umanesimo*. Salerno: Edisud Salerno, 2010.

Thompson, E. P. *Customs in Common: Studies in Traditional Popular Culture*. New York: New Press, 1993.

———. *The Making of the English Working Class*. New York: Pantheon, 1963.

Thompson, Mark Christian. *Black Fascism: African American Literature and Culture between the Wars*. Charlottesville: University of Virginia Press, 2007.

Tomasi, Mari, *Like Lesser Gods*. Milwaukee: Bruce Publishing, 1949.

Twain, Mark. *Adventures of Huckleberry Finn*. Edited by Thomas Cooley. New York: W. W. Norton, 1998.

———. *Pudd'nhead Wilson and Those Extraordinary Twins*. Introduction and notes by Darryl Pinckney. New York: Barnes & Noble Classics, 2005.

United States Census Bureau. *2010 American Community Survey*. http://factfinder. census.gov/faces/tableservices/jsf/pages/productview.xhtml?pid=ACS_10_1YR _B04006&prodType=table.

———. *2010 Census Briefs: The Black Population*. https://www.census.gov/prod/ cen2010/briefs/c2010br-06.pdf.

Vecoli, Rudolph J. "Are Italian Americans Just Plain White Folks?" *Italian Americana* 13.2 (1995): 149–61.

———. "The Making and Un-Making of the Italian American Working Class." In *The Lost World of Italian American Radicalism: Politics, Labor, and Culture*, edited by Philip V. Cannistraro and Gerald Meyer, 51–76. Westport, CT: Praeger, 2003.

Verga, Giovanni. *I Malavoglia*. Milan: Arnoldo Mondadori Editore, 1989.

Von Drehle, David. *Triangle: The Fire That Changed America*. New York: Grove, 2003.

Wald, Alan M. "Willard Motley (July 14, 1909–March 14, 1965)." In *Writers of the Black Chicago Renaissance*, edited by Steven C. Tracy, 250–72. Urbana: University Illinois Press, 2011.

Ward, Theodore. "Five Negro Novelists: Revolt and Retreat." *Mainstream* (Winter 1947): 100–110.

Warner, Ralph. "'Blood on the Forge' Is Story of Negro Brothers." *Daily Worker*, November 8, 1941, 7.

Warren, Kenneth W. *Black and White Strangers: Race and Literary Realism*. Chicago: University of Chicago Press, 1993.

———. *What Was African American Literature?* Cambridge, MA: Harvard University Press, 2011.

Warren, Robert Penn. *All the King's Men*. Orlando, FL: Harcourt, 2005.

Washington, Booker T. *Up from Slavery*. Edited by William E. Andrews. New York: Oxford University Press, 1995. First published in 1901.

Washington, Booker T., with Robert E. Park. *The Man Farthest Down: A Record of Observation and Study in Europe*. Garden City, NY: Doubleday, Page, 1912.

Watson, Bruce. *Sacco and Vanzetti: The Men, the Murders, and the Judgment of Mankind*. New York: Viking, 2007.

Whitman, Walt. *Leaves of Grass*. New York: Aventine, 1931.

The Wild One. Directed by Lásló Benedek. Columbia Pictures, 1954. Film.

Wirth, Thomas H. Introduction to *Gay Rebel of the Harlem Renaissance: Selections from the Work of Richard Bruce Nugent*, 1–61. Foreword Henry Louis Gates Jr. Durham, NC: Duke University Press, 2002.

Wolff, Daniel. *4th of July, Asbury Park: A History of the Promised Land*. New York: Bloomsbury, 2005.

The Wolf of Wall Street. Directed by Martin Scorsese. Paramount Pictures, 2013. Film.

Wright, Morris. *Man and Boy*. New York: Alfred A. Knopf, 1951.

Yutang, Lin. *Chinatown Family*. Edited by C. Lok Chua. New Brunswick, NJ: Rutgers University Press, 2007.

Zandy, Janet, ed. *Calling Home: Working-Class Women's Writing: An Anthology*. New Brunswick, NJ: Rutgers University Press, 1990.

———, ed. *Liberating Memory: Our Work and Our Working-Class Consciousness*. New Brunswick, NJ: Rutgers University Press, 1995.

———. Introduction to *What We Hold in Common: An Introduction to Working-Class Studies*, edited by Janet Zandy, xiii–xv. New York: Feminist Press of the City University of New York, 2001.

INDEX

Page numbers in *italics* indicate illustrations.